The Gospel According to Dan Brown

Many writers have shown The Da Vinci Code *to be fiction, not truth. But that is not enough. It is precisely as a work of fiction that Dan Brown's book has so much power and impact. Here, Jeff Dunn and Craig Bubeck engage Brown's stories—not just* The Da Vinci Code *but his other novels as well— showing the mythology and the worldview they convey. The authors bring to light Brown's conspiratorial thrillers, comparing them to the gospel stories of Jesus Christ and challenging all to seek the truth.*

GENE E. VEITH, PH.D.
CULTURE EDITOR, *WORLD MAGAZINE,*
EXECUTIVE DIRECTOR, CRANACH INSTITUTE, CONCORDIA THEOLOGICAL SEMINARY
AUTHOR, *THE SOUL OF THE LION, THE WITCH, AND THE WARDROBE*

Dunn and Bubeck leave the strictly factual analysis of Dan Brown's stories to others and go straight for the jugular—i.e., the worldview that Brown promulgates so powerfully by means of his mythos. In so doing, they show us why all the fuss about The Da Vinci Code *really matters. A valuable contribution to an important ongoing dialogue.*

JIM WARE
AUTHOR, *GOD OF THE FAIRY TALE;*
COAUTHOR, *FINDING GOD IN THE LORD OF THE RINGS* AND
FINDING GOD IN THE LAND OF NARNIA

The most obvious virtue of this book is its scope—it is a marvelous collection of wide-ranging information. A second distinctive excellence is its literary focus, which brings a fresh slant to the current ferment over The Da Vinci Code *phenomenon. The authors pursue their task with an impressive analytic rigor.*

LELAND RYKEN, PH.D.
AUTHOR, *HOW TO READ THE BIBLE AS LITERATURE,*
COAUTHOR, *A READER'S GUIDE THROUGH THE WARDROBE*
CLYDE S. KILBY PROFESSOR OF ENGLISH, WHEATON COLLEGE

Jeff Dunn and Craig Bubeck have taken a novel approach in analyzing Dan Brown's writings. Using their knowledge of how literature works, they compare the gospel stories of the Bible and Brown's myths. They show that we are in two very different literary worlds and that the two messages are equally different and indeed irreconcilable. Serious students of the Da Vinci phenomenon would do well to consider what these authors have to say.

PETER JONES
COAUTHOR, *CRACKING DA VINCI'S CODE*

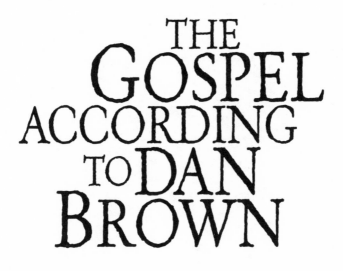

THE GOSPEL ACCORDING TO DAN BROWN

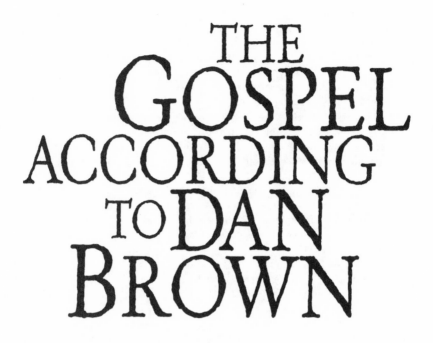

THE GOSPEL ACCORDING TO DAN BROWN

JEFF DUNN &
CRAIG BUBECK

Victor®

COOK COMMUNICATIONS MINISTRIES
Colorado Springs, Colorado • Paris, Ontario
KINGSWAY COMMUNICATIONS LTD
Eastbourne, England

Victor® is an imprint of
Cook Communications Ministries, Colorado Springs, CO 80918
Cook Communications, Paris, Ontario
Kingsway Communications, Eastbourne, England

THE GOSPEL ACCORDING TO DAN BROWN
© 2006 by Jeff Dunn and Craig Bubeck

The Web addresses (URLs) mentioned throughout this book are solely offered as a resource to the reader. The citation of these Web sites does not in any way imply an endorsement on the part of the authors or the publisher, nor do the authors or publisher vouch for their content for the life of this book.

Cover Design: BMB Design
Cover Photo Credit: The Last Supper © Planet Art
Cover Photo Credit: Dan Brown © AP

First Printing, 2006
Printed in Canada

1 2 3 4 5 6 7 8 9 10   Printing/Year   10 09 08 07 06

All Scripture quotations, unless otherwise noted, are taken from the *Holy Bible, New International Version®. NIV®*. Copyright © 1973, 1978, 1984 by International Bible Society. Used by permission of Zondervan. All rights reserved. Scripture quotations marked MSG are taken from *THE MESSAGE*. Copyright © by Eugene H. Peterson 1993, 1994, 1995, 1996, 2000, 2001, 2002. Used by permission of NavPress Publishing Group; TLB are taken from *The Living Bible*, © 1971, Tyndale House Publishers, Wheaton, IL 60189. Used by permission; NLT are taken from the *Holy Bible, New Living Translation*, copyright © 1996. Used by permission of Tyndale House Publishers, Wheaton, IL 60189. All rights reserved; NKJV are taken from the *New King James Version*. Copyright © 1982 by Thomas Nelson, Inc. Used by permission; and KJV are from the King James Version of the Bible. (Public Domain.) All rights reserved.

Hardcover:
ISBN-13: 978-0-7814-4440-8
ISBN-10: 0-7814-4440-3

Paperback:
ISBN-13: 978-0-7814-4501-6
ISBN-10: 0-7814-4501-9

LCCN: 2006929257

*To my wife, Kathleen, who is living proof that the soul-mate myth is
a very literal reality, composed by God*
—C. B.

*To my long-suffering wife, Kathy, whose love for me
is a truly great work of art*
—J. D.

Contents

Acknowledgments

Our deepest thanks to the editorial team of Cook Communications, whose vision and patience has made this book happen. Special thanks in particular to Dan Benson, the director of this orchestration; to our managing editor, Lora Schrock, whose skill as an editor is perhaps only surpassed by her uncanny ability to crack a scheduling whip with grace and mercy; to Jennifer Lonas for her additionally keen editorial insight and wisdom; to Phyllis Williams for employing her stylizing magic; to Mary McNeil for her further eagle-eyed editorial analysis; to Nancy Kopper for her excellent indexing work; to Emily Garman and Jack Campbell for their sharp attention to detail; and to Karen Athen for her artful design of the interior.

Our sincere gratitude and kudos likewise go to the Cook Communications marketing team, for their excellence in cover design and promotional work, and also to the sales team for their passion and integrity. What an incredible privilege to work alongside such great professionals and even greater friends. But most of all, we thank and praise our living, personal God who has granted us the honor to be handlers of his truth, fumbling as we are. May truth be found in—and perhaps sometimes in spite of—these finite pages.

We Don't Hate Dan Brown

In spite of what you may think, we are not Dan Brown haters. (We don't even know him, though we think we'd like to.) We'll never argue that he is evil or a tool of the Devil because he has written books that criticize the church or question Christianity. As a matter of fact, we are glad for his books, especially for the attention they've drawn to some long-standing challenges to the Christian faith.

With so many books already on the market either defending or refuting Dan Brown's theories, why did we decide to write *The Gospel According to Dan Brown*? More important, why are you reading it?

The answers to both questions are of eternal importance. It is not simply a matter of whether you like Brown's writings or agree with his theories—it is vital you understand this. Dan Brown is presenting what appears to be an entirely new worldview, a different kind of "gospel" that is easy and somewhat exciting to embrace. However, it is in fact a very old worldview in brand-new clothes. Brown wants to let you in on a great secret—and don't we all like to think we know something others don't? It's fun and conspiratorial and, according to Brown, will even make you more spiritual.

The problem is this: Brown's theology is very different from what we read in the Bible. As a matter of fact, it's impossible to hold both Brown's views and those in the Bible at the same time. That is why our examination is necessary. We are going to lay out all of Brown's claims and his gospel messages in his gospel stories—and compare them with those of the Bible. And there's one principle we're going to be unswerving about: You will need to choose which gospel to believe. You can't hold on to both.

That's our agenda—that you *choose wisely*. And, yes, we do believe there is a wise choice to be made. But before you slam this book shut and put it back on the shelf as just one more conservative-Christian, agenda-driven critique, consider this: Every book has an agenda. Actually, that's the purpose of a book. Dan Brown has an agenda in his stories—a spirituality he is advocating. And we have an agenda too. In fact, every author has an agenda (and really, it isn't an evil thing), but most important is how that agenda is presented. We will try to present our agenda in this book as reasonably and objectively as possible. But as reasonable and objective as we try to be, we also believe that the questions we'll examine are important on a deeply personal level and should concern all of us. We believe that the choice you make about which gospel to accept will determine whether you survive the spiritual storm that's now barreling down upon us or get washed away by the popularity of the gospel being preached by Brown and others.

A Hurricane Named Da Vinci

Storm? What storm?

On August 29, 2005, one of the most powerful storms ever recorded struck the Gulf Coast of the United States just east of New Orleans. Hurricane Katrina devastated large parts of Louisiana, Mississippi, and Alabama, leaving close to two thousand people

Critical Decisions

Rescue workers say many holdouts have insisted on staying in their homes or makeshift residences rather than obey the mandatory evacuation order [New Orleans Mayor Ray] Nagin first put into effect on August 28, the day before Katrina crashed ashore. Some said they were concerned about their property being looted, while others were unaware of [the] disaster's full extent, worried about their pets or concerned that conditions would be even worse in shelters.

"New Orleans," pars. 14–15

Before Katrina hit the Gulf Coast on Sunday, August 28, Debbie said she hadn't paid much attention to the warnings and didn't want to evacuate without the family's pets. "I never once dreamed ... I just thought it would be a little wind and rain and then it would just blow over."

Pangyanszki, par. 15

dead, hundreds missing, and hundreds of thousands homeless. While warnings had been posted several days before the hurricane made landfall, many of those who died chose to ride out the storm in their homes, thinking it really wouldn't be all that bad. Their choice was the wrong one.

Today another storm has struck, not just in America, but all over the planet. It wasn't forecast on The Weather Channel. CNN didn't have crews onshore to announce its arrival. But it is deadly nonetheless. And Dan Brown's best-selling novels are at the storm's leading edge.

The storm we're talking about is spiritual in nature, which gives it eternal importance. This storm threatens to sweep away all who are not firmly anchored, those whose lives are built on sand rather than bedrock. The winds in this storm howl, "The true Jesus isn't the Jesus you think he is," "The ancient texts are the work of men with political motives," and "There are secrets the church is hiding from you."

Many people won't recognize this cultural phenomenon as a storm. In their little neck of the woods, it still might seem like a refreshing breeze at first, something to be enjoyed and sought after—just like the minutes before Katrina hit, when the sea was calm and people were relaxing in their homes.

And then they died.

A spiritual storm is coming your way, and it's inevitable. At the eye of this storm is this message: What the church has taught you about Jesus is wrong.

Perhaps you've been chasing this storm for some time, even reveling in it. Along with Brown, you may think it really began some seventeen hundred years ago when Nicene Council Christians hijacked the real Jesus and followers were swept away by the fantastic notion that he was actually God. To you, the world is finally coming to grips with reality—and embracing an authentic spirituality. You might argue that in the scope of the past two thousand years of church history, what we know as Christianity has merely been the eye of the storm—a calm of false hope for a few centuries—and now the other edge is bearing down on contemporary culture.

Others would like to think they do believe in biblical Christianity. But this recent Dan Brown wave ... well, it's powerful. Many who call themselves Christians but are not anchored in their faith will be swept away. In fact, many, after reading *The Da Vinci Code* and Brown's other books, have already been washed off their sandy foundations.

And finally, some grounded Christians are just now realizing a storm has hit but still don't know what it's all about. Maybe this book is even tapping you on the shoulder and drawing your attention to what's going on outside the relatively secure walls of your church. You don't particularly want to go running outside out into the thick of it, but it's starting to worry you. You're wondering if you should batten down the hatches of your church or your family.

The Gospel According to Dan Brown is a call for you to check your moorings. On which gospel are you anchored? Which gospel will your kids embrace? Are you prepared for this spiritual storm that is even now at your personal shore?

Why Another Dan Brown Book?

It seems you can't even turn around in a bookstore today without finding a book by or about Dan Brown. The publishing industry loves the former school teacher from New Hampshire for creating an insatiable desire for books about his books.

So, why are we adding to that growing list? Is our book really necessary? Yes—and here's why.

While most other Dan Brown–related books focus solely on his mega-best-selling *The Da Vinci Code*, our book looks at the whole body of his fiction, starting with the 1996 release, *Digital Fortress*. We will provide plot summaries of these four novels, complete with spoiler warnings and look at the common threads throughout his writings—what we call his gospel. We will also compare these four novels to books of the Bible and the Christian gospel.

A Force to Be Reckoned With

A few years ago, Dan Brown was a relatively unknown author who had three works of fiction in print at the end of 2002—*Digital Fortress*, *Angels & Demons*, and *Deception Point*. None had sold more than a few thousand copies. But Jason Kaufman, Brown's editor at

Doubleday, felt there was something special about the author's fourth manuscript.

Kaufman convinced his marketing team to take a chance and send out ten thousand advance copies of *The Da Vinci Code*. The gamble paid off. After its release in March 2003, *The Da Vinci Code* immediately soared to the top of major best-seller lists, where it has remained for nearly three years. By the beginning of 2006, more than twenty-five million hardcover copies of *The Da Vinci Code* were in print worldwide, ironically putting it in direct competition with another all-time best seller: the Bible.

The publishers of Brown's other novels rushed to rerelease his earlier works in both paperback and hardcover to take advantage of his success. For a while, Brown even pulled off the unthinkable: His books occupied the top four slots on the *Sunday Times* best-seller list at the same time. And that was before the illustrated versions of *The Da Vinci Code* and *Angels & Demons* were released.

Nearly two dozen books written to debunk *The Da Vinci Code* followed. (We were the editors of one such book—*Cracking Da Vinci's*

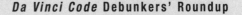

Da Vinci Code Debunkers' Roundup

- *Breaking the Da Vinci Code* (Darrell L. Bock, Nelson) distinguishes fictitious entertainment from the historical elements of the Christian faith. Bock's research uncovers the origins of Da Vinci's codes by focusing on the 325 years following the birth of Christ.
- *Cracking Da Vinci's Code* (James L. Garlow and Peter Jones, Victor) engages the suspense novel's teachings by comparing it with a more accurate Christian theology and history while tracing Brown's hypothesis back to its roots, revealing pagan influences in today's culture and the church.
- *The Da Vinci Codebreaker* (James L. Garlow with Timothy Paul Jones and April Williams, Bethany) is a dictionary-style guide with hundreds of historically and theologically correct answers to the most-asked questions about people, locations, events, and definitions.
- *The Da Vinci Deception* (Erwin W. Lutzer, Tyndale) examines the blurred "facts" behind *The Da Vinci Code* from a Christian perspective and clarifies the issues involved in the deception.
- *Truth and Fiction in The Da Vinci Code* (Bart Ehrman, Oxford University Press) purports that it isn't defending a particular theological view. Debunking the historical inaccuracies in Brown's book, Ehrman argues that readers should not try to learn history from speculative fiction.

Code by James L. Garlow and Peter Jones—which to date has sold nearly half a million copies.) Several nonfiction books have also been written to support Brown's claims. Bookstores have even devoted entire sections to Brown and his theories. In May 2006, *The Da Vinci Code* was released as a big-screen movie directed by Ron Howard and starring Tom Hanks. Brown's fifth novel has not even been published, but several books already have been written to solve its mysteries.

There is no question that Dan Brown has become an industry unto himself, a powerful marketing force to be reckoned with.

What's in a Gospel?

Is there more to Brown's fiction than just a story? Do we really believe he's preaching a gospel? And what do we mean by "gospel," anyway?

When Christians speak of *gospel,* they usually mean one of two traditional senses of the word: the gospel as truth and the gospel as story. The first sense is that "good-news" *truth* (John 3:16), which proclaims God loves us, and if we believe in his uniquely begotten son, Jesus Christ, we'll have eternal life. That's the Truth of all truths as far as Christians are concerned.

More Good News

The word *gospel* morphed into its present-day English form from the Old English word gōdspel (*gōd* meaning "good," and *spel* meaning "news or tidings"). It is a direct translation from the New Testament Greek word *euaggélion*, meaning "good news" or "tidings," which is also the root word of *evangelical* and *evangelism.*

Even so, this ultimate good-news truth is generally *not* what your friend means when he or she declares, with right hand raised, "I swear; it's the gospel truth!" Ironically, it isn't the "good news" sense of the word *gospel* but rather the "truth" sense that our culture has adopted. (After all, your friend with raised hand might be bearing the bad tidings that the one-of-a-kind antique you just bought at an expensive store is going on sale at Kmart.) Our society has attached "gospel" to a wide array of truth messages, some more true than others.

Allusions to this factoid-type of gospel pop up regularly in our culture, often with the formula "the gospel according to [fill in your favorite sage]." A quick Web search reveals literally hundreds of book titles that play on this theme: *The Gospel According to Peanuts, The Gospel According to Disney, The Gospel According to Harry Potter, ... The Simpsons, ... Tolkien, ... Tony Soprano, ... Superheroes, ... Oprah, ... Zen*—and many more.

And now we have *The Gospel According to Dan Brown*.

All these books borrow from the original Christian claim to absolute, irrefutable truth—some good-humoredly, some cynically, some even with a promise of good news, and some with comparably zealous claims of spiritual truth. But all are not so subtly alluding to Christianity's gospel message with its claim to the ultimate good-news truth.

When we titled this book *The Gospel According to Dan Brown,* we took that into consideration. Brown presents a message he believes is true—truer, in fact, than that claimed by mainstream Christianity. And he has declared his commitment to spreading his gospel. We'll examine that gospel in depth in subsequent chapters, comparing and contrasting the Bible's claims of gospel truth with Dan Brown's, and we'll get down to the basics of what we mean by "truth" for that matter.

The second meaning of the word *gospel* is not as widely known, but it's still dear to the hearts of Christians. It's the gospel as *story*—the "old, old story" that forms the very foundation of the Christian faith. The first four books of the New Testament (Matthew, Mark, Luke, and John) are actually called Gospels. That's because these historical narratives—the gospel stories—are the vehicles for the good-news message of Jesus Christ. Without the gospel stories, the message is meaningless, because the message at its heart *is* the story. You can't call yourself a Christian if your belief in God isn't fundamentally informed by the greatest of all stories: the gospel of Jesus, the Christ.

This Book Is for You

In all of his stories, Dan Brown is putting forth a gospel message that he says you can build your life on. But you need to ask yourself whether you're building on a solid foundation or one made of sand. Our hope with this book is to help you ensure the soundness of your foundation.

In chapters 1 through 4 we'll examine the power of story (Brown's and the Bible's), why taking story seriously actually is key to having a strong foundation, and how our perception of truth is defined by our worldview. Chapters 5 and 6 compare Brown's gospel messages of survival of the fittest and the power of deception in *Digital Fortress* and *Deception Point*, contrasting those values against the biblical gospel stories' values of sacrifice and a very personal truth.

Chapters 7 and 8 go deep into Brown's second-most successful novel, *Angels & Demons*, exploring the differences between Brown's mysterious and unknowable gnostic God that is the sum total of everything that exists and the Bible's personal, knowable God who created everything that exists. And then finally we examine Brown's magnum opus, *The Da Vinci Code,* with its worldview of pagan-gnostic enlightenment, comparing it to the Bible's gospel story of light in the darkness.

Our purpose in this book is not to criticize Brown for the literary license he takes in saying that Jesus may have been married. We aren't concerned that what he calls "fact" has actually been proven to be fiction. Nor are we accusing Brown of being misinformed because he calls the artist "da Vinci" rather than the traditional reference "Leonardo."

As we've already stated, we don't hate Dan Brown. But we are concerned for those who have read his theology and are now building their lives on its foundation. And we're concerned for Brown himself. We want to dialogue with those who wonder whether to believe his view of history—because what each of us believes matters. Our beliefs shape our actions and, eventually, the outcome of our lives.

This book is for you, even if you're sure of your beliefs but don't see any problem with enjoying Brown's books as simply escapist fiction. After all, they're just stories, aren't they?

This book is for you if your friends have read Brown's novels and are engaging you in discussions about the divinity of Jesus and the role of women in the church. Are you prepared to answer their questions?

Most of all, this book is for you if you haven't yet decided which gospel to believe or why having solid beliefs is necessary at all. It is for you who, in spite of the warnings that have been issued, choose to ride out the storm. We don't want you to be swept away. You need to build your house on solid rock. This is your invitation to begin building.

A gospel storm is blowing on your shores. But it's not too late to anchor yourself to the real truth.

1

"It's Just a Story"

Jane sips her latte, fingering with her free hand a frayed rip developing along the bottom corner of the book's well-worn jacket. "I don't understand what all the hubbub is about." She glances up at Susan, who looks disapprovingly at her across the small round table. "Interesting plot, okay characters, some provocative theories. I thought it was a good read. What's the big deal?"

Susan rolls her eyes upward, her own coffee cup suspended in her hand. "It's heresy, Jane. It's a pack of lies, and you shouldn't be supporting it by reading it."

"So you haven't read it?" Jane smiles carefully, just enough to ease the tension.

"No, but—"

"Susan, trust me, because I *have* read it. All the media noise is just that. There are some unorthodox theories in it, I admit. But did you know Brown says he's a Christian? I don't think he's the Antichrist, and I don't think people should judge Brown or the book, *especially* if they haven't read it."

Jane finishes her drink, then leans forward. "It's pure fiction, and that's how any serious thinker should categorize it. Come on, it's just a story!"

Susan glances over at the mostly empty tables around them. "Okay."

Jane picks up the book, turns it over once, and then points it at Susan. "*You* should read it."

What Do You Mean by "Just"?

"It's *just* a story."

If you've ever discussed *The Da Vinci Code* with someone and your conversation came around to the controversy surrounding it, that comment almost certainly was made. Whether you're a devotee of the novel or a conservative Christian ready to denounce it, you've probably formulated the same summary dismissal: It's just a story, and we shouldn't be taking it so seriously.

However, the book continues to sell in the millions, and the movie has only further popularized its subject matter. In fact, the book you're holding admittedly is riding on the coattails of *The Da Vinci Code*'s success, offering yet another perspective on what Dan Brown has established through story—a gospel message that is here to stay, no matter how much the Christian community might wish otherwise.

Maybe We "Just" Don't Get It ...

Using the word *just* in regard to Brown's novels proves that we don't understand the importance of the issues he has raised. Consider how this engaging suspense thriller revolving around a hidden code in a Leonardo da Vinci painting has spawned some fairly intense debates. "Why all the hubbub?" we ask. It is, after all, "just" a story, right?

Because many excellent books deal with this very question, we won't reinvent the well-worn wheel of separating fact from *Da Vinci Code* fiction. But we are going to challenge you to consider this question from a different perspective.

Dismissing any work of fiction as "just a story" reveals an ironic disconnect from reality, especially present reality. Today's postmodern culture is rediscovering that story is a valid way of perceiving reality. This approach isn't new; it was just somewhat lost on progressive thinkers of the past century.

The Bible reminds us, "There is nothing new under the sun" (Eccl. 1:9), and story is a means of understanding the world that is

What's Real?

Besides being complicated, reality, in my experience, is usually odd. It is not neat, not obvious, not what you expect.... Reality, in fact, is usually something you could not have guessed. That is one of the reasons I believe Christianity.
—C. S. Lewis, *Mere Christianity*

as ancient as humanity itself. From the beginning of time, humans have imparted truths about their existence from generation to generation through the power of stories—stories that many today would write off as "just" myths.

"Seek the Truth"

Do stories really proclaim what an author thinks is truth, or are stories only entertainment? Dan Brown's premier gospel story proclaims without reservation that it is very much about a truth. *The Da Vinci Code* movie transparently implores viewers to "seek the truth." And the success of both the book and the movie illustrates that the power of story hasn't faded. Story actually appears to be a more serious force to contend with today than it was in the past. To the chagrin of many historians, theologians, and scientists, this novel has proven that the masses prefer truths in story to the supposedly indisputable truths staked out by their respective disciplines.

True Myth?

Some of you may say, "I took my share of literature classes in college, (I'm glad they're behind me too), so I know stories contain meaning, even truth. But come on. We're talking myths here. By definition, *myth* means something didn't really happen. Zeus didn't really throw lightning bolts. That's because the story is a *myth*."

You might also say this is true of Brown's novels: "The events in *Angels & Demons* and *The Da Vinci Code* never really happened. They are like the Greek myths in this way, at least—they're *fictional*. They are made up!"

Most people certainly will agree that fiction and myth both refer to stories about events that never actually happened. But are fiction and myth truly the same thing? If not, in what respects do they differ? And more important, is there any such thing as true fiction or a true myth? To answer these questions, we need to look more closely at how myth is defined.

Myth as Lie

For the most part, the word *myth* refers to something "false" or "unreal," or even to an outright "lie." But the editors of *Webster's* unabridged dictionary even seemed to struggle over the ambiguity, almost apologetically acknowledging that the definition "varies considerably in its denotation and connotation, depending on the persuasion of the user" ("myth," *Webster's*).

Most people would agree with the venerable *Webster's* first attempt at a definition: "a person or thing existing only in imagination or whose actuality is not verifiable." Similarly, they'll often use the word in the sense that the dictionary further defines it: to disparage a "story, belief, or notion commonly held to be true but utterly without factual basis."

For example, in *The Da Vinci Code,* Brown's main character, Professor Robert Langdon, laments for good reason the holocaust against witches: "During three hundred years of witch hunts, the

Itching Ears

For the time will come when men will not put up with sound doctrine. Instead, to suit their own desires, they will gather around them a great number of teachers to say what their itching ears want to hear. They will turn their ears away from the truth and turn aside to myths.

—Apostle Paul in 2 Timothy 4:3–4

Church burned at the stake an astounding five *million* women" (125). However, the alleged facts in Langdon's statement are themselves actually drawn from a very popular myth—a conspiracy story commonly held to be true, but utterly without factual basis. As Garlow and Jones explain, it was "secular courts, not church courts, [that] handed down the majority of capital sentences. Those found guilty of witchcraft by the church were usually given nonlethal penalties" (65). And furthermore, Oxford University scholar Robin Briggs clarifies:

A potent myth has become established, to the effect that nine million women were burned as witches in Europe; gendercide rather than genocide. This is an overestimate by a factor of up to 200, for most reasonable modern estimates suggest perhaps 100,000 trials between 1450 and 1750, with something between 40,000 and 50,000 executions, of which 20 to 25 percent were men.

Myth as Truth

Webster's offers yet another slant on the meaning of *myth*—a definition that clearly has a spiritual sense:

[A myth is] a story ... that ostensibly relates historical events usually of such character as to serve to explain some practice, belief, institution, or natural phenomenon, and that is especially associated with religious rights and beliefs.

Even though this definition gives the more original sense of the word, most of us have never given much thought to it. But we need to. This is the only sense in which myth may be considered true. After all, *myth* in this sense isn't some academic distinction. Brown's own gospel myth shows that practically enough. He has brought this sense of myth very much into the forefront of our culture, and that is what accounts for his great success. Brown's novels not only want to explain human practices, institutions, and even natural phenomena, but they also take a stab at explaining our "religious rights and beliefs."

What else would make *The Da Vinci Code* so popular (at least by marketing standards)? It isn't merely that it's "just" a great story. What Brown has ably tapped into is really very simple: It's the ancient power of myth to impart its message at a level much more deeply, much more profoundly, and much more spiritually

History and Myth

Karen Armstrong notes that archaeological studies of ancient graves consistently portray five defining and informative characteristics of myth. All of these elements characterize both Brown's and the Bible's gospels:
1. [Myth] is often rooted in an experience of death.
2. It is often accompanied by ritual sacrifice.
3. It is about extremity beyond human experience.
4. It tells us how to behave physically and spiritually.
5. It speaks of another plane of existence that somehow supports ours (3–4).

than anything we could ever hope to accomplish by another means.

Dan Brown's Gospel Myth

Certain ancient texts, such as *The Gospel of Thomas, The Gospel of Mary Magdalene,* and *The Gospel of Truth,* tell a very different story from the Bible's Gospels. And contemporary books, such as *The Gnostic Gospels* by Elaine Pagels and *Holy Blood, Holy Grail* by Michael Baigent, Richard Leigh, and Henry Lincoln, have popularized these competing ancient gospel accounts that were, until recently, largely inaccessible.

Dan Brown's modern-day myths are effectively furthering these ancient gospel messages, communicating a very different truth from the Christian Gospels and all in a form that just about anyone can understand and enjoy.

In the following chapters, we'll carefully examine each of Brown's gospel stories and compare them to the Bible's gospel stories. We will discuss their historical and factual accuracy in some instances, but as we mentioned in the previous chapter, our primary purpose in this book is not to separate fact from fiction. Rather, we want to carefully examine the religious worldviews presented in each story. These worldviews will help us understand each story's message much more than analyzing the factual and historical minutiae. Life is about much more than details, and stories try to imitate life.

One Is All and All Is One

So what's the truth behind the reality in Dan Brown's novels? His gospel stories and the Bible's gospel stories each represent two essentially irreconcilable worldviews: pagan monism and biblical theism. (Please see the sidebar on page 29 for more information on these terms.) Brown's religious worldview is pagan monism.

As we explore each of Brown's novels, we will show that his worldview is clearly rooted in monism, a philosophical belief that says there is essentially only one kind of substance or ultimate reality (think *mono* = one + ism). For the monist, an independent Creator-God who originated the creation can't exist because creation in the strictest sense never was created; it always has existed and is continually evolving. So the common concept of gods and goddesses would be mere manifestations (children, as it were) of the one substance or unified whole, as you yourself would be.

C. S. Lewis—an Oxford professor, converted atheist, and beloved

Monism versus Theism

- Monism: "Reality is one unitary [organic] whole with no independent parts." Everything shares the same divine nature.
  - ✓ Pantheism: "Equates God with the forces and laws of the universe." God is in everything and everything is God.
  - ✓ Polytheism: "Belief in or worship of more than one god."
  - ✓ Paganism: "Polytheistic belief in which nature and its forces are worshipped as divine."
- Theism: "Belief in the existence of one God as the creative source of man and the world who transcends yet is immanent in the world."

author of both philosophy and fantasy—used a helpful analogy to distinguish pantheism, the belief that everything is God, from biblical theism. In *Mere Christianity,* he wrote that a pantheist believes God is the painting, and there has never been, nor will there ever be, anything else in existence but the painting—anything we want to call a god is just a part of or a different view of the painting. But, according to Lewis,

> The Christian idea is quite different. They think God invented and made the universe—like a man making a picture or composing a tune. A painter is not a picture, and he does not die if his picture is destroyed.... [Christianity] thinks God made the world—that space and time, heat and cold, and all the colours and tastes, and all the animals and vegetables, are things that God "made up out of His head" as a man makes up a story. (44–45)

Irreconcilable Differences

So we have two competing stories before us—Brown's gospel and the Bible's—both claiming to be true. These two gospels tell very different stories about the same characters and events. Just as the conflicting stories of two courtroom witnesses recounting a story can't both be true, neither can these conflicting gospels. Each side supports its respective viewpoint and accuses the other side of conspiring to fool you. There is no avoiding the irreconcilable differences here. The hard reality is, someone—either Dan Brown or the Christian church—isn't telling the gospel truth.

Yet as Brown would have it, Christianity is an evolving story and therein an evolving truth. His gospel story changes with the times. As his *Angels & Demons* protagonist, Vittoria Vetra, proclaims with impassioned conviction, "Religions evolve! The mind finds answers, the heart grapples with new truths" (535).

Despite Brown's well-intentioned aspirations for an evolving religious unity in the world, his gospel cannot reasonably be an evolved form of the ancient Christian gospel any more than darkness can evolve from light. You can't have both. Either the light switch is turned on or it's off; either there is a separate Painter (or Author) or there is only the painting.

As for monism and the argument that its newer pagan manifestations are more evolved forms of Christian belief, consider its historical roots. Monism really has been the major competition against biblical theism since the very beginning of religion. According to the biblical account, it was this worldview that essentially brought about the rift between God and humanity. After all, the Eden crisis wasn't simply about the temptation to eat a forbidden fruit. The heart of the matter was the prospect of being our own gods (Gen. 3:5)—of spreading the wealth of deity, as it were, among all people. So, rather than created beings who would submit to a ruler God, each of us becomes a proletariat god—a comrade within the egalitarian whole that together makes up God.

The rest of the Bible is about the struggle between a vast majority who preferred variations on the monist be-your-own-god theme and a small remnant who clung to the very unpopular theistic notion of just one God, separate from creation. Some claim that monism is simply a more evolved form of theism, but the truth is, these worldviews are ancient adversaries that came into existence at roughly the same time. To this day these same worldviews compete for our hearts and minds. As Drs. Jim Garlow and Peter Jones write plainly in *Cracking Da Vinci's Code,*

> Two views of religion are warring in our day, and simply pretending otherwise won't make it go away. There might be hundreds of factions (religions) with their unique little agendas, but ultimately they all will eventually align themselves under two fundamental alliances: pagan monism and biblical theism. (223; see also Jones's *Stolen Identity*, 19–20)

These are the worldviews that Christianity and Dan Brown are preaching—the context in which their gospel stories take place.

Christianity's Gospel Myth

For Christians, God is more than the Author of history; he must also be the Author of the great gospel myth. We realize that equating the gospel with myth may cause many a Christian to squirm uncomfortably because it evokes all the misconceptions about myth that we just looked at. But this discomfort often stems from a neurotic distrust of story. After all, no true believer wants the gospel story of Jesus Christ to be relegated to "just" a story.

And yet the Christian gospel is arguably the best example of myth in all of human history. Like Brown's novels, it too is a great story of humanity that explains a religion's practices, beliefs, and institutions, as well as natural phenomena. With all the religious traditions and speculations that abound in today's world, it would be good to summarize the plot of the Christian gospel myth so that we can operate on the same playing field when we discuss the Christian gospel with others.

Once Before a Time

In the beginning God created everything, and it was good. (Nowhere does the Bible say God created evil.) He created people in his own image, which meant giving them freedom of choice.

Tempted by the prospect of becoming like God, humans chose to break free from him by disobeying his one command. This choice to separate from God ushered death and evil into the human race, the natural consequences of separation from infinite life and goodness. Evil is the absence of God.

The rest of humanity's story throughout the Old Testament essentially repeated this tragic theme: Humans were born into darkness and tried to be their own light, their own gods. God intervened in a few lives, but the separation still existed.

The Gospel Story Plot in the Bible

Background Context:
- God first created the world and everything in it. Then he created humans in his image (with the ability to choose).
- But humans chose to rebel against their Creator and become their own gods.
- The Old Testament recounts the stories of God's pursuit of humanity to bring them back into relationship with him.
- The Old Testament also promises that a Messiah will one day come to deliver humankind from sin and death.

The Gospel's Plot:
- The Author of history became a character in his own story—Jesus Christ (the only Son of God) was born into the world as the promised Messiah, and he grew up in a humble Jewish family.
- In his early thirties, Jesus began preaching and teaching that the only way to God was by believing in him, Jesus.
- Jesus was tried and crucified for claiming to be God.
- Jesus rose from the dead after three days, proving that death is conquered through him.
- Jesus told his followers to spread the good news that everyone who believes in him can be restored to fellowship with God.
- When Jesus left the earth and returned to heaven, he then fulfilled his promise to send the Holy Spirit to live within those who believe in him.
- The rest of the story: The church is God living inside people rather than alongside them.

Then in the New Testament, God, the Author of history, stepped into the story himself. The eternal Creator took on human flesh and became a baby boy—Jesus, the Christ. He became a character in the story in order to bridge the gap separating humans from himself. Jesus grew up like any other Jewish citizen in the Roman world, and when he was in his early thirties, he started telling people he was the prophesied Messiah.

At the climax of the story, Jesus was crucified because he claimed to be God's Son, making himself out to be equal with God. And because he was God the Son—not separated from his Father by sin—his death was the only legitimate substitute for the death that should come upon those separated from God. When God the Son—the sinless, and therein immortal, human—took on human sin by dying, he bridged the impassable gap.

But tragedy was transformed into victory when Jesus rose from the dead three days later. Jesus' death and resurrection had bridged the gap between God and humanity, and death and sin were conquered. And since Jesus conquered the power of sin and death, he promises that those who believe in him will also overcome sin and death one day.

The gospel story ends with an open-ended proposition: The risen Jesus told his followers (later called "Christians"—those belonging to Christ) to tell this story all over the world so that everyone has the opportunity to cross over the gap to God. The rest of human history is about individual stories and whether people will respond to God's offer to bring them back into relationship with him—out of darkness and into his light. (See 1 Peter 2:9.)

Never the Twain Shall Meet

Dan Brown sees reality and spirituality from a monistic perspective, but the Bible's gospel story is decidedly theistic in its worldview. In Brown's view, God and his creation are one and the same. But from a theistic perspective, God is separate from his creation, and he brought it all into being. He is the Master Painter who made the painting. But then he (as God the Son) stepped into the painting and became part of it himself.

It's worth noting that the incompatibility of monism and theism is also why so many of the increasingly popular, ancient gnostic gospels could never be included in the canon of the Bible. They represent the diametrically opposing monistic worldview, while the Bible is absolutely consistent in its theistic worldview—God is the separate Creator, C. S. Lewis's Artist.

Likewise, with Brown's reliance on the gnostic canon and its monist worldview, there is naturally a world of difference between his and the Bible's respective gospels of the origins of things. The pagan scientist, Vittoria Vetra, aptly sums up the issue for Langdon early on in *Angels & Demons*: "The Bible, of course, states that God created the universe … God said, 'Let there be light,' and everything we see appeared out of a vast emptiness. Unfortunately, one of the fundamental laws of physics states that matter cannot be created out of nothing" (68). The solution she would offer to the creation *ex nihilo* dilemma is that matter actually originated out of energy, and that "pure energy" is the eternally existent "father of creation" (72).

Brown tells us that only the *painting* has always existed; the Bible's gospel tells us that only the *Creator* has always existed and that he created this painting—this story we call reality—relatively recently.

The Myth That Became Reality

The Bible's gospel is truly a remarkable story in spite of all the cultural baggage many of us naturally associate with Christianity. In fact, it's such a remarkable story that many ancient myths predating Christianity foreshadowed the story of Jesus in their own savior-god stories.

Skeptics point to this as evidence that Christianity merely mimicked a tried-and-true theme—as in Robert Langdon's "Transmogrification" theory (see following sidebar). But Christians believe something far more fantastic, yet reasonable: that theirs is the myth that has actually come true. This myth, God's myth, is the very thing for which all other myths in centuries past have yearned and cried out—as if they knew what it must take to right what has always been wrong. In a sense, the apostle Paul spoke to this in his great theological letter to the Romans:

> We know that the whole creation has been groaning as in the pains of childbirth right up to the present time. Not only so, but we ourselves, who have the firstfruits of the Spirit, groan inwardly as we wait eagerly for our adoption as sons, the redemption of our bodies. (8:22–23)

For Christians who understand the Bible's gospel, it doesn't matter which ancient religion or cult might claim first dibs on the

Langdon's "Transmogrification"

The vestiges of pagan religion in Christian symbology are undeniable. Egyptian sun disks became the halos of Catholic saints. Pictograms of Isis nursing her miraculously conceived son Horus became the blueprint for our modern images of the Virgin Mary nursing Baby Jesus. And virtually all the elements of the Catholic ritual—the miter, the altar, the doxology, and communion, the act of "God-eating"—were taken directly from earlier pagan mystery religions (232).

—Dan Brown, *The Da Vinci Code*

savior-god-become-man myth. Christians believe God authored the whole of human history from Eden on, and all other stories—even the pagan myths—are various strains of "groaning" for the promise of deliverance from evil, from death, from all that is clearly wrong with the world. One reason no new myths really exist "under the sun" is because God created the sun, and all stories that follow originate from the one he originated.

In Genesis 3, God confronted Adam and Eve and spelled out the consequences of their great rebellion and spiritual separation from God (known as original sin). Directly addressing the Serpent who, as the Tempter, presented the be-like-God option to Adam and Eve in the first place, God promised to "put enmity between you and the woman, and between your offspring and hers" (v. 15).

But this prophecy had a clear double meaning when God further specified, "[The woman's offspring] will crush your head, and you will strike his heel." Christians know this to be more than a petty enmity between women and snakes. It is the titanic struggle between God and his created being Satan, who rebelled for the same reasons that swayed Adam and Eve: He wanted to be like God.

There would come a day when the Serpent would strike God's heel through a Roman cross, but that same event would bring a crushing blow upon the first rebel and all his followers. Christians have been celebrating the anniversary of that day of Jesus' resurrection ever since, for two thousand years—it's Easter. Paul, at the end of his letter to the Romans, carried forward the image of Jesus' crushing blow, accomplished through his church, and culminating one day in a great final victory: "The God of peace will soon crush Satan under your feet. The grace of our Lord Jesus be with you" (16:20).

The grace Paul speaks of in his closing blessing to the Roman Christians sums up the end of the Christian story. But it begins when God himself took the strike to his heel by stepping into history as Jesus the Son, and through his death and resurrection dealt the crushing blow to the Enemy. Christians believe God wrote the myth into reality, and all others that precede and follow it are pale imitations yearning for the real thing.

Historical Myth

C. S. Lewis believed in the Christian myth with all of his soul. In his autobiography *Surprised by Joy,* he recounted his progression from atheism to general theism to a personal faith in Christ. Then he described a crystallizing moment:

> Early in 1926 the hardest boiled of all the atheists I ever knew sat in my room on the other side of the fire and remarked that the evidence for the historicity of the Gospels was really surprisingly good. "Rum thing," he went on. "All that stuff of Frazer's about the Dying God. Rum thing. It almost looks as if it had really happened once." (178–79)

In another of his nonfiction classics, *God in the Dock,* Lewis expounded more directly on the importance of understanding this Christian myth. He would never have accepted any of our "just a story" marginalizing:

> The heart of Christianity is a myth, which is also a fact. The old myth of the Dying God, without ceasing to be myth, comes down from the heaven of legend and imagination to the earth of history. It happens—at a particular date, in a particular place, followed by historical consequences.... Those who do not know that this great myth became Fact when the Virgin conceived are indeed to be pitied. But Christians also need to be reminded ... that what became Fact was a Myth, that it carries with it into the world of Fact all the properties of a myth. (66–67)

Lewis would undoubtedly have counted Dan Brown's fictional character Robert Langdon among those ignorant ones who are "to be pitied." In *The Da Vinci Code,* Langdon and his British royal historian and mentor, Sir Leigh Teabing, are ironically two more of the "just a story" types who just don't get it. Neither of them will entertain and perhaps cannot even fathom the possibility of a myth that becomes reality. They much prefer their own seemingly saner countermyths of grand conspiracies to deify a historical Jesus that in their reality would have been merely a "great and powerful man" (234). Teabing's protests betray a somewhat pitiful arrogance (by Lewis's standard, anyway):

> "My dear," Teabing declared, "until *that* moment in history [the Nicene Council], Jesus was viewed by His followers as a mortal prophet … a great and powerful man, but a *man* nonetheless. A mortal." (233)

You might more easily forgive the contempt these characters have for the supernatural in favor of the commonplace if they weren't so hypocritical in their devotion to the myth of their own historical Jesus. For example, Teabing's account of the Nicene Council conspiracy, which most real-world scholarship refutes, is more or less presented unapologetically in *The Da Vinci Code* as a real history suppressed by third-century power brokers.

Teabing pronounces,

> History is always written by the winners. When two cultures clash, the loser is obliterated, and the winner writes the history books—books which glorify their own cause and disparage the conquered foe. As Napoleon once said, "What is history, but a fable agreed upon?" (256)

Somehow it doesn't seem to occur to Teabing or Langdon that this same maxim has to apply to what they themselves are claiming as history. Presumably theirs is the really, *really* true history. And certainly, the two of them have agreed upon their fable.

Circular Reasoning

Christians are fond of summarizing C. S. Lewis's classic apologetic defense of the biblical, historical Jesus found in *Mere Christianity*: Jesus had to have been a lunatic, a liar, or Lord. As Lewis candidly put it,

> You can shut Him up for a fool, you can spit at Him and kill Him as a demon; or you
> can fall at His feet and call Him Lord and God. But let us not come with any patro-
> nising nonsense about His being a great human teacher. He has not left that open
> to us. He did not intend to. (55–56)

Yet for many with postmodern (or "Teabing-esque") sensibilities, there should be a fourth option: Jesus as *legend*. Jesus can remain a great human teacher in history who has simply been given mythic god stature over the centuries, much like the embellishments bestowed upon historical figures such as King Arthur or Daniel Boone.

However, many people do believe history can be trustworthy. And for these folks, it matters a great deal that there are so many scholars who agree that the Bible's four Gospels stand up to all academic standards of historical reliability, better than nearly any other verifiably historical documents known to man ... if only it weren't for the pesky matter of this God-man doing those supernatural miracles.

Strangely, Teabing would still like to appeal to the believers in history as well, especially with his cute quip, "The Bible did not arrive by fax from heaven.... It has evolved through countless translations, additions, and revisions. History has never had a definitive version of the book" (231). It's a nice sound bite, echoed in the movie as well, but it will fall flat on the ears of any serious student of biblical history.

Complete manuscripts of the New Testament dating as far back as more than 1,700 years exist today, and certain portions of the New Testament still exist dating back as far as the AD 200s. What's remarkable about all of these ancient documents is actually the opposite of what Teabing asserts—they're amazingly consistent with contemporary translations, with only occasional minor variants in language. One would assume Teabing's (and apparently, Brown's) version of history to be the case under any normal circumstance, but the Bible is remarkably exceptional (miraculous, some would say) when it comes to its verifiable, historical consistency.

But if Teabing's premise that you can't trust any history is true, then Teabing, Langdon, and Brown have no business appealing to history at all. By their circular reasoning, they end up refuting their own arguments for a truer history of Jesus—Nicene conspiracy and all. But then that runs counter to the common wisdom of the millions who love *The Da Vinci Code* for the very reason that it presents historical "facts" throughout its fiction.

History in the Eye of the Beholder

History is a fiction with the truth left out.

—American proverb

History is written by the winners.

—George Orwell, *As I Please*

If all records told the same tale—then the lie passed into history and became truth. "Who controls the past," ran the Party slogan, "controls the future: who controls the present controls the past...." All that was needed was an unending series of victories over your own memory. "Reality control," they called it: in Newspeak, "doublethink."

—George Orwell, *1984*

Nowhere is salvation conceived of as a flight from history as in Greek thought; it is always the coming of God to man in history. Man does not ascend to God; God descends to man.

—George Eldon Ladd, *The Last Things*

Ask the former generations
  and find out what their fathers learned,
for we were born only yesterday and know nothing,
  and our days on earth are but a shadow.
Will they not instruct you and tell you?
  Will they not bring forth words from
their understanding?

—Job 8:8–10

The Gospel Choice

Which gospel story should we choose to believe in—Brown's or the Bible's? Which story is the true, the better story?

While *myth* in common lingo refers to a lie, *myth* in its deeper and original sense (and for the sake of our discussions in this rest of this book) refers to a story that communicates a proposed message of truth about the human experience. It could be said (based upon Teabing's assessment, anyway) that myth might well be more reliable than history. Brown's novels are gospel myths communicating their versions of monist truth; the Christian gospel myth consistently presents the Bible's gospel truths.

The differences between the two gospels are indeed irreconcilable. In which gospel will you place your faith?

2

Stranger Than Fiction

"The system is screwed up. He killed my son. He should have gotten at least 15 to 20 years," [the victim's father] said yesterday. "They're worried about jailing the drug dealers, but these killers are slipping through the system."

The plea is an anti-climactic end to a tumultuous three-week trial last year that included conflicting eyewitness accounts of the shooting, morbid rap lyrics, and a disputed motive.... Prosecution witnesses testified that Wilson [the victim] had a gun, but never removed it from his waistband, while defense witnesses said the victim pulled the weapon and pointed it at Flemming [the accused's cousin].

Although the gun Wilson supposedly brandished was never recovered from the scene of the murder, a jury of 10 men and two women could not decide whether the shooting was justified. After 14 hours of deliberations over four days, the trial ended in a hung jury. (Daly, pars. 6–7, 10)

This news story about a hung jury at a manslaughter mistrial is just one among thousands of all-too-common cases that cause us to sadly shrug our shoulders and admit that the truth may never be known. In our postmodern era, that has increasingly become a problem with history, hasn't it? You can never know for certain what actually happened unless you witnessed events yourself. And even then, contradictory eyewitness accounts repeatedly show that they too can be subject to debate. And that's assuming all the witnesses involved have honest intentions.

Increasing our doubts about knowing the truth are those more sinister reasons for distrusting historical accounts. In *The Da Vinci Code,* the historian Teabing makes an ironic pronouncement: "History is always written by the winners.... 'What is history, but a fable agreed upon?'" (256). This sounds a bit like the equally cynical appraisal by Vladimir Lenin: "Speaking the truth is a petty-bourgeois prejudice. A lie, on the other hand, is often justified by the end" (qtd. in Berzins). But really, who knows whether Lenin actually said this? Perhaps this quote too was a fable agreed upon by the USSR-era winners.

Whether history is recounted by Teabing, Dan Brown, or the Bible's gospel writers, we must still choose what to believe *by faith*. It might be a matter of choosing the most reasonable faith, but it is faith nonetheless. Obviously, even seeing is a matter of believing when it comes to history, because we still have to rely upon others who claim to have seen what happened. They might have been unreliable conspirators for all we know. We still must have faith in the storytellers.

We all have to ask ourselves, can we know a true history? And more fundamentally, can we know that there is such a thing as truth?

How Do You Define Faith?

Now faith is being sure of what we hope for and certain of what we do not see.
—Hebrews 11:1

What Is Truth?

This question—What is truth?—is at the crux of the debate surrounding Brown's novels, especially *Angels & Demons* and *The Da Vinci Code*. Brown proposes worldviews and so-called historical facts in these novels that are in direct opposition to those of biblical Christianity. And we must decide which gospel to believe—Brown's or the Bible's. Both gospels lay claim to eyewitness accounts, but as we've had to admit, that's no certain proof of anything. And in that case, Brown can't claim that his novels contain any definitive historical facts either.

Speaking to the New Hampshire Writers' Project in May 2004, Brown shared why he is cautious about making any dogmatic claims:

> The world is a big place. And now, more than ever, there is enormous danger in believing we are infallible, that our version of truth is absolute, that everyone who does not think like we do is wrong, and therefore an enemy. ("NH Writer's")

That's not to say Brown's novels don't make factual claims. As pointed out in the introduction, plenty of published voices readily distinguish the valid Brown facts from some of his invalid fabrications. But many postmodern readers don't really care to be confused by the facts.

As condescending as that may sound, it's really not intended that way. The real confusion here is between fact and truth. Dan Brown's novels lay claim to several facts about the existence of historical evidence or scientific phenomena, and we can leave those to the PhDs out there to prove or disprove. Brown also uses the terms *facts* and *truths* interchangeably. But the truths that he preaches require some faith too, just as the Christian doctrines of Christ's deity and resurrection do.

Nothing but the Truth

Truth is a word that understandably makes any sincere skeptic a bit nervous. The truth has been abused, distorted, and misconstrued so much throughout history (as Brown's novels are quick to point out) that some people question whether there really is such a thing. Nevertheless, a difference must exist between fact and truth.

Facts must be objectively and indisputably verifiable, and therein as universally free from faith as $2 + 2 = 4$; but truth must be discerned and believed in, and it is often come to by interpreting the facts. Truth requires faith, even when it is a reasoned faith; facts pretty much require our senses and maybe some basic analysis. In essence, a fact is something that has objective reality; it's concrete and can be measured in some way. So by this definition a fact may always be considered truth. But the real question is, *Is truth always fact?*

Imagine a courtroom in which a person on the witness stand raises his hand and repeats the oath, "I swear to tell the truth, the whole truth, and nothing but the truth, so help me God." And he just might do well to take that last part about God's help seriously as he faces the lawyers' interrogations. It's not going to be easy to accurately report everything he's going to be asked to remember.

But why would it be so hard? If he's honest and he's just recounting the facts, then there shouldn't be any debate, right?

Actually, why does there even need to be a trial at all? Can't we simply accept the facts the witness supplies?

To understand the distinction between fact and truth, consider whether this witness can be truthful and yet inaccurate in his recollection of the facts. You don't have to watch many TV courtroom dramas to catch on pretty quickly that witnesses don't always interpret circumstances correctly. The facts themselves may be irrefutable, but the witnesses' recollections of those facts certainly aren't. Conflicting eyewitness testimonies are actually fairly common in today's courtrooms. In the U.S. legal system, a judge and a jury sort through the facts, trying to get down to the truth of the matter—because there is a difference.

Defining Terms

Webster's draws just such a distinction. *Fact* is defined as "a thing done" or "something that has an actual existence" and an "objective reality." Facts themselves are not up for debate. The sun has risen every day since the dawn of human history (or more literally, the earth has rotated on its axis in such a manner as to produce the effect of a sunrise in your little spot of the world). This is a fact.

Whether the sun will rise tomorrow is a matter of interpreting the facts. Not to worry. It's very reasonable to believe that it will, but because it hasn't occurred yet, tomorrow's sunrise is not yet "a thing done" or something that actually exists. Tomorrow's sunrise is not a fact—it's debatable.

But on the definition of *truth, Webster's* gets a bit fuzzier. It uses language that smacks more of the subjective and interpersonal—words like "*relationship, conformity,* or *agreement* with fact." The deeper you get into the definition (and it's a long one), the more you realize that most attempts at describing *truth* get at the human factor of the equation, but only in so much as it is "in accord with what is fact."

Descriptive terms such as *conception, judgment, statement, proposition, belief,* or even *opinion* all bring to mind people who are contemplating, tossing around, and responding to the facts very subjectively. So while facts are about the existence of things independent of human influences (the sun also rises every day on Mars), truth is more about a personal relationship to the facts (that the rising sun makes you wonder if there was a Designer of it).

Truth can be understood by finite humans in terms of its conformity with objective fact. But it is more than the facts. Truth is also personal.

Just the Facts, Sir

In Brown's *Angels & Demons* we are ushered into the novel with certain preliminary "facts": The European nuclear research institute mentioned in the novel—the *Conseil Européen pour la Recherche Nucléaire* or CERN—actually exists. You can "observe" it for yourself on its Web site. Recently the lab succeeded in producing the first particles of antimatter, which is "identical to physical matter except that it is composed of particles whose electric charges are opposite to those found in normal matter" (xi). But by the next paragraph on this page in the book, readers move into "facts" that have been laced with some decided interpretation and innuendo—looking much more like arguments for truth than nondebatables. For instance, Brown says that "antimatter is the most powerful energy source known to man" because "it releases energy with 100 percent efficiency" (xi). Scientists at CERN qualify this "fact" with a less-than-enthusiastic response: "Depends what you mean by efficient ... in *fact* we have to use hundreds of times more energy to create the matter/antimatter pairs" (CERN, pars. 35, 37).

And as for Brown's claim that a "droplet [of antimatter] could power New York City for a full day," he neglects to mention the fact that it would take billions of years to create such a droplet. Indeed, the real CERN physicists point out that they'd be happy to be able to power a light bulb for five minutes with all the antimatter they've ever produced, even if it were possible to contain it (see CERN).

The facts about the existence of CERN and antimatter are indisputable, but whether deadly "larger quantities" of antimatter are a real threat to or salvation for humanity ... well, there's the rub. It makes for a nice thematic device in Brown's novel (salvation versus destruction; angels versus demons), but is it fact, let alone true?

DisCERNible Details

- Contrary to Brown's claims in *Angels & Demons,* CERN is not a Swiss institute but an intergovernmental organization funded by twenty European member states.
- There are no redbrick buildings at CERN, and its architecture does not look like that of an Ivy League school.
- In 1995 CERN was the first laboratory in the world to produce anti-atoms.
- CERN's Large Hadron Collider will be the largest particle accelerator in the world when it's completed in 2007. The collider is being built one hundred meters below ground in a circular tunnel with a circumference of twenty-seven kilometers.
- Dan Brown states correctly that the Word Wide Web was invented at CERN in 1989 by British scientist Tim Berners-Lee.
- CERN does not own any aircraft, let alone an X-33.
- CERN's scientists fight stress not by playing in a wind tunnel but rather by jogging on the CERN campus or skiing in the nearby Jura Mountains.

—From the CERN Web site: www.cern.ch

Truth from Fact

Another well-known story that poignantly makes the distinction between fact and truth is the account of Jesus before the Roman governor Pilate in John 18.

Jesus has become a political hot potato, and Pilate is trying to get to the bottom of the Jewish leaders' demand for Jesus' execution.

> "What is it you have done?" [Pilate asked].
>
> Jesus said, "My kingdom is not of this world. If it were, my servants would fight to prevent my arrest by the Jews. But now my kingdom is from another place."
>
> "You are a king, then!" said Pilate. (vv. 35–37)

The cynicism must have been dripping in Pilate's voice—the irony of the allegation clearly isn't lost on him.

> Jesus answered, "You are right in saying I am a king. In fact, for this reason I was born, and for this I came into the world, to testify to the truth. Everyone on the side of truth listens to me." (v. 37)

And then imagine the climax of this scene: The camera zooms in on Pilate as he turns away, eyes glancing quickly out a window, and then there's a long, awkward silence.

Finally Pilate sniffs as his gaze falls to the floor, and he mumbles,

"What is truth?" (v. 38)

What is truth? That is the bottom line of our examination of Brown's books. And it is the ultimate question each of us must answer.

The *fact* of the matter was that the Jewish leaders were accusing another Jew of a crime that didn't warrant execution under Roman law. Another fact was that a lot of political unrest existed under Pilate's watch. And one more important fact was that whatever anyone was saying, this lowly Jewish rabbi was not even pretending to be a political candidate for king of the Jews, let alone Rome. Pilate knew these indisputable facts.

But the *truth* of the matter was a bit more complicated. Jesus used the word *truth* to mean something completely different from Pilate's meaning. He told Pilate he was born into this world to testify to the truth. It was his message, and it was his story. You'd have to have been following Jesus' story—his ministry—leading up to this moment to get it. It's the essence of what Christians call the "gospel," the good news.

We don't know that Pilate got it, really. He didn't show any signs of getting it. He knew the facts, but he hadn't followed the story. But Jesus points out some people had been following it—his disciples, who had been living his story with him. These are the ones who listened to him—"everyone on the side of truth" (v. 37).

Now you have to ask yourself, who was confused by the facts: Pilate or the disciples who'd been following Jesus' story along with him? Which of these resonates more deeply with your soul: the truth that Pilate had Jesus executed because it was politically expedient or the truth from Jesus' own perspective about his crucifixion? His perspective is reflected in one of the most beloved gospel passages, and it is the definition of what *he* meant by the truth for which he entered into this world:

For God so loved the world that he gave his one and only Son, that whoever believes in him shall not perish but have eternal life. For God did not send his Son into the world to condemn the world, but to save the world through him. (John 3:16–17)

From Jesus' perspective, as recorded in John's gospel, the truth was that God had sent his one and only Son to earth to save all who would simply place their faith in him. But from the perspective of the Jewish leaders, Jesus was a heretical blasphemer for that very same reason: He claimed the title of "Christ, the Son of God" (Matt. 26:63–66). According to the Gospels, it was a fact that Jesus claimed to be God. (See John 8:54–59; 10:22–38.) As to whether it was true, that's the proposition of the whole gospel story.

But the distinction is clear: one fact—the biblical Jesus claimed he was the Christ, the Son of God—but two arguments as to the truth about his identity and purpose.

True to Life

And that brings us back to the challenge of choosing between Dan Brown's gospel stories and the Bible's gospel stories. Both have their own set of facts that serve as an interesting study in and of themselves. For instance, Brown's gospels present a set of facts, such as the founding of the Priory of Sion in AD 1099, the existence of Vatican City, a contemporary sect called Opus Dei, and an artist named Leonardo da Vinci. Likewise, the Bible's Gospels present a set of historical facts: the Roman occupation of Palestine, the historic city of Jerusalem, a first-century rabbi named Jesus, and his followers who would later be called Christians.

From the observable facts, both gospel stories build arguments for their unique truths. But as we have seen, Brown's monistic worldview and the Bible's theism are diametrically opposed. And yet, according to *Webster's* definition, truth must line up with or conform to the facts. The jury must decide which witness's account is true to the facts. We need to decide which gospel story is true to life.

But packaging and presenting a story in a palatable and entertaining form doesn't necessarily make it true to life. Aesop's fables present wise principles in story form, but are the stories true to life? Not really—and that's not their goal. Dan Brown's stories are more than just fables presenting some presumably wise and moral principle. Brown's stories attempt to mimic life. They go beyond the observable facts we experience daily and they seek to interpret those facts at a deeper, more subjective level. They seek to impart truth, to imitate the human experience—what it's like to love and be loved, to have a meaningful existence, and what it's like to die as well.

This is why the protest for Dan Brown's stories being merely fictional stories must fall apart. And this is why much of the debate over the accuracy of his facts can become a distraction. Dan Brown's novels are gospel stories that would proclaim *truth.*

The Magic of Story

Stories are about creating worlds that imitate the world as we know it. The job description of story is fundamentally to imitate life. Whether the characters are talking farm animals, elves and hobbits, priests and scientists, or Dr. Robert Langdon, stories at their core are about imitating the human experience. Accepting this job description of story—imitating life—is a crucial premise to our having any worthwhile discussion about Brown's novels.

The magic of stories has always been their ability to enable us to experience life vicariously, seeing through the characters' eyes, reaping all the benefits of adventure, joy, and truth without suffering the consequences of bad choices and evil circumstances. In story we can go through the school of hard knocks without getting knocked so hard.

The tools stories use have been around for as long as stories have been told: *plot, setting, imagery, characters,* and *theme.* Think of it in terms of your own body. It takes many parts to make up a whole body. In fact, medical science has labeled these parts and has described them in intricate detail to make it easier to identify and diagnose problems. For instance, if you say you're having a hard time with something you ate, your doctor will examine not only your stomach but your entire digestive system. If you say your arm has hurt ever since you slipped and fell on the ice, your doctor will look at your arm and your skeletal system.

Doctors recognize that the parts and systems of the human body are interrelated and interdependent, integrated into a living, organic whole, and that in order to understand and treat the constituent parts, they must understand and examine the whole body. It's the same with story. When we look at its constituent parts, we always do so with an eye toward understanding the whole. *Plot* is the skeletal system of the story—the story line, which is populated by *characters* and takes place at a certain time in a *setting.* In chapters 5–10 we'll offer detailed *plot summaries* of all Brown's novels, which will serve both as a review and a tool for understanding Brown's gospel message as a whole.

On Stories

To be stories at all they must be series of events: but it must be understood that this series—the plot, as we call it—is only a net whereby to catch something else.... If the author's plot is only a net, and usually an imperfect one, a net of time and event for catching what is not really a process at all, is life much more?
—C. S. Lewis, *Of Other Worlds*

But to talk intelligently about *Angels & Demons,* for example, we also have to be able to understand the flesh-and-blood *characters* of Langdon, Vittoria, Ventresca, and the Hassassin. We need to know who these people are and what they believe about their own worlds.

To understand the characters' worldviews, we also need to understand the *setting* of the story, the worlds in which the characters live and breath. In *Angels & Demons,* the setting shifts back and forth between the CERN science community and the Vatican, and it is only by viewing these worlds in which the characters live and interact that we can understand their worldviews.

To believe in the fictional world, we need to be able to visualize it through *imagery*. We learn best through story when we're allowed to experience it vicariously. When the setting is more real because we can see it through descriptive language, because we can see Simon's ghostly face, because we can hear the rasp of the Hassassin's voice, or because we can virtually touch Sophie's hair—that's when story is at its strongest, when it shows rather than tells.

These story elements—characters, setting, imagery, and plot—are all critical to understanding story because they are all critical to understanding life. You're the main protagonist in your own life story, but many other characters also come in and out. Your life is occurring in a time and place—a setting—both of which have a significant impact upon your life. You also see and understand your life through your five senses, and your life is occurring in a timeline, a sequence of events—a plot.

The Stuff of Life

All of these tools of story—and a few more—combine to help us recognize what is commonly called the *theme* in a story. Too often the term *theme* suggests impositions of messages that we and sometimes the authors themselves never saw coming. At its most basic level, theme is simply about repetition. If something happens more than once, it's a theme; the more it happens, the stronger the theme is.

Using our medical analogy, if you had a headache once last week, the reason might be because you didn't get enough sleep. But when you tell the doctor you've had a headache every day for a week, well, now it's a theme, and your doctor will need to diagnose what it means.

In *Angels & Demons* you might notice a theme ringing pretty consistently within the first few pages. The scene begins with Langdon's dream of a young woman joking at his expense that she should have married a "younger man," and then that woman is replaced by an old man "with rotting teeth" and a "lonely grimace." The novel ends with a variation on this same dream.

An *Angels & Demons* Dream

High atop the steps of the Great Pyramid of Giza a young woman laughed and called down to him. "Robert, hurry up! I knew I should have married a younger man!" Her smile was magic.

He struggled to keep up, but his legs felt like stone. "Wait," he begged. "Please ..."

As he climbed, his vision began to blur. There was a thundering in his ears. I must reach her! But when he looked up again, the woman had disappeared. In her place stood an old man with rotting teeth. The man stared down, curling his lips into a lonely grimace. Then he let out a scream of anguish that resounded across the desert.

—Dan Brown, *Angels & Demons*

The dream sets us up to notice other language evoking old age and loneliness: Langdon's home is "deserted" and more like an anthropology museum packed with religious artifacts, including "a young warrior's symbol of perpetual youth" (5). Langdon's reflection in a window suggests to him the image of an "aging ghost." As we put together all of these descriptions, we start to see a theme forming—mortality. And just in case we weren't getting it, the theme is explicitly identified for us: Langdon is acutely aware of being a "youthful spirit living in a mortal shell," although he is only forty years old.

It's one thing to identify a story's theme, but what we do with it is quite another matter. After all, if story imitates life, then figuring out how to interpret a story's themes is akin to interpreting themes in your own life. For that matter, it might even touch on interpreting the very meaning of your life (yikes!). Interpreting life is not easy and is often messy, but that's also what makes story worthwhile.

Instead of seeing that story imitates life, those who protest that Dan Brown's novels are "just stories" infer that stories don't imitate life, or that if they do, life is pretty meaningless and there's no use talking about it. But we believe your life does have meaning, and so must stories that imitate it.

True Fiction

Your worldview naturally affects how you see the world. This is why story for the sake of story alone cannot make it true or worthwhile. Not all stories agree, and surely not all stories are true. In fact, some stories are constructed purposefully to deceive.

White-supremacist racism and extremist violence are two hallmark themes of the novel *The Turner Diaries*, which was brought to the public spotlight because it allegedly inspired Timothy McVeigh's bombing of the Alfred P. Murrah Federal Building in Oklahoma City. Some will argue that the plot, setting, and characters of such a story might imitate certain lives and certain worlds. But in a sense, McVeigh's world imitated the novel—the U.S. Department of Justice and other government agencies consider it "the bible" of right-wing militia groups, and the FBI believes it provided the blueprint for the Oklahoma City bombing.

But is the story "true"?

We must measure the quality of a story by the standard of human experience—how true it is to reality and facts, but also how its reality is informed by truth.

Getting Back to Our Roots

Despite what Dan Brown's characters repeatedly argue, Christians were largely responsible for ushering in the age of scientific rationalism. During this period, Christian theologians developed apologetics (defending the faith by reason) into a refined science, placing more emphasis on the reasons for believing than on faith itself. Its followers, who themselves were fully credentialed, readily embraced the wondrous logic of God's creation according to their particular academic discipline. Despite what Brown often portrays in his novels, to this day there are many experts in almost any scientific field who are Christians and yet have no problem demonstrating the reasonableness of their faith through their profession.

But by the twentieth century, while Western culture (and by default, Western Christianity) had developed a broader view of science, it had also developed a narrower, more utilitarian view of story. Christians even came to distrust stories, viewing them as myths, fables, and fairy tales with pagan origins—nothing that mature, reasonable Christians should indulge in.

At one time Christians owned story much as they did the rest of the arts. The works of the three great Johns of Western literature—

God of the Fairy Tale

"Cinderella" and "The Little Mermaid" and "The Wild Swans" and "The Bremen Town Musicians," when viewed through Christ-colored glasses, have such an authentic aura of the gospel about them.... These tales are remarkably like the stories Jesus told. For Jesus never engaged in mere moralizing. He hadn't the slightest interest in turning His listeners into nicer people or more productive citizens. His parables were never intended to inspire one to greater thrift, industry, responsibility, or patriotism. Instead, they take us by the throat, turn us on our heads, and rattle us to the core.

—Jim Ware, God of the Fairy Tale

Donne, Milton, and Bunyan—are still relevant to believers and non-believers today. But an uncertainty about story persists among many believers today—a distrust of anything that falls short of overtly allegorical preaching.

This kind of pious pragmatism is an affront to the very nature of our Creator-God. Taking this stance undermines the very gospel these Christians would preach, because the God of Christianity is the proto-Author of the human story, and therefore the gospel story.

Christians believe God spoke creation into existence, and by all accounts in Genesis 1, "It was good," even "very good." And yet God didn't seem to have any explicitly pragmatic purpose for creating other than it was just plain good to create. Believe it or not, nowhere does the Bible say that God began this human story for the purpose of saving souls. It doesn't even say he created so that he could have more souls. The only explicit motive we can see in the Bible for God's creativity was simply that it was good.

Then the Author of creation did a really good thing: He created humans uniquely in his own image—"in the image of God he created him; male and female he created them" (Gen. 1:27). Clearly, bestowing his "image" on this part of his creation had nothing to do with human physical appearance or gender, because God is spirit, not human. (See Num. 23:19; John 4:24.) But what, then, did it have to do with?

Wake-Up Call

Most Christians accept that they were created in the Creator's image, but some resist connecting the dots—that is, they refuse to accept that humans themselves were created to be creators. But that's what it actually means to be created in God's image. Anyone who has a mature Christian worldview understands that the act of creating a real story—one that authentically imitates life—is a holy act. When done well, story is about imitating the Creator, the Author of history.

When *The Da Vinci Code* first came out, most Christian churches shrugged their collective shoulders and considered it as just fictional entertainment not worthy of response. They found it hard to believe that anyone could be persuaded by the obviously transparent attempts to repackage the very old and always readily available early-church heresies as evidence for supposedly newly uncovered religious conspiracies.

But now that the movie has been released, the church is beginning to actively engage *The Da Vinci Code* story, and Christian leaders are coming to grips with the power of story to win minds, hearts, and even souls. And as Brown's gospel story continues to increase in popularity, it is also proving to be a powerful apologetic for the pagan-monist worldview. Many rank-and-file believers are wondering whether some of Brown's gospel is true or whether truth even matters. Can't we all just get along and enjoy a good yarn?

Why Can't We Just Get Along?

Many people think Christians are really the problem when it comes to getting along. To be sure, we have all witnessed hostile encounters between Christians and non-Christians over issues of faith and have at times been embarrassed by the behavior of those who claim to follow Christ. And yet believers can and must in good faith agree to disagree with pagans and monists as well as others who hold different religious worldviews. However, we should still try to get along with those of different faiths, treating them with kindness and respect and loving our "enemies" as Jesus commanded (Matt. 5:43–48).

Yet no honest Christian would embrace or endorse the idea that there are many paths to God. We call this unpopular exclusiveness "the scandal of the cross," because it is scandalous to the rest of the world. Brown's stories, on the other hand, have greater appeal, because at least on the surface they seem to be much more inclusive.

But consider exclusivity from the perspective of God's story. Humanity had broken its relationship with God—defied him to his face by effectively saying, "Thanks, but we prefer to be our own gods." Evil, pain, suffering, destruction, and death are all the by-products of this great divorce, as C. S. Lewis called it. As we saw in the previous chapter, the Christian gospel recounts the story of God's gift of salvation, which he offered when he stepped into human history to bring people back into relationship with him. He did this by becoming a man and dying for each human being—past, present, and future.

All anybody needs to do is accept the gift. Yet even though Jesus died for them, most people would still respond with something like "Umm, no thanks. You're not the god I'm looking for. I'll make my own way into eternity." Is it so scandalously exclusive for God to more or less say, "Fine. Good luck with that eternity thing. Because—as you wish—you aren't going to spend it with me?"

This really is why Christians cannot "get along" with Brown's premise that Jesus was a great teacher whose message was "hijacked" by his followers. And for that matter, Christians can't accept Brown's gospel because the Bible's gospel story has just too many impartial witnesses who heard Jesus say things like "I am the bread which came down from heaven" (John 6:41 NKJV) and "He who eats My flesh and drinks My blood abides in Me, and I in him" (John 6:56 NKJV).

But Jesus also said something that was so outrageous, so maddening to the religious leaders of the day, that if it were not really true, the gospel writer would never have included it in his book for fear of death. Jesus looked at the Jews around him and said, "Most assuredly, I say to you, before Abraham was, I AM" (John 8:58 NKJV). Jesus used the unspoken name of God (I AM), which in itself was a great offense to the Jews. But he did more than just speak the unspeakable; he applied that name to himself. He was, with that simple phrase, declaring that *he* was the everlasting God.

Not only would Jesus have been mad to say such a thing if it were not true, but also John would have been equally as crazy to write it down. Sure, start up your own religion if you want, but don't go saying or writing things that are utterly blasphemous to the

Jesus' Seven "I Am's" in the Gospel of John

1. "I am the Bread of Life" (6:35).
2. "I am the Light of the World" (8:12).
3. "I am the Gate for the sheep" (10:7; cf. v. 9).
4. "I am the Good Shepherd" (10:11, 14).
5. "I am the Resurrection and the Life" (11:25).
6. "I am the Way and the Truth and the Life" (14:6).
7. "I am the true Vine" (15:1; cf. v. 5).

—John Walvoord and Roy Zuck, *The Bible Knowledge Commentary*

Jews. That's a great way to get killed. And in Jesus' case, that is exactly what happened.

Becoming a follower of Jesus in the first through third centuries was not exactly a way to ensure long life. Jewish religious leaders who sought to protect the integrity of their beliefs persecuted Christians. Men like Saul of Tarsus (whose life we'll examine a little more closely in chapter 11) went from town to town looking for Christians, dragging them from their homes and taking them to court or, worse, to their deaths. Saul, of course, later had an encounter with the risen Jesus and became a hunted man himself. He is known better today as the apostle Paul.

Soon after the gospel stories and their sequel, the book of Acts, Roman rulers found Christians a convenient group to persecute for shortcomings in the empire. So the question is this: If the early believers simply followed a "great teacher," why did they cling to their beliefs in the face of death? And why would they have invited trouble by assembling writings that included such inflammatory books as John? If these first followers of Jesus did not truly believe he was the risen God he said he was, then they died cruel, hideous deaths for nothing and must have been incredibly foolish.

But if their belief in Jesus was valid, then it is still valid today. And if that is so, then we each must decide whether to become a Christian or to renounce the gift of salvation Jesus offers.

This is the scandal of Christianity. Regardless of your persuasion, you can appreciate why some of Brown's characters would resent this exclusive demand. When Jesus said, "I am the way and the truth and the life. No one comes to the Father except through me" (John 14:6), he was drawing a clear line in the sand, with the promise that he is the only guaranteed way to God.

If you're offered a gift that's sacrificial, no less, and you don't want the gift in the first place, you're really going to resent it. Even so, Jesus made it very clear there's no use wasting your time looking for another gift. His is the only one, and it's absolutely sufficient. The only option available to every human being is whether to accept it.

That's Jesus' story, and true Christians are sticking by it.

3

The Tales of Two Storytellers

He's a storyteller, a man who weaves loose plotlines together to teach a lesson. The stories aren't complicated, and we really don't get to know his characters in depth. But the lessons these stories teach, oh, they've stirred up a number of controversies.

His stories captivate his audience, which is huge, reaching around the world, as his writings have been translated into many languages. This audience, numbering in the millions, has been changed through these stories. And this, in turn, has upset many religious leaders. Books have been written about this storyteller in an effort to debunk his stories and turn people back to what the religious scholars call "truth." Yet in spite of these protests, the storyteller's audience continues to grow, and lives continue to be changed.

The storyteller's name?

Jesus of Nazareth.

You were expecting Dan Brown? Certainly similarities exist between the two. Both teach by telling stories. Both have attracted large numbers of followers and large numbers of critics. Both discuss the interaction between God and humans. Their stories, while differing in their means and ends, are intended to make readers and listeners think.

And while Jesus never mentioned Dan Brown in his gospel stories, Brown tells us what he thinks of Jesus in his novels. He refers to Jesus, through the character Sir Leigh Teabing in *The Da Vinci Code*, as a great prophet (233). Jesus was a great prophet and teacher. And like the other Jewish teachers, or rabbis, of his day, Jesus used stories to convey *truth* to his students, who were also known as *disciples*, which means "learners."

Jesus knew—just as Brown knows—the power of story, of allowing his disciples to place themselves in the tale and consider how they would react and respond. Jesus used stories that were familiar to his hearers, stories that rabbis had told for generations. But he told them differently.

Stories That Nudge and Twist

One day, as Jesus taught from a boat, his disciples asked why he didn't use some other kind of lesson plan. What was up with story after story?

Jesus replied,

> You've been given insight into God's kingdom. You know how it works. Not everybody has this gift, this insight; it hasn't been given to them. Whenever someone has a ready heart for this, the insights and understandings flow freely. But if there is no readiness, any trace of receptivity soon disappears. That's why I tell stories: to create readiness, to nudge the people toward receptive insight. (Matt. 13:11–13 MSG)

In Jesus' day, many rabbis taught with stories that began, "There was a man who had two sons ..." The younger son was almost always a con man, the one who broke the rules. The older son was the righteous one who worked hard to please his father. And the father of these two boys was strong and upright, even in the midst of the younger son's lawless ways.

When Jesus started a particular lesson with "There was a man who had two sons ..." (Luke 15:11–32), those listening had a good idea where this story was going. The younger son, said Jesus, demanded his share of the inheritance and ran off with it to have some fun.

The fact that the father gave his son the money would have scandalized those listening. The son's demand for his inheritance was the same as saying to his father, "I wish you were dead." According to Jewish standards, the father should have exploded with anger at this horrible request. He would have been justified in punishing his rebellious boy while the upright older son

Gospel Stories

Jesus told stories a lot. The gospels of Matthew, Mark, and Luke record dozens of stories Jesus told to illustrate and teach his message. They're called parables or short stories and were used to illustrate moral principles. Following is a list of Jesus' parables as recorded in the New Testament Gospels:

- The lamp under a bowl
  Matt. 5:14–15; Mark 4:21–22; Luke 8:16;11:33
- The wise and foolish builders
  Matt. 7:24–27; Luke 6:47–49
- The new cloth/new wine with old garment/ old wineskins
  Matt. 9:16–17; Mark 2:21–22; Luke 5:36–38
- The sower and the soils
  Matt.13:3–8, 18–23; Mark 4:3–8, 14–20; Luke 8:5–8, 11–15
- Matthew 13 recounts several short parables of Jesus:

°The mustard seed	vv. 31–32; also told in Mark 4:30–32 and Luke 13:18–19
°The yeast	v. 33
°The valuable pearl	vv. 45–46
°The net	vv. 47–50
°The owner of a house	v. 52

- The lost sheep
  Matt. 18:12–14; Luke 15:4–7
- The unmerciful servant
  Matt. 18:23–35
- The workers in the vineyard
  Matt. 20:1–16
- The two sons
  Matt. 21:28–32
- The tenants
  Matt. 21:33–44; Mark 12:1–11; Luke 20:9–18
- The wedding banquet
  Matt. 22:2–14
- The fig tree
  Matt. 24:32–33; Mark 13:28–29; Luke 21:29–31
- The faithful and wise servant
  Matt. 24:45–51; Luke 12:42–48
- The ten virgins
  Matt. 25:1–13
- The talents/minas
  Matt. 25:14–30; Luke 19:12–27
- The sheep and goats
  Matt. 25:31–46
- The growing seed
  Mark 4:26–29
- The watchful servants
  Mark 13:34–37; Luke 12:35–40
- The moneylender
  Luke 7:41–43
- The good Samaritan
  Luke 10:30–37
- The friend in need
  Luke 11:5–8
- The rich fool
  Luke 12:16–21
- The unfruitful fig tree
  Luke 13:6–9
- The lowest seat at the feast, the great banquet, and the cost of discipleship
  Luke 14:7–33
- The lost coin
  Luke 15:8–10
- The prodigal son
  Luke 15:11–32
- The shrewd manager
  Luke 16:1–8
- The rich man and Lazarus
  Luke 16:19–31
- The master and his servant
  Luke 17:7–10
- The persistent widow
  Luke 18:2–8
- The Pharisee and the tax collector
  Luke 18:10–14

The apostles were selective about which stories they recorded in the Gospels, and John didn't record any of Jesus' parables in his gospel. Undoubtedly Jesus told many more parables, because he clearly loved to teach through story.

watched. Immediately, Jesus shocked his audience with a twist in his story.

The audience listened to the story of this immature son as he squandered his inheritance on "wild living" (v. 13). When his money ran out, he was forced to take a job feeding pigs. (*Serves him right,* Jesus' audience must have been thinking.) Finally, the boy had had enough. He decided to return home and ask his father for a job. Whether he was truly repentant or this was just another con he was trying to pull, Jesus didn't say. But his listeners probably had a good idea that it was the latter. And no doubt they also thought they knew what would happen next. They had heard variations of this story many times before. The father would tell his no-good son to hit the road and never show his face at the family estate again. The elder son would congratulate his father for taking a firm stand for family values and for not allowing his sinner son to get away with his actions.

The Twisted Plot Jesus Wove

But Jesus' message was different. The father saw his son approaching in the distance and ran toward him—a shocking development since Jewish fathers stood their ground while their sons ran to them. He grabbed the boy, embracing him in a strong show of unconditional love. Then he ordered his servants to slaughter a cow and prepare a feast in honor of his son's return.

Even more shocking, he took his own family's signet ring—the seal of the father, the symbol that the wearer was the legal representative of the family and the owner of all the family's possessions—and put it on this "sinner."

The elder brother's shock at his father's gracious treatment of the younger son would have been mirrored in Jesus' audience. What kind of story was this? Why was the father not standing up for the law and Jewish traditions? Even today, some reading this story might be inclined to tell the father, "You're an idiot! Get a clue. This kid's just using you again."

In telling the tale with this twist, Jesus went against the religious teachings of that time, never mind the sensibilities of pretty much all times. What would be the result? He would be denounced in the synagogues as a teacher to stay away from. Parents would warn their children against his radical ideas. If there had been a publishing industry at the time, no doubt several dozen books would have been released to debunk Jesus' teachings. He was irresponsible with his words and dangerous with the way he changed the stories that had been accepted for so long.

Brown's Twists and Turns

If Jesus could twist familiar stories to make his point—and today millions follow him as their Savior—why are we concerned when Dan Brown twists stories to make a point? Why are we worried that millions might follow Brown's teachings? Is it merely that we Christians don't like the competition?

The answer to that question lies in the distinction between what Brown believes to be truth and what Jesus believed and taught about truth. And that doesn't just include abstract concepts about truth. As we saw in the previous chapter, truth has a personal dimension to it. Before we jump to conclusions, though, we need to recognize that Jesus' understanding of truth may not be exactly what many of us want to think it is. It actually relates to his biography, not just his message.

If the biblical Jesus is who he claimed to be, he is not only a parable teller, but he is the Author of the great story of humanity—of history. And according to orthodox Christianity, Jesus is also the inspirational Author behind the authors of the Bible (more on that later). With that kind of résumé, it might not seem fair to compare Dan Brown with him. But on the other hand, Jesus' Authorship is essentially what Brown is questioning through his storytelling. And that question is really the premise for our comparisons between Jesus' gospel stories and Brown's.

Who Is Dan Brown?

In many regards, the contemporary Dan Brown is harder to know than the historical Jesus. A great deal of eyewitness, firsthand accounts have been written about the man Jesus, but Brown has purposed to keep out of most public scrutiny. One thing we do know about Brown from his writings is that he is a seeker of truth.

In a 2003 New Hampshire public radio interview, Brown has made public some of his background. He recalls how his parents hid his Christmas and birthday presents and made up riddles and puzzles for Brown to solve in order to find them. "I grew up in a house of mathematics, music, and language," said Brown. "And codes and ciphers really are the fusion of all of those languages. I think people enjoy a treasure hunt."

Brown was born on June 22, 1964, in Exeter, New Hampshire, to Richard and Constance Brown. Richard was a renowned mathematician whose skills brought him to the attention of the National Security Agency (NSA). Offered a position with the super-secret government agency, he chose to remain a teacher at the exclusive Phillips Exeter Academy.

Constance was trained in sacred music and performed as a church organist. Dan attended Sunday school and church with his parents and spent parts of his summers at church camps.

But in a talk Brown gave at the May 2004 New Hampshire Writers' Project, he recalled the struggle he experienced in his upbringing over the dichotomy between scholarship and religion.

> I was lost from day one. Where science offered exciting proofs of its claims, whether it was photos, equations, or visible evidence, religion was a lot more demanding, constantly wanting me to accept everything on faith. Faith takes a fair amount of effort, especially for young children and especially in an imperfect world. ("NH Writer's")

The Life of Brown—the Early Years

The combination of Brown's love of codes and puzzles with his background in science and religion is what makes his novels so unique. It seems that most of Brown's life has been defined by a search for truth. And the twists and turns in his novels reflect that same search, causing the reader to constantly ask, "Whom can I trust to tell the truth?"

In *Angels & Demons*, Ventresca (the *camerlengo* presiding over the election of the new pope) initially seems to be one of the few trustworthy characters committed to truth above all; yet by the end of the novel it becomes evident that he has been living a profound lie. Truth to Brown appears to be fluid, changing from one character to the next.

The Great Impersonal Truth

"Whether or not you believe in God," the camerlengo said, his voice deepening with deliberation, "you must believe this. When we as a species abandon our trust in the power greater than us, we abandon our sense of accountability. Faith ... all faiths ... are admonitions that there is something we cannot understand, something to which we are accountable.... With faith we are accountable to each other, to ourselves, and to a higher truth."

—Dan Brown, *Angels & Demons*

While Brown is confident in asserting the validity of his "facts," at the 2004 New Hampshire Writers' Project he shared why he cannot accept a single concept of truth. On his Web site (Danbrown.com), he quotes himself from that conference as he explained that our religious inclinations are cultural rather than a search for true truth. For instance, if we were born in Tibet, we would more than likely be Buddhist according to Brown. But since we have been raised in the Western world, we are Christian. "We worship the gods of our fathers," he explains.

Raised in the West, Brown says that he is naturally a Christian. His Web site records the critical question posed to him directly at the conference: "Are you a Christian?" Brown's answer was direct: "Yes." Even so, he would not go so far as to say that there is any foundation upon which he has built his beliefs.

Faith is a continuum. We all fall on that line wherever we may fall. And by attempting to classify, and rigidly classify, ethereal concepts like faith, we end up debating the semantics to the point where we entirely miss the obvious. That is, that we are all trying to decipher life's big mysteries. Where did we come from? What happens when we die? Where are we going? What does all of this mean?

And each of us must follow our own path to enlightenment. ("NH Writer's")

Dan Brown's definition of *faith*—that it is a continuum on which each of us occupies different points and that declaring any one definition of faith as truth is simply an argument over semantics—is itself a diversion employing semantics.

Obviously faith can be placed in anything. The question of truth is really about the object of that faith—is the person or thing in which faith is being placed reasonably explained according to the facts and is it true to life? Surely the objective of a faith in, say, Hitler has a different value than faith in the biblical Jesus. Even faith in objective, amoral issues can be on a continuum of either more or less reasonable: Your faith in the sun's rising tomorrow would be far more reasonable than your faith in winning a lottery.

The Life of Brown—Today

Life became more interesting for Brown when he entered a courtroom in England in late February 2006 to face charges that he plagiarized *The Da Vinci Code* from a book titled *Holy Blood, Holy Grail*. Brown had been acquitted in 2005 of similar charges brought by Lewis Perdue, author of *Daughter of God* and *The Da Vinci Legacy*.

But the case in England had an ironic twist to it. *Holy Blood, Holy Grail* was written by Michael Baigent, Richard Leigh, and Henry Lincoln. (Lincoln, who was in poor health at the time of the trial, was not a plaintiff in this case.) If you rearrange the letters in "Baigent," you get "Teabing"; and then Richard Leigh's last name becomes Teabing's first. Of course, Leigh Teabing is one of the main characters in *The Da Vinci Code*. And one of the books in Teabing's study—he mentioned it by name to Langdon and Sophie—was *Holy Blood, Holy Grail*.

Baigent's book sold moderately well after its release in 1982 and created some mild discussion about the authors' thesis; namely, that Jesus and Mary Magdalene married and had children. Their ancestors supposedly went on to form the Merovingian line of French kings and should be recognized as the true royalty in France today. Protecting this great secret was a society known as the Priory of Sion. Another figure mentioned prominently in *Holy Blood, Holy Grail* is a priest by the name of Saunière, which is also the name of the Louvre curator who is murdered at the beginning of *The Da Vinci Code*.

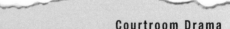

Courtroom Drama

On April 7, 2006, British High Court judge Peter Smith ruled in favor of Dan Brown's publisher Doubleday in the plagiarism case brought by the authors of *Holy Blood, Holy Grail.*

"It would be quite wrong if fictional writers were to have their writings pored over in the way DVC has been pored over in this case by authors of pretend historical books to make an allegation of infringement of copyright," Smith said in his decision. Calling their book "pretend" history added insult to defeat for the plaintiffs.

In an interesting twist, Smith devised and included his own code in his seventy-one-page verdict. He capitalized seemingly random letters, and put other letters and words in italics where it did not seem to make sense. After a few days several people came forward with the solution. The code read, "Jackie Fisher who are you Dreadnought."

Judge Smith is a fan of nineteenth century British admiral John "Jackie" Fisher, who modernized naval vessels and designed the Dreadnought, considered Britain's first modern battleship.

One significant difference between the two books is the outcome of Jesus' crucifixion. The authors of *Holy Blood, Holy Grail* claim not only that Jesus did *not* resurrect but also that he never died on the cross. They theorize that Jesus' crucifixion was an elaborately staged hoax: He was strapped to a cross for a few hours, then he was taken down and smuggled out of Israel where he lived a long life. His wife and child (or children) made their way to France, where they became the bloodline of Jesus, or the true Holy Grail.

In *The Da Vinci Code*, Jesus actually did die on the cross, but the resurrection is cast in doubt. It is metaphorical according to Robert Langdon as he speaks with Sophie:

> Sophie, *every* faith in the world is based on fabrication. That is the definition of
> *faith*—acceptance of that which we imagine to be true, that which we cannot
> prove. Every religion describes God through metaphor, allegory, and exaggeration,
> from the early Egyptians through modern Sunday school. Metaphors are a way to
> help our minds process the unprocessible. The problems arise when we begin to
> believe literally in our own metaphors. (341–42)

Yet just before the plagiarism trial began, Brown said that he would not deny Jesus' death and resurrection: "The resurrection is perhaps the sole controversial Christian topic about which I would not dare write; suggesting a married Jesus is one thing, but undermining the resurrection strikes at the very heart of Christian belief" ("Dan Brown Witness," par. 209). Perhaps he was establishing a strategic distinction between his novel and *Holy Blood, Holy Grail*. Or perhaps he was speaking ambivalently about the hard reality that Christianity is meaningless if there was no resurrection, noncommittally affirming what the apostle Paul declared to the Corinthian believers:

> If Christ has not been raised, then your faith is useless.... And if we have hope in
> Christ only for this life, we are the most miserable people in the world. (1 Cor.
> 15:17, 19 NLT)

Or perhaps Brown believes in a heterodox gnostic interpretation (more on gnosticism in future chapters) in which a man named Jesus (not God the Son) had died on the cross, and the "Christ" spirit left him to ascend to the gnostic Father. Only Brown—and God—know.

The Authors of the New Testament Gospels

The Bible's New Testament contains four different gospel accounts of Jesus' life: Matthew, Mark, Luke, and John. Theories abound—some conspiratorial, some with more scholarly merit—as to the true authorship of these Gospels and many other books of the Bible. Naturally, authorship of any ancient text is hard to prove definitively, but as we have seen, so is most all of history by today's postmodern standards. Just as scholars question the authentic authorship of Homer's poetry or Shakespeare's plays, skeptics will always want to challenge the authorship of the Bible.

Nevertheless, just as with Homer and Shakespeare, it is reasonable to at least grant the benefit of the doubt to Christian scholarship and tradition in assigning authorship to the real, historical figures of Matthew, Mark, Luke, and John. A great deal of excellent ancient and modern scholarship affirms these authorships that must be taken as, in any case, a matter of faith.

The first three gospels are often called the Synoptic Gospels because they tell the same story about Jesus with very similar language, information, and sequences of events. The word *synoptic* can be broken down into *syn* (together with) and *optic* (seeing).

John's gospel, on the other hand, focuses on different events in Jesus' life and seems to organize them somewhat by themes rather than by linear chronology. By all scholarly standards, the four independent gospel voices present a remarkably consistent historical figure named Jesus, seen from different perspectives.

Matthew

Matthew's gospel was written, by most biblical scholarship's account, somewhere between AD 50 and 70. The author, for whom the book was named, was one of the inner circle of twelve Jewish disciples whom Jesus called to follow him. (See Matt. 9:9–13.) He was a tax collector whose life changed profoundly when Jesus called him, because most decent Jews despised tax collectors, and for good reason. They were essentially traitors and informers who had abandoned their own people, much like the French Vichy government under Nazi rule.

Tax collectors often extorted their own people, overcharging taxes due to Rome and lining their own pockets. When Matthew left his work to follow Jesus, no doubt his reputation as a tax collector dogged him at least for some time. In Mark and Luke, Matthew is referred to by his other name, Levi. And as one of the Twelve, he would have been an eyewitness to Jesus' ministry.

If a conspiracy arose to assign authorship to Matthew when he didn't write this gospel, it's strange that he would have been chosen above the other disciples. He was a relatively unknown and rarely mentioned apostle; Andrew or his brother Peter would have seemed more authoritative, or perhaps one of the two sons of Zebedee.

Mark

Most biblical scholars agree that Mark is one and the same person as John Mark (*John* would have been his Jewish name and *Mark* his Latin name). He's mentioned several times in the book of Acts and in the Epistles, those letters in the latter half of the New Testament that the apostle Paul wrote to the early church. Mark was a young second-generation Christian who had known the disciples firsthand and accompanied Paul on his missionary journeys. He was also closely associated with Peter, and strong evidence shows that he would have been with Peter in Rome during the last days of Peter's life.

Good scholarship makes a strong case that Mark's gospel was written within the first century AD, just decades after Jesus' death—most likely just shortly before AD 70 and the destruction of Jerusalem.

Luke

Luke was most likely a Gentile (a non-Jew) by birth, apparently well educated in Greek culture and a physician by trade. He, like Mark, was a close companion to Paul on his early missionary trips. He wrote not only the gospel of Luke but also its companion, the book of Acts, which recounts the early church's growth and outreach.

Like Mark, Luke would also have written his gospel account within decades of Jesus' death. And while he acknowledged that many others had written of Jesus' life (see Luke 1:1), he didn't suggest that he had relied on such accounts for his own writing. Rather, he insisted that he researched carefully and drew directly from firsthand eyewitness accounts. (See v. 2.)

John

John's gospel is a firsthand eyewitness account of Jesus' story. John was one of the Twelve called by Jesus, and he was a very close friend to him. In apparent humility, John never mentioned his own name throughout the gospel but rather deferentially referred to himself as "the disciple whom Jesus loved," as if to say that Jesus' love was what defined him. If John did indeed write the gospel, then it would make perfect sense that he would have maintained anonymity. If he wasn't the author, then it would be hard to explain why a disciple who was so close to Jesus was singled out to remain anonymous.

Like the other gospels, many scholars place the authorship of John's gospel within the first century following Jesus' death, around the late 80s. But some more recent scholarship makes a strong case for authorship between AD 50 and AD 70, again, just decades after the death of Jesus.

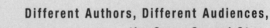

Different Authors, Different Audiences, the Same Gospel Story

- **Matthew**—This gospel's emphasis and audience was Jewish. Matthew emphasized Christ's lineage as "the son of David, the son of Abraham" (1:1). Throughout the text, a number of Old Testament prophecies are quoted and referred to as "fulfilled." Several other thematic elements build upon Matthew's clear message that Jesus is the Messiah who came to conquer the world for God's kingdom, not through military might, but through peace.
- **Mark**—Because of Mark's emphasis on discipleship and suffering, some argue that he may have been writing to Roman Christian audiences who were facing persecution, as well as non-Christian Roman audiences who might turn from Caesar worship to Jesus the Messiah. He apparently drew from authoritative sources and recorded them in the literary form of a gospel text.
- **Luke**—Luke was a Gentile convert whose emphasis upon the universal message of the gospel seems especially personal. Being the thorough, analytical researcher that he apparently was, Luke presented the most comprehensive account of Jesus' life. His gospel accounts also included frequent references to outcasts from Jewish society.
- **John**—This gospel's approach to Jesus' story is different from the Synoptic Gospels, suggesting that it was written independently of the others and that John's purpose was to present Jesus' story less chronologically and more thematically. The gospel's format and style appears as if it would appeal more to Greek thinkers and serve as a response to false teachings that were developing in the early church. Clearly the major theme and purpose of John's gospel was to help people understand the meaning of Jesus' life so that they may believe in him.

In the Spirit of the Word

Whenever we as Christians discuss the authorship of any portion of the Bible, it's important we understand that our faith is based upon the conviction that the Scriptures are uniquely inspired by God. We believe that God is not only the Author of history but the Author of all the canonical Scriptures.

How exactly God authored his Word through men has been the subject of a great deal of debate and speculation, especially during the last century. But we believe this is exactly what happened. As Christ followers we accept by faith Paul's emphatic premise: "All Scripture is God-breathed" (2 Tim. 3:16; see also 1 Thess. 2:13 and 2 Peter 3:15–16).

We believe that God's impact upon the writing of the Bible is much greater than that of Shakespeare's figurative muse. We likewise believe that this is how the Bible could remain so coherently consistent in its message, even though it was written by many different authors, in three different languages, and over the span of several centuries.

Furthermore, it seems not only reasonable but also to be expected that God would direct and protect the canonization of select books of the Bible in later centuries. If God had a direct hand in the Bible's development, he would certainly have had a hand in its preservation.

Skeptics like Brown's characters Teabing and Langdon would scoff at the idea; but if, as they say, history is so uncertain and unknowable, then why would such an explanation be implausible? That is, of course, if you're a theist. But if you believe, as a monist does, that God is everything—rather than a separate person—then inspiration that is any more special than Shakespeare's would be hard to swallow. Getting to know the coauthor of the Bible—God— well, that's a tall order. Yet from the Christian perspective, that is exactly the reason the Gospels were written. If God the Son, the Creator of the universe, became a man and lived among us, then that means the Author of all history, who is also the Author of the Bible, became a character in history and in the Bible. And if that's true, then all we need to do to know the Gospels' Author is to get to know Jesus.

The Tales of Two Storytellers

Who Is Jesus?

When Jesus called people to him, he did so most often with a simple two-word phrase: "Follow me." This call, however, was anything but simple. The path Jesus walked—and called his disciples to walk with him—was one of hardship, rejection, suffering, and death. He did not promise his followers wealth and riches. He did not say there would be political victories. He did not offer a better life now. There was no "continuum" of faith as Brown suggests. There's always been only one way to be a follower of Jesus, and that's to follow on his terms.

Truth Is a Very Personal Thing

Brown's understanding of truth varies significantly from the Bible's consistent teaching about it and from the truth teachings of Jesus. However, Jesus did preach a very personal truth. That's because when it comes to Jesus' take on truth, the question is not which truth to follow but rather which person. That's where the roads of Brown's gospel of Jesus and the Bible's gospel of Jesus diverge. It's not merely a question of whether the message of the Bible's Jesus is the only way; the real issue is whether the *person* of Jesus Christ is the only way—the only one to follow and the only one who can truly save.

Amazingly, Jesus really didn't say he had come to teach *about* objective truth; he said he *was* Truth—"I am the way and the truth and the life" (John 14:6). Because Jesus claimed to be the embodiment of truth, that would mean everything he said and did was the truest of true. But the truly radical proposition of Christianity is that this God-the-Son Jesus *is himself Truth*.

This point is one that Christians and those who agree with Dan Brown butt heads over. Because for Christians it's not just a matter of assenting to our version of truth; it's a matter of knowing Truth personally—then the rest will follow. And when it comes to talking about a person, we can't define who a person is or isn't according to our own standards or preferences. Modernists and postmodernists may disagree on the relativism of truth, but they must agree on the absoluteness of any individual's personality—of who you and I are as unique, self-aware individuals.

For better or for worse, a person is who he or she is. And like him or not, Jesus is who he is—or as God said to Moses, "I AM WHO I AM" (Ex. 3:14 NKJV). When Dan Brown and so many others challenge Christians to compromise the truths of Scripture and accommodate other truths, what they're really asking Christians to do is to change the person Jesus himself claimed to be into someone entirely different.

That's the really hard thing about authentic Christianity: It's not merely some propositional theory to accept or reject. It's about a person—*the* personal Truth who became a flesh-and-blood human. This is why people must decide whether to become a Christian or acknowledge their faith is in something else than the one personal God and Creator, Jesus the Christ—they really should come up with another name for their particular faiths, for that matter. Monism might be a good start because the essence of the monist worldview is that all paths are one and the same. But remember, Christians by definition are theists who believe in a separate God who created the world and intervenes in it. And the ultimate intervention by God himself is defined by the gospel story of Jesus the Christ, who said, "I am the only way—if you know me, you know God the Father" (John 14:6–8, author's paraphrase).

That is Jesus' truth: knowing God the Father personally by knowing God the Son personally. And as absolutely uncompromising as that might seem, it's really no less reasonable than the conditions of your relationship with your best friend. For a friendship to be real, it too must be uncompromisingly based upon knowing and accepting your friend for who he or she is. You can't have a real relationship with anyone, let alone God, if you're going to operate on the premise that your friend is who you want him or her to be. Your friend is who your friend is, not some contrivance inside your head. (And if he or she is a contrivance inside your head, well, then a good therapist might do better at helping you sort that one out.)

Granted there is the reality that you're always getting to know your friend better and better, and so there is the prospect of changing and increasing knowledge of that person. But you're not the one defining who that person is. The essence of who is that person isn't what's changing; it's your knowledge of that person that grows.

That's why we Christians tend to scratch our heads when skeptics argue, "Well, my God would never cause pain." From a theist's perspective, that makes no more sense than saying to your friend, "Well, you're my friend, so you can never cause anyone pain."

What If God Were ... Alive?

An "impersonal God"—well and good. A subjective God of beauty, truth and goodness, inside our heads—better still. A formless life-force surging through us, a vast power which we can tap—best of all. But God Himself, alive, pulling at the other end of the cord, perhaps approaching at an infinite speed, the hunter, king, husband—that is quite another matter. There comes a moment when the children who have been playing at burglars hush suddenly: was that a real footstep in the hall? There comes a moment when people who have been dabbling in religion ("Man's search for God!") suddenly draw back. Supposing we really found Him? We never meant it to come to that! Worse still, supposing He had found us?

—C. S. Lewis, *Miracles*

Your relationship with a person doesn't define that person. That person just *is*. To a theist's way of thinking, and a Christian's in particular, God just is.

Monists will readily embrace a theology that has them defining God on their terms, because monists are part of God and God is part of them. But as appealing as that may seem, there really can't be any kind of personal relationship with such an all-things-are-god God—no more than you might have a relationship with a toaster, which to a monist is technically part of God too. (But if you do have a relationship with your toaster ... yeah, the therapist thing again.)

The Christian proposition is necessarily and fundamentally about intimate relationship with a very personal, love-defining God. So when Dan Brown calls himself a Christian, is that what he means? Can there really be, as Brown says, many different definitions of what it means to be a Christian? Are you a Christian if you simply call yourself one?

What's in a Name?

Shakespeare wrote about an identity crisis of similar sorts in his great work *Romeo and Juliet.* Wishing with all of her heart that her beloved Romeo did not bear the family name of her father's enemy, she muses, "What's in a name? That which we call a rose / By any other name would smell as sweet" (2.2.43).

We can, as Brown put it, debate over the semantics of what's in a name like *Christian.* But lovers of Christ know that, finally, who we call a Christian, by any other name would smell as sweet ... because that name is Christ. Christians are followers of the Christ—Jesus— who scandalously insisted that he personally is the only way to God. There is no quibbling over semantics on this point. It's what the Jesus of the Bible proclaimed, and it's what those who would be Christians must believe.

The term *Christian* was first used for the followers of Jesus at Antioch in the middle of the first century. (See Acts 11:26.) The suffix *-ian* means "belonging to the party of." Thus, believers in Antioch were recognized as being of the "party" of Christ. Something in their way of living and believing made them identifiable as Christians, a group distinct from other Jews. It was not just that they had been born in a certain land at a certain time as Brown suggests.

The word *Christos,* or Christ, is the Greek word for "anointed one"; from the Hebrew we have the equivalent, "messiah." This name was used in Jesus' time of someone the Jews thought would be their prophesied deliverer from oppression. And when Jesus came on the scene, some believed that he might save them from Rome's oppressive rule.

But Jesus made it clear this was not the reason he'd come. As we read in the previous chapter, Jesus told the Roman governor Pilate, "My kingdom is not of this world. If it were, my servants would fight to prevent my arrest by the Jews. But now my kingdom is from another place" (John 18:36). Jesus never expressed the slightest interest in setting the local political systems right. The kingdom he was about was God's, not this world's.

But if Jesus wasn't interested in an earthly kingdom, what would he deliver the Jews from? In what sense was he the *Christos*—the anointed deliverer? Jesus was constantly calling people to repent, which means to turn away from and renounce something. He called people to turn away from the kingdom of this world and be united with God's kingdom, with Jesus himself. He came to deliver people from their hopeless state of separation from God, to deliver them from sin, not Rome.

Therefore, anyone claiming to be a Christian must belong to *Christos* (the deliverer from the terrible state and effects of being separated from God). If that is not what Dan Brown and any other would-be Christians believe, then they shouldn't really call themselves Christians—any more than a tulip should be called a rose.

The Sweet Perfume

But thanks be to God, who made us his captives and leads us along in Christ's triumphal procession. Now wherever we go he uses us to tell others about the Lord and to spread the Good News like a sweet perfume. Our lives are a fragrance presented by Christ to God. But this fragrance is perceived differently by those being saved and by those perishing. To those who are perishing we are a fearful smell of death and doom. But to those who are being saved we are a life-giving perfume.
—Apostle Paul, 2 Corinthians 2:14–16 NLT

Yes, a tulip is a tulip regardless of what one calls it. It doesn't do any good to call a tulip a rose because a rose is easily distinguished by its sweet smell. Authentic Christians have the distinctively sweet smell of *Christos*—their one-and-only, anointed God-the-Son deliverer. And this they believe is because the Christ has transformed them into real roses.

The Personal Jesus—Then

Not everyone in Jesus' day could accept his terms of transformation, though. In the book of Luke, we read of some who found Jesus' conditions too demanding:

On the road someone asked if he could go along. "I'll go with you, wherever," he said.

Jesus was curt: "Are you ready to rough it? We're not staying in the best inns, you know."

Jesus said to another, "Follow me."

He said, "Certainly, but first excuse me for a couple of days, please. I have to make arrangements for my father's funeral."

Jesus refused. "First things first. Your business is life, not death. And life is urgent: Announce God's kingdom!"

Then another said, "I'm ready to follow you, Master, but first excuse me while I get things straightened out at home."

Jesus said, "No procrastination. No backward looks. You can't put God's kingdom off till tomorrow. Seize the day." (9:57–62 MSG)

Some think that to follow Jesus means to work hard at obeying certain rules and regulations or living by a list of dos and don'ts. Just such a person approached Jesus to see what rules were most important to follow. Jesus told him to keep the commandments. The young man asked, "Which ones?" (Matt. 19:18). After all, the Jews had a list of 613 laws in the books of Moses. Some were certainly more important than others. What did Jesus think were the most important laws?

Jesus replied, "Do not murder. Do not commit adultery. Do not steal. Do not testify falsely. Honor your mother and father. Love your neighbor as yourself."

"I've obeyed all these commandments," the young man replied. "What else must I do?"

Jesus told him, "If you want to be perfect, go and sell all you have and give the money to the poor, and you will have treasure in heaven. Then come, follow me." But when the young man heard this, he went sadly away because he had many possessions. (Matt. 19:18–22 NLT)

Jesus was not saying that all his followers must take a vow of poverty; what he was saying is that totally forsaking all—possessions, family, status, ambition—is key to being his disciple.

There is yet another requirement Jesus set forth for being his follower, one that demands the ultimate sacrifice: "If anyone desires to come after Me, let him deny himself, and take up his cross daily, and follow Me" (Luke 9:23 NKJV). To follow Jesus—to be a Christian—we must be willing to leave our families, to lay aside all our possessions, and be ready every day to die. This kind of Christianity—the kind Jesus was calling people to—was hardly a continuum.

The Personal Jesus—Today

It's rather ironic that Brown would like to relegate Christianity to a Western-only religion. Paul, following Jesus' cue, preached the gospel to non-Jews in increasingly distant and foreign regions. (See Matt. 28:19–20; Acts 1:8; Rom. 15:20; 2 Cor. 10:16.) Christianity originated as a Jewish sect in the Middle East, and because of the absolute universality of Jesus' gospel truth, it spread in just two millennia from Jerusalem to Judea to Samaria and finally throughout the world.

Today millions of committed Christ followers in Asia, Africa, and the Middle East would object to the inaccurate and stereotypical description of Christianity as a Western religion. Christians of every nationality know they are not of this world (see John 15:19; 17:14–16); they know that region and culture are fundamentally irrelevant to the one-way faith in Jesus Christ. After all, would a true God relegate truth to a particular region or culture?

For Christians in the United States, Brazil, Cuba, North Vietnam, and North Korea; for the followers of the *Christos* in Canada, South Africa, Egypt, Iraq, and Iran; for those in Mexico, China, Australia, and the United Kingdom who know the way to God through Jesus alone; for every believer in Austria, Germany, France, Romania, Russia, and Yugoslavia—for literally every nation in every corner of the world there are those who know Jesus is the Christ, the living Creator, God the Son.

Of course, many people say they're Christians, ardent followers of Christian traditions and principles, and yet they would never claim to have a personal relationship with a personal God. Perhaps to them such a faith suggests psychosis or, at best, egocentricity.

But a remnant of Christ followers, who actually number in the millions, really do believe they have a personal relationship with Jesus. To these believers, this personal kind of relationship with their God is no opiate. They know it to be the reason for their existence. They know it firsthand to be the meaning of life and why they were created.

These believers know the gospel stories of Matthew, Mark, Luke, and John. They have read in their own languages the parables of Jesus, and they have come to believe that the Bible is more than an anthology or great Jewish literature handed down through the centuries. They know that God himself was guiding its unique writings. They know this to be true through faith.

They have friends and loved ones who, like Dan Brown, are seekers who want to believe that faith is a continuum and is relative to different religions. They pray that these friends will come to know not merely the abstract concept of truth but also the literal person of Truth. Some Christians may express their faith a little awkwardly, some a little too fervently or even disrespectfully, and some may try to explain in simplistic terms the meaning of an infinitely complex but truly personal God.

It's a strange thing, this Jesus himself being Truth. But Christians believe that if such truth is stranger than fiction, it's also a far, far better thing.

4

The Gospel of Conspiracy

Here are the facts.

Just after midnight on August 31, 1997, Diana, Princess of Wales, former wife of Prince Charles, walked through the kitchen of the Ritz Paris to a waiting Mercedes. With her was Dodi al-Fayed, her boyfriend, and Trevor Rees-Jones, her bodyguard. Behind the wheel was Henri Paul.

Dodi sat directly behind Henri Paul, the driver; Diana was on his right. Rees-Jones, seated in the front passenger seat, was the only one to fasten a seat belt. As soon as the doors closed, the car sped off into the night, first heading south on Rue Cambon, then along Rue de Rivoli, which took them past an Egyptian obelisk at the Place de la Concorde. By the time they reached the Point de l'Alma tunnel, Paul was up to at least sixty miles per hour, probably a bit faster. Trailing a quarter mile behind was the paparazzi, hoping to get a shot of Diana with her lover.

But something happened in the tunnel. By one account, Paul attempted to pass a slower-moving car and lost control. Another unverified story says the car was sideswiped by an unidentified vehicle. What is known is that the right rear of the Mercedes hit the tunnel wall, sending the car into a spin. Paul attempted to correct by turning hard to the left, but the Mercedes hit the concrete barriers that separated the lanes, giving Paul and the other occupants no chance.

The engine was pushed straight back into Henri Paul and Dodi. Princess Diana was near death. Rees-Jones was badly injured but would survive. It was just a few minutes shy of 12:30 a.m.

A few minutes after Diana's death was announced, the conspiracy theories began to circulate. They ranged from the almost believable (Diana was killed because England's monarchy could not tolerate the idea that she might marry al-Fayed, a Muslim) to the less-than-believable (Diana faked her death to get away from the limelight). Another story claimed that strobe lights flashing inside the tunnel had blinded the driver. But the most fantastic theory could be found on Ru Mills' Web site.

Ru Mills, the pseudonym for Rayelan Allan, said she received a phone call the night of Diana's death informing her that the Point de l'Alma tunnel was built on an ancient pagan site where people worshipped the goddess Diana. This pagan site, said the source, was a direct portal to the throne of heaven. According to Mills, *pont* is translated as "bridge" and *alma* as "soul"—thus, the Bridge of Souls.

Mills says she did more research and discovered that this place was where kings in the Merovingian line assembled for battle, and that those who died in battle there ascended directly to heaven. Further research showed that Diana was of Merovingian descent. The Merovingians, according to Mills, are the true kings of Europe, descendants of Jesus and Mary Magdalene and King David. She concluded that Princess Diana was sacrificed on the altar of the goddess Diana to take her place as queen of heaven and rule over the earth. There is more to this theory, but we think you get the point.

It's surprising that Dan Brown hasn't weaved this into another Robert Langdon novel. Surely he could find clues pointing to Diana's ritual sacrifice in some fifteenth-century artwork, couldn't he? And what about the Egyptian obelisk the Mercedes passed just before it crashed?

The conspiracy theories surrounding Diana's death continue to capture the imagination nearly a decade later. But conspiracy theories are nothing new. In the Bible Absalom conspired against his father, King David, and stole the throne for a period of time. The Jewish leaders of Jesus' day conspired with Pontius Pilate to say that the disciples had stolen Jesus' body as a way to cover up the resurrection. Mad emperor Nero concocted a tale to blame the burning of Rome on the Christians. And, of course, there is the whole "who killed JFK?" thing.

Some conspiracy theories are relatively harmless, like the one that said the Canadian rock band Klaatu is actually the Beatles reunited. Other rumors, however, can create a great deal of discomfort, mistrust, and hardship. For instance, a rumor circulated following Hurricane Katrina that government officials deliberately flooded certain sections of New Orleans inhabited by African Americans. Residents who believed this rumor, or suspected it might be true, found it easy to rationalize the looting that destroyed many businesses.

Anatomy of a Conspiracy

We humans are curious. "That's just how it is" has never been a good enough explanation for what we don't understand. We couldn't see across the ocean, so we built boats that allowed us to explore beyond the horizon. We didn't know what was on top of the mountains, so we found a way to climb up to see for ourselves. Even the moon begged us to find a way to explore its surface.

When we read, hear about, or experience something we don't understand, we search for an explanation. Sometimes it is a simple matter, especially if it only involves one of us. ("I don't understand how my checking account can be overdrawn. Oh, wait. I forgot to enter this withdrawal. Now I see.") But when the situation is more complex and involves many people—and maybe even takes place over a period of many years—the facts are not as easily discerned. This is where conspiracy theory enters the picture.

A good conspiracy theory seeks to explain something we may not have even known needed explaining. It will try to impose order on a chaotic situation, even if the explanation stretches credulity to the breaking point. For instance, we can't understand how Lee Harvey Oswald could have gotten off that one lucky shot from such an awkward angle at the Texas School Book Depository, so we come up with a theory that involves more than one gunman, the CIA, the Cubans, the Mafia, Lyndon Johnson, and extraterrestrials. Thus, a conspiracy theory is born.

Conspiracy theories are typically intricate, complicated explanations for events that are difficult, if not impossible, to understand. After all, if you can understand the theory, where is the conspiracy? A conspiracy theory should contain many different "arms" in its explanation of the event—thus the commonly used term *octopus theory*—because if one arm of the octopus theory is shown to be false, the other arms, or aspects, of the theory continue to function. If someone attempts to disprove the conspiracy theory, other clues will show it to be true. The more leads or arms to the theory, the better.

The best conspiracy theories are those that affect the largest number of people. The larger the conspiracy, the more impossible to prove it is true or false.

Of course, the capstone to conspiracy theory is this: Even if undeniable proof exists that part of the theory is false, those who cling to belief in the conspiracy will say that "they"—a mysterious group of powerful people—have covered up the truth. "They" control society in general and thus are able to hide their activities and true intentions even from those who think they know the truth. Of course we have proof that the conspiracy does not exist. That's what "they" want us to believe.

Who Are "They"?

Conspiracy theorists generally agree that a group of wealthy, influential people control—or attempt to control—the world's economic, political, cultural, and religious affairs. Most of these groups, according to the theories, have been organizing for centuries, preparing for the day when they will step out of the shadows and exert their total control over the world. These groups include

- the Illuminati
- the Freemasons
- the Council on Foreign Relations (CFR)
- the Trilateral Commission
- the Vatican
- the Institute of International Bankers

Each organization desires, of course, the establishment of the New World Order. They communicate with one another with secret handshakes, code words, signs in artwork and architecture, even symbols on paper currency. They have infiltrated governments, religious organizations, the intelligence community, major corporations, and—most important—the media. Thus, when it is reported on radio or television, in magazines and newspapers, or on legitimate Web sites that these organizations are not what some people think they are, the response of those looking for conspiracy is "Of course that's what 'they' would say. 'They' are in the media, too."

These groups are popular in fiction, too. In *Angels & Demons*, Langdon listens to the Hassassin reveal his diabolical plan:

> *Jesus,* Langdon thought, *they've got someone on the inside.* It was no secret that infiltration was the Illuminati trademark of power. They had infiltrated the Masons, major banking networks, government bodies. In fact, Churchill had once told reporters that if English spies had infiltrated the Nazis to the degree the Illuminati had infiltrated English Parliament, the war would have been over in one month. (152)

A key attribute of conspiracy is the inability to disprove anything, even the most ridiculous of claims. Former BBC sports reporter David Icke has unique ideas about world history and where civilization is headed. A visit to his Web site shows his interest in the Illuminati, Freemasons, bankers, and mind control—the usual suspects. But he throws in an unusual twist by saying that reptilian humanoids are actually controlling our world. Some of these reptiles masquerading as humans include, according to Icke, George W. Bush, Queen Elizabeth, Henry Kissinger, and Kris Kristofferson. (We always did suspect ol' Kris was not one of us.)

You think Icke is crazy? You think there is no way reptiles could take on human form and rule our nations? Go ahead—prove him wrong. Even if you were to conduct a complete physical on each person listed and show with lab work and X-rays that they appear human, Icke would say that these reptiles are really, really good at what they do and can completely change their physiological makeup to fully match that of humans.

See what we mean?

Theories like those put forth by Icke are fairly easy to dismiss, but others are not. Even when we have historical records proving, for instance, that the Illuminati ceased to exist by the end of the eighteenth century, we have statements like those of Dan Brown in *The Da Vinci Code* that "… history is always written by the winners" (256). Thus, historical fact itself is cast aside as unreliable since "they" control the writing of history. So, just who can be trusted?

Perhaps the better questions to ask are "Why do we not want to trust those who appear trustworthy?" "What is the attraction of believing the unbelievable?" "Why do people cling to conspiracy theories?" and "Why invent fear?"

We live in an era of unsurpassed safety. Most contagious diseases have been eradicated or can be controlled through medication. Heart surgery is almost as common as tooth extraction. Seat belts and air bags can help us survive car crashes.

We no longer have to stumble in the dark when it comes to knowing what is happening in our world. Communication is almost instantaneous thanks to e-mail, cell phones, and the Internet. When severe weather threatens, we can tune in to our weather stations ahead of time so we won't be taken by surprise. This instant communication should make us feel more secure, but somehow it doesn't.

Marc Siegel, an internist and medical-school professor, wrote in his book *False Alarm: The Truth About the Epidemic of Fear:*

> At a time in history when there are no true scourges, the population is controlled through fear. Rather than enjoy the safety that our technological advances have provided us, instead we feel uncertain. Respiratory masks and other paraphernalia meant to shield us actually spread panic more effectively than any terrorist agent by sending the message that something is in the offing. Our personal fear alerts are turned on all the time. Fear is not intrinsically pathological, it is a reaction to the pathology of our times. (21)

Fear is not unique to humans. Animals, even plants, experience fear when real danger is near. Only humans, however, react to *imagined* fear. We invent our own dangers and then react to them. We have no proof that "they" are out to get us or that "they" even exist. Yet we expend a tremendous amount of energy worrying that unseen powers are controlling our environment, economy, educational systems, and entertainment enterprises.

Admit it—how will you ever be able to again look at a Kris Kristofferson album cover and not wonder if he's a lizard in disguise?

Since September 11, 2001, our fears have been on overdrive. The constant reminders in the media that we may experience another terrorist attack at any moment have us watching with suspicion those who are different from us. And let's face it: Fear sells. If we had nothing to be concerned about, would we watch the evening news every night? Would we be compelled to buy the magazines and books that warn us of coming dangers? Media companies play on our imagined fears, running out the next crisis as soon as worries over the last one start to wane.

Siegel offers insight into this heightened state of fear:

> The sense of fear in the United States today seems greater than at the height of the Cold War, when the Soviet Union was a more tangible threat, with an enormous arsenal of nuclear weapons aimed at us. Why? The greatest reason for the change is the growing fracturing and parceling of information into hyped media sound bites. No matter how safe we are, all we need to hear is the word *danger* or *threat,* and the cycle of worry starts. When one cycle is extinguished, another one takes its place.
>
> In the post-9/11 world, the only cable station that doesn't scare us is the cartoon channel, which lacks headlines or news updates of any kind. However, in January 2004, I even noted on the cartoon channel a shift in the wrong direction, when "Grandpa" on *Hey, Arnold!* told the other characters that they'd better "watch out for weapons of mass destruction." (59)

Even with all the real dangers in our world, we find time and energy to invent conspiracies so we have more to be afraid of. And the main focus of our fears is that we don't know who is in control or what "they" are doing.

Dan Brown's Conspiracy Theories

This is precisely what Dan Brown capitalizes on in his novels. In *Digital Fortress* he makes us wonder if the NSA is monitoring our e-mails or phone conversations. Then we must spend time after reading *Deception Point* considering whether to trust government agencies, such as NASA, to tell the truth. Maybe the moon landing was an elaborate hoax after all. (This is another conspiracy theory that just won't go away.) And if NASA is lying, maybe the Centers for Disease Control and Prevention are lying about the dangers of the chemicals sprayed on apples.

We then have organized religion—specifically the Roman Catholic Church—to watch. What is it hiding from us? How is it manipulating science? What parts of history has the church changed to its own advantage? And since we can't trust the church, we also wonder whether we can trust the God we learned about in church.

Do you see where Brown's gospel is leading?

On his Web site, Brown responds to the question "Would you consider yourself a conspiracy theorist?"

> Hardly. In fact, I'm quite the opposite—more of a skeptic. I see no truth whatsoever in stories of extraterrestrial visitors, crop circles, the Bermuda Triangle, or many of the other "mysteries" that permeate pop culture. However, the secret behind *The Da Vinci Code* was too well documented and significant for me to dismiss. ("NH Writer's")

If Brown is such a skeptic when it comes to conspiracies, why then such a fascination with secret societies? He discussed his interest in all things secret during his plagiarism trial:

> I have asked myself why all this clandestine material interests me. At a fundamental level my interest in secret societies came from growing up in New England, surrounded by the clandestine clubs of Ivy League universities, the Masonic lodges of the Founding Fathers, and the hidden hallways of early government power. I see New England as having a long tradition of elite private clubs, fraternities, and secrecy—indeed, my third Robert Langdon novel (a work in progress) is set within the Masons. I have always found the concept of secret societies, codes, and means of communication fascinating. In my youth I was very aware of the Skull & Bones club at Yale. I had good friends who were members of Harvard's secret "finals" clubs. In the town where I grew up, there was a Masonic lodge, and nobody could (or would) tell me what happened behind those closed doors. All of this secrecy captivated me as a young man. ("Dan Brown Witness," par. 55)

Brown the "skeptic" seems to show quite a bit of interest in those with whom he has either had personal experience or learned of through research. The secret behind *The Da Vinci Code*—the conspiracy theory formulated by the church to hide evidence that Jesus and Mary Magdalene were married—was so believable to him that he had to pursue it. And he acknowledges that his next Robert Langdon novel will have the Harvard professor entering the secret realm of the Masons. Yet Brown isn't a conspiracy theorist? He also said at his trial that "many of the aforementioned themes from *The Da Vinci Code* fall in a category I often call 'secret history'—those parts of mankind's past that allegedly have been lost or have become muddied by time, historical revision, or subversion" (par. 82).

Sure sounds a lot like a conspiracy theory, doesn't it?

Brown's *Angels & Demons* centers on a plot of the Illuminati, a clandestine organization that was founded in 1776 in Bavaria but by most accounts ceased to be a viable group only a decade later. Yet Brown doesn't let facts get in the way of a roaring good conspiracy theory. And, of course, he has an explanation for why we don't hear of the Illuminati today.

> Secret societies like the Illuminati go to enormous lengths to remain covert. Although many classified intelligence reports have been written on the brotherhood, few have been published. Conspiracy theories on the Illuminati include infiltration of the British Parliament and U.S. Treasury, secret involvement with the Masons, affiliation with covert Satanic cults, a plan for a New World Order, and even the resurgence of their ancient pact to destroy Vatican City. Separating Illuminati fact from fiction can be difficult on account of the massive quantities of misinformation that has been generated about the brotherhood. Some theorists claim this plethora of misinformation is actually generated by the Illuminati themselves in an effort to discredit any factual information that may have surfaced. ("NH Writer's")

Even though Brown says he's not a conspiracy theorist, his writings suggest the opposite. For example, in *Angels & Demons*, Langdon reflects on what he believes to be the significance of satanist symbolism:

> Satanists historically were educated men who stood as adversaries to the church…. The rumors of satanic black-magic animal sacrifices and the pentagram ritual were nothing but lies spread by the church as a smear campaign against their adversaries. (37)

Conspiracy again raises its head when the Hassassin accuses the camerlengo and the Catholic Church:

> For two millennia your church has dominated the quest for truth. You have crushed your opposition with lies and prophecies of doom. You have manipulated the truth to serve your needs, murdering those whose discoveries did not serve your politics. Are you surprised you are the target of enlightened men from around the globe? (152)

Conspiracy is a main attribute of Dan Brown's gospel.

Christian Conspiracy Theories

Christians aren't exempt from becoming conspiracy theorists themselves. As a matter of fact, some make a career of promoting the conspiracy *du jour* in books, magazines, radio, and television. Several popular Christian authors continue to push ideas of a one-world government ruled by international bankers who are part of a secret society, such as the Illuminati. Much of the time Christian conspiracy is advanced under the banner of end-times prophecy. Proponents of these theories link current events to biblical passages, trying to prove that Jesus is returning soon.

The Bible does make it clear that Jesus will return to rule on earth. There is coming a time, according to the Bible, of intense spiritual persecution, when Christ followers will suffer greatly. But nowhere in Scripture do we find any admonition to be afraid of these coming times or to root out secret plots or reveal hidden one-world government plans. Christians who fall prey to conspiracy theories simply have not read—or obeyed—scriptural commands, such as,

- Don't be like this people, always afraid somebody is plotting against them. Don't fear what they fear. Don't take on their worries. If you're going to worry, worry about The Holy. Fear GOD-of-the-Angel-Armies. (Isa. 8:12–13 MSG)
- He who fears the LORD has a secure fortress, and for his children it will be a refuge. The fear of the LORD is a fountain of life, turning a man from the snares of death. (Prov. 14:26–27)
- The fear of the LORD leads to life: Then one rests content, untouched by trouble. (Prov. 19:23)

- I'm speaking to you as dear friends. Don't be bluffed into silence or insincerity by the threats of religious bullies. True, they can kill you, but *then* what can they do? There's nothing they can do to your soul, your core being. Save your fear for God, who holds your entire life—body and soul—in his hands. (Luke 12:4–5 MSG)

Are conspiracy theorists trying to get us to fear unseen persons who may or may not be trying to take over our world when Scripture clearly tells us to fear only God?

The Conspiracy Industry

Whether or not he intended to, Dan Brown lit a fire under the conspiracy industry. Books such as *Holy Blood, Holy Grail*—published nearly twenty years before *The Da Vinci Code*—have suddenly found themselves on best-seller lists. Ancient theories of a Jesus and Mary Magdalene union, John the Baptist as the real Messiah, and similar ideas have come to the forefront after years of being relegated to self-published books and graveyard-shift radio programs.

One of the authors of *Holy Blood, Holy Grail*, Michael Baigent, put a fresh coat of paint on that book's ideas in a new book titled *The Jesus Papers*. Released the same day *The Da Vinci Code* came out in paperback, *The Jesus Papers* was an instant best seller. Claiming to have seen documents that proved Jesus faked his crucifixion, Baigent couldn't produce any real proof, but he continued to stoke the conspiracy fires.

Holy Blood, Holy Grail was built on documents that "proved" the existence of the Priory of Sion, but the Priory was exposed as fraudulent in a French court in the early 1990s. Still, this did not stop Lynn Picknett and Clive Prince from releasing *The Sion Revelation: The Truth About the Guardians of Christ's Sacred Bloodline*. Christopher Knight and Robert Lomas, both Freemasons (or so they say), unlock the "truth" with *The Hiram Key: Pharaohs, Freemasons, and the Discovery of the Secret Scrolls of Jesus*.

All these books and many others have received renewed interest since *The Da Vinci Code* was published. The thought that "they"—in this case, religious leaders—are hiding the truth about Jesus from the rest of us is somehow very intriguing. It also allows those with shallow commitments to Christ and the church to forsake Christianity. After all, if Christianity is just a part of a conspiracy, then why bother with it? Not going to church is more convenient than going. Not reading or obeying the Bible is easier than reading and obeying. The books by Brown, Baigent, and others offer freedom from following Jesus. They expose the plot by religious leaders to mislead the gullible public and call into question what Christianity has always held as the truth.

Conspiracy theories are very good at questioning what is assumed to be true, but they're not so good at providing solid answers to build one's life on.

Unless, of course, the answer really is Kris Kristofferson.

5

The Fortress Mentality—
Survival and Sacrifice

(DIGITAL FORTRESS)

A U.S. government agency is equipped to intercept and read your e-mail and monitor other Internet activities. Its members have found a way to break the encryption codes of software programs that give you the illusion that your online communications are private. The president has authorized them to do whatever it takes to interpret communications that may lead to the prevention of terrorist activities and other crimes. This agency is among the most secretive in the U.S. intelligence community, yet it may be the most intrusive into your private life.

Is this information from recent headlines or is it the imagination of a fiction writer?

A NASA scientist has made a startling and potentially life-changing discovery, yet the president, through other agencies and individuals, is seemingly putting a gag on this scientist, preventing him from disclosing this vital information.

Breaking news or the plot of a novel?

The National Security Agency (NSA) is a very real government agency that gathers and processes information. With thousands of agents worldwide, the NSA monitors communications via satellite, telephone, radio, and the Internet. They received unwanted attention late in 2005 as the news broke that President George W. Bush had authorized the NSA to intercept private citizens' e-mail and phone communications as part of the war on terrorism.

Whether the president's actions were right or wrong, one thing is certain: The super-secret NSA is now a little less mysterious than before. We now know that it has the technology to read the e-mail and instant messages we think are private. Its ability to decipher codes and break security measures is unparalleled. Nothing sent over the Internet is completely secure any longer.

The NSA is also the focus for Dan Brown's *Digital Fortress,* a novel that explores the agency's ability to break codes and read e-mail. Released in 1998, *Digital Fortress* seems right at home in today's headlines. Brown's characters and plotline, seemingly far-fetched when the book was first released, are eerily similar to current events.

Likewise, *Deception Point,* published in 2001, echoes the *New York Times* headlines of January 29, 2006, when NASA scientist James Hansen said the Bush administration had tried to stop him from speaking publicly about the dangers of greenhouse gases and global warming. *Deception Point* also deals with the politics of a NASA discovery, the attempts to verify it, and the subsequent cover-up to hide the discovery—again, mirroring real-life news.

In the next two chapters, we'll examine more closely Brown's two lesser-known novels—which don't feature Robert Langdon—and the gospel he presents in them. We'll look at Brown's main characters, the plotlines (we'll give you a clear "spoiler warning" in case you haven't read the novels yet), and the reasons the books were written. Then we'll compare Brown's gospel story with that of the book of Mark from the New Testament. We chose Mark because it most closely resembles the characteristics of a modern novel with its fast-paced, action-packed plot and compelling characters. The philosophy Brown teaches is ancient, and seen through the light of an ancient book like the two-thousand-year-old gospel of Mark, we can better understand the foundation it's built on.

But first, let's go back and see how Dan Brown the teacher became Dan Brown the best-selling author.

Background Music

Dan Brown taught at Phillips Exeter Academy in the 1980s, but this was not his ideal job. He considered himself to be an aspiring songwriter-musician who was struggling to really come into his own. Then in the spring of 1991, Brown left New Hampshire for Los Angeles to network with the musical community.

He joined the National Academy of Songwriters, an organization that offered musicians and songwriters help in their careers. Blythe Newlon, artist-development director for the academy, took a liking to Brown and was soon booking shows and auditions with record-label executives, even though it was not a part of her job. She even arranged for one of the top record producers at that time to produce the self-titled album *Dan Brown* using some of the best studio musicians in Southern California

"We fully expect Dan Brown will someday be included in the ranks of our most successful members," Newlon wrote in a press release, invoking "talents like Billy Joel, Paul Simon and Prince" (qtd. in Rogak, 22). She, of course, was right. Brown is certainly one of the most successful members of the National Academy of Songwriters—but that success isn't based on his musical talents.

Brown's recording career never really got off the ground. While he received a few nice write-ups for his album, Brown never felt at home in the spotlight. In order to sell his music, he needed to get out of the studio and hit the road. Performing in bars and clubs held little appeal for Brown, who relished the time he spent in private composing and recording music. Shortly after the release of *Dan Brown,* he decided to move back to New Hampshire to resume teaching at Phillips Exeter—and he didn't move by himself. He and Blythe Newlon had become lovers, and she agreed to go with Brown to keep the creative team together. But just what were they going to create?

Before Brown released his first novel, *Digital Fortress,* he produced another music album—*Angels & Demons*. While *Dan Brown* (the album) had featured a well-known producer and some big-name musicians, *Angels & Demons* listed only Brown as writer and producer. Only one other musician was given credit on this album—his backup singer, Blythe. Brown mixed the album using software on a Mac computer (something that's often done today but was done only by amateur engineers in the mid-1990s). Not surprisingly, *Angels & Demons* didn't sell any more copies than the previous album did. Brown, it seems, was ready to move on from his music career to writing books.

A Different Tune

If we were to gauge Brown's success based on his first two published works, we would conclude that Brown the writer had no more illustrious prospects than Brown the singer. The book *187 Men to Avoid: A Survival Guide for the Romantically Frustrated Woman* was a humorous look at dating from a woman's viewpoint. The author is listed as Danielle Brown, a pseudonym for Dan. And 1998 saw the equally forgettable *The Bald Book* with Blythe listed as the author. (Blythe and Dan married shortly after moving to New Hampshire.) In actuality, both books were written by Dan Brown, although neither one is listed on his Web site.

Then came a serendipitous moment that opened the door for Brown to pursue a career as a serious novelist. Before he and Blythe moved back East, they flew to Tahiti for a vacation. While on the beach, Dan found a discarded copy of Sidney Sheldon's *Doomsday Conspiracy*. Flipping it open to the first page, he began to read. Brown recalled,

> I read the first page … and then the next … and then the next. Several hours later, I finished the book and thought, "Hey, I can do that." (Glaister, par. 1)

He could indeed.

We don't know whether this was the first of Sheldon's books that Brown had read, but it was *Doomsday Conspiracy* that set the course for *Digital Fortress, Angels & Demons, Deception Point,* and *The Da Vinci Code*. A quick read of Sheldon's 1992 sci-fi/suspense story reveals that many of the story lines, character sketches, and even character names in Brown's books are heavily influenced by *Doomsday Conspiracy*.

1. *The grand conspiracy.* In *Doomsday Conspiracy* a group of twelve men know a great secret that will affect the entire earth. The men are driven to protect and manipulate this incredible secret for their own selfish gain.

We see this same type of grand conspiracy at work in each of Brown's novels—an organization has a secret to protect at all costs: the NSA in *Digital Fortress,* NASA in *Deception Point,* and the Roman Catholic Church in *Angels & Demons* and *The Da Vinci Code.*

Digital Fortress Plot Summary—the Beginning

1. Ensei Tankado lies dying on the street in Seville, Spain. As he clutches his chest with one hand, he holds out his other deformed hand, with three fingers extended. On one finger is an engraved gold ring. But before he knows whether his message is understood, Tankado dies.

2. Susan Fletcher is summoned to the National Security Agency (NSA) headquarters for an emergency meeting with her boss, Commander Trevor Strathmore. Susan, an NSA cryptographer, learns Strathmore is concerned that their secret supercomputer, TRANSLTR, has been working for more than fifteen hours to decode a message when the average time is six minutes. The message was sent by Tankado, who had sworn to destroy TRANSLTR. Strathmore and Susan run programs to see why the computer has stalled on this message. The unbreakable message is named Digital Fortress.

3. Meanwhile, David Becker—Susan's fiancé—has been sent to Spain by Strathmore in an attempt to recover a passkey that will decode Tankado's message, which Strathmore thinks would be among the deceased Tankado's personal effects. Though David doesn't work for the NSA (he's a linguistics professor at Georgetown), he speaks Spanish, which is enough for his simple job: Go to the morgue in Seville where Tankado's body is and recover all of his personal effects. Then bring everything back to Washington.

4. When David arrives at the morgue in Seville, Tankado's body is lying naked on a cold slab. David puts Tankado's wallet, passport, and other personal effects in a box and is about to head back to the airport when he notices that Tankado's hand is sunburned, except for a band around his ring finger. The policeman who has escorted him to the morgue says that a Canadian tourist told the police that as Tankado was dying, he held up his hand with this ring and kept pushing it into the faces of those who had gathered to help. He seemed to be begging the tourist to take it, and the officer thinks the tourist must have it now. So David rushes off to find the tourist and, hopefully, the ring.

5. Strathmore tells Susan that Tankado had been e-mailing information about Digital Fortress to NDAKOTA@ara.anon.org. Susan sets off to trace this e-mail address. Could it be her fellow code breaker, Greg Hale? Hale has come in on his day off and is showing unusual interest in Susan's activities. At the same time, technician Phil Chartrukian finds Strathmore to alert him to a new danger: TRANSLTR may have a virus.

6. David finds the tourist who was with Tankado when he died, but the tourist didn't take the ring. He tells David that a German tourist and his escort took it. David tracks down the German and his escort, only to find that they had given the ring to a teenage girl with red, white, and blue hair. So David takes off in search of the girl. What he doesn't know is just after he leaves each of these people connected with the missing ring, an assassin follows behind to kill them.

7. Susan discusses the purpose of TRANSLTR with Greg Hale. She says that it is necessary to intercept and read e-mail in order to "guard the gate" of our nation. Hale asks, "Who will guard the guards?" Later, Hale leaves and Susan checks his computer. On it she finds e-mails from Tankado to NDAKOTA. It appears that Hale is not only NDAKOTA but is Tankado's partner.

8. Chad Brinkerhoff is the administrative aid to the NSA director. Working late on a Saturday, he notices a serious problem with the daily budget report. Consulting with Midge Milken, the NSA internal security analyst, Chad determines that TRANSLTR hasn't broken any codes that day and is stuck on one code. But when Chad calls Strathmore, Strathmore assures him that TRANSLTR is working just fine—breaking codes right on schedule. Chad and Midge begin to investigate.

9. Phil Chartrukian decides to investigate in the sublevels of the Crypto floor. He opens a recessed door in the floor and begins to descend to where TRANSLTR is powered. Greg Hale watches him descend.

10. While in the bathroom, Susan hears men's voices through the floor vent. It sounds like Phil arguing with someone about TRANSLTR and how it has a virus. Then she hears a scuffle and a hideous scream. After that, the lights in the bathroom flicker and go out. Susan is in complete darkness.

Continued on page 99

2. *Impersonal controlling force.* In both *Doomsday Conspiracy* and Brown's novels, the main characters must reveal or destroy a specific object in order to "win." A vegetablelike female alien is the object Sheldon presents in *Doomsday Conspiracy*. Brown starts with a supercomputer called TRANSLTR in *Digital Fortress,* then he follows with a fossil-laden meteorite in *Deception Point,* a container of antimatter in *Angels & Demons,* and the Holy Grail in *The Da Vinci Code.*

3. *The cover-up.* The twelve men who guard the great secret in *Doomsday Conspiracy* destroy anyone who might have even a glimpse of the truth. To them, human life is a cheap commodity, and they are willing to kill to protect the status quo. This scenario is repeated in each of Brown's novels: An organization tries to cover up "leaks" by employing trained assassins to terminate those who may have knowledge of the secret. Cold-blooded killing is rampant in all of these books.

4. *Innocent seekers of truth.* In Sheldon's novel, Commander Robert Bellamy is ordered by the NSA deputy chief to find witnesses to the crash of a top-secret weather balloon. Bellamy quickly discovers that something much more sinister is afoot and seeks the truth. His ex-wife (and still the love of his life), Susan Banks, is also drawn into this search.

Brown employs couples in each of his books to seek out the truth even as they are running from those who want to kill them. These couples are innocently drawn into the conspiracies and have only the purest of motives in their quest for the truth. Or so we are to think.

5. *And the bad guy is ... surprise!* Just when you think you know whom you can and can't trust, the tables turn. In *Doomsday Conspiracy,* Robert Bellamy trusts a fatherlike figure, only to learn that this person has ordered Robert's death. Likewise, in each of his novels, Brown coaxes us into trusting a harmless, helpful figure before revealing that this is the very person who has initiated all the violence we have witnessed.

6. *Shallow Hal ... and Robert, Susan, Dustin ...* The characters in *Doomsday Conspiracy* are extremely shallow. By this we mean that we only get to see one side of them. Robert Bellamy is driven in his

Digital Fortress Plot Summary—the Conclusion

(**Spoiler Warning**—ending of the novel is revealed on this page.)

11. David tracks down the girl with the colorful hair to a punk club outside of the town of Seville but learns that she left for the airport to return home to the United States. He tries to find a ride but ends up buying a scooter and races to the airport where he finds the young girl, now back to her normal hair color, with the ring. After a long ordeal, David retrieves the ring. But before David can leave the airport, the assassin corners him in a bathroom stall. David manages to escape, but with the assassin hot on his heels.

12. Susan looks into the sublevels and sees Phil Chartrukian's body, as well as Greg Hale hiding. She and Strathmore close the trap door and think they've caught Tankado's associate. They then begin to erase all traces of Digital Fortress.

13. Back in the Crypto office, Susan makes her way in the dark to her computer. But someone else is there with her—Greg Hale. He wasn't trapped in the sublevels after all. Hale begs Susan to help him get out of NSA. He says he saw Strathmore kill Chartrukian. Susan doesn't believe him and, after another struggle, escapes to find Strathmore. When she does, Strathmore says he needs to talk with Susan—that he hasn't been totally honest with her.

14. After Strathmore's admission that he was trying to put a "back-door" code in Digital Fortress, he and Susan race to find the passkey in Hale's computer. But Susan finds more; she discovers that Digital Fortress is not an unbreakable coded message but a trick to introduce a virus into TRANSLTR. The computer overheats and starts to shut down its security. Soon, hackers will be able to have access to top-secret information in the computer's main data banks.

15. The assassin is closing in on David. The chase takes them to a Catholic mass, where David escapes through a back door. The assassin believes he has David cornered in a tower and sends an e-mail to the one who sent him to Seville, saying David has been killed. But just as the assassin advances, David trips him down the long flight of stairs and kills him. David is then met by men with guns who force him into their van.

16. Susan and Strathmore find that they cannot abort the Digital Fortress program. Susan goes to the sublevel to shut down TRANSLTR manually. But before she reaches the shut-off panel, she hears a gunshot. Returning to the top level, she finds Greg Hale dead with a suicide note next to his body. Strathmore's pager goes off, and Susan reads "DAVID BECKER—TERMINATED." She now knows that Strathmore is behind it all. Strathmore tells Susan he loves her, has always loved her, and begs her to come with him. Susan runs up the stairs, just as TRANSLTR explodes, killing Strathmore.

17. The virus has infected the main data bank. Susan races to help keep the firewalls protecting this sensitive data from being breached. A transmission from Spain comes in. Two undercover agents have David in their van—alive. David reads the inscription from Tankado's ring—it's Latin for "Who will guard the guards?" But it's not the passkey—it doesn't stop Digital Fortress. The agents play back video they took of Tankado as he lay dying in Seville. He was holding up his hand with the ring, but it was not the ring he was calling attention to. It was his three fingers—the number three.

18. The number three is the passkey that restores the firewalls protecting the top-secret material. David flies home, and he and Susan prepare for life together.

vocation but empty in his soul. Susan Banks is kindhearted but needy. Monte is a manipulator, and Dustin even more so. Each of the people we spend time with in this book are portrayed as two-dimensional—clichéd with little sophistication.

In *Digital Fortress* and *Angels & Demons,* Brown's characters portray these same traits; they are very shallow and two-dimensional. Good guys are always good; bad guys are always bad. We are not meant to get to know any character well, as that would slow down the plot. Above all, Sheldon and Brown weave plots but don't create realistic characters.

7. *The name game.* Brown took more from *Doomsday Conspiracy* than just the inspiration to become a fiction writer. He also took many of the names Sheldon gave his characters. Could Robert Langdon (of *Angels & Demons* and *The Da Vinci Code* fame) be the namesake of Robert Bellamy? Perhaps Susan Banks suggests Brown's Susan Fletcher *(Digital Fortress)*? Okay, Robert and Susan are common names, and the fact that Brown uses these names in his novels may be just a coincidence. But the more blatant allusion to Sheldon's character Janus in Brown's *Angels & Demons* should make us take another look at the similarities between Brown's and Sheldon's works.

Janus is the nickname for the mastermind behind the conspiracy and cover-up in Sheldon's work, an uncommon but useful name for such a character. In mythology, Janus is the Roman god of gates and doors, of all beginnings and endings. You can no doubt guess that Brown thought the name would be appropriate or at least convenient as the nickname for the mastermind behind the conspiracy and cover-up in *Angels & Demons.*

The day Brown found that discarded Sidney Sheldon novel was the day he began to become a best-selling author. He found his role model in Sheldon. His first four novels mimic Sheldon's style, pace, story lines, characterizations, and even names. Brown didn't set out to challenge orthodox Christianity the day he finished reading *Doomsday Conspiracy,* nor did he determine to advance his own religious agenda on that day. He had a much more down-to-earth motivation when he said, "I can do that": He wanted a creative outlet, a way to make money other than by teaching. He hadn't found it in songwriting. And he knew it wouldn't come from writing novelty books. But after reading Sheldon's novel, Brown had an epiphany: He would become a novelist. He had the inspiration; now he just needed a story.

Conspiring Events

Inspiration for Brown's first novel came in 1995 in the form of the U.S. Secret Service on the campus of Phillips Exeter. A student at the private school had e-mailed a friend saying how he hated then-president Bill Clinton and thought Clinton should be shot. Federal agents swarmed on campus and pulled the disgruntled student aside for questioning. The agents quickly determined the student wasn't a serious threat, packed up, and left. But the incident stirred Brown's curiosity. Just how did the Secret Service learn the contents of the student's private e-mail?

Brown began to research just how this could happen and learned of an intelligence-gathering agency he had never before heard of: the NSA.

"The more I learned about this ultra-secret agency," said Brown, "and the fascinating moral issues surrounding national security and civilian privacy, the more I realized it was a great backdrop for a novel. That's when I started writing *Digital Fortress*" ("NH Writer's").

Breaking into the Fortress

Digital Fortress features two primary settings: NSA headquarters in Fort Meade, Maryland, and Seville, Spain. Susan Fletcher is a programmer and code breaker for the NSA. Trevor Strathmore, her boss and the deputy director of the NSA, asks Susan to come to the NSA building on a Saturday—a rare occurrence—to help with an emergency situation.

A code that was loaded into the NSA's supercomputer, TRANSLTR, has now been running for more than an unheard of fifteen hours and is threatening to breach the highly secret data stored in the computer. Upon arrival Susan learns that Strathmore has sent David Becker, Susan's fiancé, to Seville to recover the passkey to the log-jamming code.

Thus begins *Digital Fortress*—and Brown's novel-writing career. Following Sheldon's model, Brown keeps his chapters short, each ending with a mini-cliffhanger to draw the reader forward in the plot. And for the most part this tactic works. The book flows quickly, changing scenes before the reader can get bored or too confused. And while Brown's descriptions of advanced technologies in *Digital*

Fortress contain many factual errors, that is not what we want to dwell on.

Mark—the Early Gospel Writings

Before we can compare Brown's gospel with the gospel of Mark, we must first travel two thousand years into the past to discover just who Mark was and why he compiled this book on the life of Jesus.

In many ways, Mark resembles the younger Dan Brown in that Mark also seemed to be searching to find out just who he really was. And like Brown, Mark seemed to stumble on something that would change his life.

We have very little direct information about Mark. When we see him, it's only a glimpse here, a brief glance there. The first time he appears in Scripture is on the night of Jesus' arrest.

Jesus and his disciples had just finished the Passover meal at the home of one of Jesus' supporters. Except for Judas, who had left the dinner to find the Jewish leaders in order to betray Jesus, they left the house and went to the garden of Gethsemane. By this time Judas had convinced the Pharisees he knew where they could find Jesus. A band of armed men followed Judas to where he had last seen Jesus. Not finding Jesus there but perhaps getting a tip on where he was headed, Judas and the band of men set out for the garden. When they arrived, Judas betrayed Jesus with a kiss, and the armed men made their move to arrest Jesus. After a brief scuffle, the disciples fled and the crowd left the garden with Jesus in custody. At this point in the story, we read the following verse, unique to the gospel of Mark:

> A young man was following along. All he had on was a bedsheet. Some of the men grabbed him but he got away, running off naked, leaving them holding the sheet. (14:51–52 MSG)

Many scholars suspect this naked young man was none other than Mark and that the home Jesus used for the Passover meal was Mark's home. This idea is strengthened when we next run into Mark in Acts 12. Peter, who is in prison, is miraculously freed by an angel.

He then goes straight to where he knows other disciples will be gathered—the home of Mary, the mother of John Mark. (See Acts 12:12.) Mark, we gather, was the son of followers of Jesus. He may have met Jesus in person, but his knowledge about Jesus really came from following other disciples.

Mark had accompanied Paul and Barnabas on a mission trip to Pamphylia, but for one reason or another chose to return home. As Paul and Barnabas prepared to go on another trip, Barnabas wanted to take Mark with them again, but Paul was against the idea of taking a quitter along. The disagreement grew so intense that Paul and Barnabas went their separate ways with Paul taking Silas with him and Barnabas giving Mark another chance. (See Acts 15:36–41.)

Later, Mark and Paul reconcile, as can be seen in the benedictions of two of Paul's letters. In his epistle to the Colossians, Paul asked them to welcome Mark when he arrives (see 4:10), and in his second epistle to Timothy, Paul told him, "Get Mark and bring him with you, because he is helpful to me in my ministry" (4:11).

But Mark's most spiritually formative time came as a disciple of Peter. Toward the end of Peter's life, he spent time encouraging the church in Rome. Mark served as Peter's interpreter and scribe, writing Peter's letters to the churches. He no doubt listened intently as Peter recounted the teachings and acts of Jesus that he had witnessed firsthand.

Whether on his own or encouraged by Peter, Mark committed these teachings to writing—teachings that had previously been passed down by word of mouth. These are the teachings that make up Mark's gospel.

Similar Audiences, Similar Approaches

Mark wrote in the same style that was typically used in oral teaching—very short, to-the-point stories that would be easily remembered and repeated. In the Jewish culture Jesus and Mark grew up in, written material was extremely rare. People learned important lessons largely from oral tradition.

We see this in Paul's first letter to the church at Corinth: "For I received from the Lord what I also passed on to you" (11:23). Later in the same epistle, Paul wrote, "For what I received I passed on to you" (15:3). The words "received" and "passed on" indicate the tradition of handing down from one person to another a lesson in spoken words.

Just What the Masses Want

Dan Brown and Mark share a similar writing style. Neither would be called especially literary, but both of their writings target a mass, popular audience. Mark wrote in a direct, forceful way with little subtlety. There was no scene setting and little character development in his stories. Whereas Matthew and Luke started off their gospels with the genealogical history of Jesus and the story of the virgin birth, Mark jumped right into John's baptism of Jesus, Jesus' temptation in the wilderness, and the calling of the twelve disciples.

The gospels of Matthew, Luke, and John include long orations by Jesus (such as the Sermon on the Mount in Matthew 5—7), but Mark's gospel has none. Mark shows us a very active Jesus who is constantly going from place to place, healing, casting out demons,

Action Scenes in Mark

- As Jesus was coming up out of the water, he saw heaven being torn open and the Spirit descending on him like a dove. (1:10)
- Immediately the Spirit drove Him into the wilderness. (v. 12 NKJV)
- Then Jesus entered a house, and again a crowd gathered, so that he and his disciples were not even able to eat. When his family heard about this, they went to take charge of him, for they said, "He is out of his mind." (3:20–21)
- When Jesus got out of the boat, a man with an evil spirit came from the tombs to meet him. (5:2)
- As soon as all the people saw Jesus, they were overwhelmed with wonder and ran to greet him. (9:15)
- He took Peter, James and John along with him, and he began to be deeply distressed and troubled. (14:33)
- Going a little farther, he fell to the ground and prayed that if possible the hour might pass from him. (v. 35)
- Very early in the morning, the chief priests, with the elders, the teachers of the law and the whole Sanhedrin, reached a decision. They bound Jesus, led him away and handed him over to Pilate. (15:1)
- Trembling and bewildered, the women went out and fled from the tomb. They said nothing to anyone, because they were afraid. (16:8)

and performing miracles. The pace is breathtaking—just like what we find in Brown's novels.

Mark's action scenes take place with great urgency and with a great display of emotion. Similarly, Dan Brown starts *Digital Fortress* with an emphasis on urgency and action.

> It is said that in death, all things become clear; Ensei Tankado now knew it was true. As he clutched his chest and fell to the ground in pain, he realized the horror of his mistake. (1)

Clutching, falling, horror—the pace is set for us in the first two sentences. And Brown doesn't let up throughout the entire story. In dialogue, characters tease, cringe, demand, stammer, probe, snap, and fire back. Sentences, paragraphs, and chapters are short. The combination of action words and short sentences makes the book feel very urgent. The style propels the reader through the book at breakneck speed.

Intriguing Plots

A key word that connects this Mark's gospel with Dan Brown's writings is *mystery*. Jesus is a mysterious figure in Mark. He speaks in parables so that only those who have entered the kingdom will understand. (See 4:11.) He does great miracles, including raising a young girl from the dead, but he strictly tells any witnesses to keep silent about what they've seen. Who is this Jesus whom Mark shrouds in a cloak of mystery? Is he similar to the mysterious figures we see in *Digital Fortress*?

In Brown's novel, we have Trevor Strathmore, NSA deputy director. Just why is he running a code that has the most powerful computer in the world tied in knots? Greg Hale is a cryptographer for the NSA with a sketchy past. Why is he at his post on a Saturday, and why does he show great interest in this particular code? Then there is the strange man in wire-rim glasses who wears a curious device on his belt with which he sends messages regarding those witnesses he has "terminated." But to whom is he sending the messages? All of these characters are involved—voluntarily or involuntarily—in a great plot and cover-up that keeps the pages of *Digital Fortress* turning.

In the very first chapter of Mark, we see what at first looks like a cover-up by Jesus. Mark gets right to the miraculous healings Jesus performed, but then he includes this mysterious passage:

> Jesus healed great numbers of sick people who had many different kinds of diseases, and he ordered many demons to come out of their victims. But because they knew who he was, he refused to allow the demons to speak. (1:34 NLT)

In the same chapter we read a similar account:

> A leper came to him, begging on his knees, "If you want to, you can cleanse me."
>
> Deeply moved, Jesus put out his hand, touched him, and said, "I want to. Be clean." Then and there the leprosy was gone, his skin smooth and healthy. Jesus dismissed him with strict orders: "Say nothing to anyone. Take the offering for cleansing that Moses prescribed and present yourself to the priest. This will validate your healing to the people." But as soon as the man was out of earshot, he told everyone he met what had happened, spreading the news all over town. So Jesus kept to out-of-the-way places, no longer able to move freely in and out of the city. But people found him, and came from all over. (1:40–45 MSG)

Why did Jesus not want others to know he had healed these people? It was certainly a sign of the Messiah to be able to heal. Didn't Jesus want people to know that he was the Christ? Why cover up who he was?

Conspiracy Theories

At the beginning of the twentieth century, German theologian William Wrede published his theory that Mark added these passages to cover up the fact that Jesus never saw himself as the Messiah. Mark, according to Wrede, needed to show a Jesus who did not use healings as a means of publicizing his true identity. Wrede makes the case that Jesus was only a prophet who, after his death, was made into something more by the writers of the gospels. This theory, of course, is echoed by Brown's character Leigh Teabing in *The Da Vinci Code*.

But there's another explanation for Jesus' wanting to keep his identity secret. At the time of his ministry on earth, the land of Israel was under Roman domination. The conditions for Jews were harsh, to put it mildly.

The Jewish Scriptures and rabbinical teachings promised that a messiah would come and lead the Jews out of bondage and into freedom. Many had come before Jesus who had claimed to be the Messiah, only to dash their followers' hopes. What the people wanted in a messiah was a political and military hero, someone to drive out the Romans and restore the Davidic kingdom to Israel.

Jesus, however, didn't come to lead a coup or revolt against the Roman authorities. He came to die a sacrificial death for the forgiveness of sins committed by all who had lived, who were living, and who were yet to live. Jesus didn't want a large following of hero seekers; thus, he kept his identity secret. He handpicked twelve men to train for a job that wouldn't begin until after his death.

For three years they walked with Jesus, watching him heal, raise the dead, walk on water, calm the storms, feed thousands with a few fish. And it wasn't until near the time of Jesus' death that they began to understand just who he was.

The key verse in the gospel of Mark is found in chapter 8. Jesus was walking with the Twelve. He had maintained his mysterious secrecy up to this point, even with his closest friends. Now he asked them who the people thought he was.

> "Well," they replied, "some say John the Baptist, some say Elijah, and others say you are one of the other prophets."
>
> Then Jesus asked, "Who do you say I am?"
>
> Peter replied, "You are the Messiah." But Jesus warned them not to tell anyone about him. (vv. 28–30 NLT)

From this point on, Jesus began to speak openly with his disciples about who he really was and why he had come. If he had started his relationship with these men by declaring that he was God and had come to die so that people could be forgiven for their sins, what do you think the response would have been? It took the disciples months or even years of following Jesus, seeing his love and compassion in action, before they were ready to accept this incredible revelation.

Of course, word had spread of Jesus' actions. Those who had only a cursory glimpse of Jesus through one of his miracles thought he was a great prophet. But Peter now knew differently. He had been with Jesus, had walked on water when Jesus called him. He, the former fisherman, had seen Jesus multiply a single fish into enough pieces to feed thousands. How could a mere man do these things? Peter was beginning to believe. Yet still Jesus wanted his identity kept secret. The time to proclaim him as King would not come until after his death and resurrection. At that time he told Peter and the others to boldly tell the truth to the entire world. (See Acts 1.)

So, yes, Jesus had a secret to keep, but his secret was for the ultimate good of all, whereas the secrets kept by Dan Brown's characters are for their own gain. Brown's characters kill innocent people in order to protect their secrets. Jesus, the only truly innocent person, died so that his secret could be revealed.

No Greater Love

This contrast between Jesus and Brown's characters reflects the same core distinctions that exist between pagan monists and Christian theists—at least philosophically and, potentially, very practically. History offers profound examples of self-sacrifice by noble pagans not only in the past but more recently as well. But if all paths to truth and enlightenment are the same, and faith is just a continuum for any individual, then why should anyone die for someone else? After all, it might seem the right choice for you, but what if it's not best for the recipient of your sacrifice? Your sacrifice could be the ultimate imposition of your truth upon another. And that person might not appreciate it or even see it as the gift you intend it to be.

It's hard to fathom anyone giving his or her life for another who didn't see things in pretty absolute terms. This is about as black and white a choice as one can make—life and death.

People who give their lives sacrificially for another do so because they love that person and know that person's life is worth preserving, even if it means the loss of their own. It's not a matter of which life is more valuable to humanity or society; it's simply an affirmation of a person's ultimate value as a human being.

Can a pagan monist philosophically justify such a sacrifice? With our worldviews decidedly formed by theistic Christianity (as if you couldn't tell), we're at a loss to answer. When we view the world through pagan monist–colored glasses, valuing and applauding self-sacrifice just doesn't seem to make much sense.

Somehow sacrificial love seems to override what should be our most fundamental, naturalistic, evolutionary instincts— self-preservation and the survival of the fittest. But then, perhaps survival of the fittest could explain a little the sacrificial drive, albeit in an amoral kind of way. Maybe there is nobility to preserving the species. Then the question becomes, is it nobler for a mother to save her child from drowning or to save herself? According to the principle of self-preservation, it could be just as noble for a mother to choose to preserve her own life over that of her drowning child if she is the most fit and has the greatest prospect of bearing more children. But then what of the mother who chooses to dive into the river, deliver her gasping child to shore, and then is washed away into oblivion? Which choice is better? Which is truer?

Or is there some universal truth that demands universal sorrow for the savior-mother, a sorrow that aches, weeps, and blesses, saying, "Well done"? And everyone knows deep within that it was love, as if there is absolutely such a thing.

All of us know human existence is about far more than the survival of the fittest and species preservation. And whether or not we'll admit it, we know there's something much greater to such sacrifice than the cold-comfort subjectivity of some relative, greater cause.

In Charles Dickens's masterpiece *A Tale of Two Cities*, a great tragic novel set during the French Revolution, the final chapter ends with one of the most well-known images of sacrificial love in all of Western literature. Sydney Carton needs only to sit back and allow circumstances to play out, and Charles Darnay, the husband of the woman Carton loves, will be executed. It isn't his responsibility; he only bears an uncanny resemblance to the man.

Yet, inconceivably, Carton uses his influence on one of the jailers to enter Darnay's cell, drug him, exchange clothes with him, and have the jailer remove Darnay to safety. In the final scene Carton calmly stands at the guillotine and declares to an indifferent mob, "It is a far, far better thing that I do, than I have ever done; it is a far, far better rest that I go to than I have ever known" (374).

Why does that resonate with each of us as true? We know it's far better because true love sacrifices all. Dickens knew this, and in his story he purposefully imitated the sacrificial death of Christ that he and all Christians know to be the supreme story of sacrificial love.

Self-Preservation or Self-Sacrifice?

The virtue of Brown's stories, however, seems to resonate more with self-preservation than with self-sacrifice. Perhaps his sensibilities are truly more consistent with pagan monism at this level as well. *Angels & Demons* presents a far, far different fate than that of Carton. The protagonists all survive, and the villains are destroyed. As Cardinal Mortati (soon to become the new pope) brings final closure to the tragic circumstances of his predecessor's death, he says, "No love is greater than that of a father for his son" (555).

The great irony of this allusion is no accident. Brown is purposefully affirming the monist worldview, which necessarily contradicts Christian self-sacrifice. The syntax of that short comment clearly mimics and contravenes Christ's famous definition of love:

> My command is this: Love each other as I have loved you. Greater love has no one than this, that he lay down his life for his friends. You are my friends if you do what I command. (John 15:12–14)

Jesus and this pope hold very different views on what is truly love. And by the pope's standard, the Christian God the Father could not be revered as supreme in his love if he sacrificed his Son for the sake of humanity. Indeed, as Brown's story is played out in a kind of perverse reversal, it's the son who sacrifices the father, but he does so out of hatred, not love. Sacrificial love is not relevant in this pagan world; it's merely a matter of bringing back balance, not freedom or truth.

Jesus insisted that there is no greater love than that of self-sacrifice. And he commanded his followers to love that same way, just as he would demonstrate on the cross. Those who would be Jesus' friends—who would be called Christians—cannot help but sacrifice for others, and they revel in expressions of self-sacrifice by others.

Brown's *Digital Fortress* gospel of self-preservation or Mark's gospel of sacrificial love—which worldview do you want to embrace?

6

The Point of Deception and Truth

(DECEPTION POINT)

The truth is out there. It's waiting to be discovered by those brave souls who are willing to risk it all. We believe in this truth. We just don't know what it is—yet. But it will be revealed to the one who's clever enough to outwit and uncover it, the person who can decipher and decode what those in power want to conceal. And we know "they" conceal the truth, don't we?

As Henry David Thoreau wrote in his journal on February 21, 1842, "There must be some narrowness in the soul that compels one to have secrets" (99). It's those narrow souls who conspire and conceal, who hold the power of the secret. But if we follow closely behind our favorite conspiracy novel's protagonist, we'll discover the truth. Before the story is done, we will have vicariously revealed the real story—and we will have acquired the secret's power for ourselves.

The Power of Hidden Truth

It's the thrill of the hunt that attracts us, no question about it. But when it comes to uncovering the secret, there's more to it than merely the good fun of solving a puzzle. For most of us, it's also about power and defeating the abuse of it.

The revelation of the power of hidden truth is what drives the plot of *Deception Point* as well as the lives of its protagonists, such as Director William Pickering.

> To call the [the National Reconnaissance Office] director a plain man was in itself an overstatement. NRO Director William Pickering was diminutive, with pale skin, a forgettable face, a bald head, and hazel eyes, which despite having gazed upon the country's deepest secrets, appeared as two shallow pools. (14)

Pickering (the equivalent of Trevor Strathmore in *Digital Fortress*) is a father figure to Rachel Sexton, the novel's heroine. He's the one to whom she looks for help and guidance in her adventure. What else do we learn in this portrait of Pickering?

> The man's quiet diligence, combined with his wardrobe of plain black suits, had earned him the nickname of the "Quaker." A brilliant strategist and the model of efficiency, the Quaker ran his world with unrivaled clarity. His mantra: "Find the truth. Act on it." (14)

Pickering is a truth seeker in a world that's constantly conspiring to conceal it. Seeking the truth (or, as Pickering describes it, "the hunt for buried or forgotten treasure" [14]) is a consistent theme throughout all of Dan Brown's novels. Each book's protagonist searches for hidden codes and clues and then acts on them the best way he or she knows how. Because, as President Zach Herney says toward the end of *Deception Point*, "There's just no substitute for the truth" (551).

Before we go dashing off with Sexton and Pickering in their particularly rigorous pursuit of truth, think back to that cynical counterpoint we discussed in chapter 2, which was spoken two thousand years ago by Pilate: "What is truth?"

And Jesus' answer was "I am."

While Brown's characters love to bandy around the word *truth*, what Pickering, Sexton, and Brown mean when they talk about truth in *Deception Point* and *Digital Fortress* is not at all the meaning Jesus had in mind. These two novels are decidedly Brown's lighter reads, filled with fun, action, and intrigue. When the characters speak of *truth*, they're generally referring to facts. They want to know the hidden details behind the conspiracy. And although Brown's gospel messages admittedly aren't as strong and clear in these two novels, we can begin to hear his message faintly whispering between the lines.

And just what is the truth that Brown sends his characters in search of? In these novels it's the *hunt* for truth that is at the heart of Brown's gospel message. With a core premise that facts are often secrets that must be revealed and that with their revelation comes personal power, these novels show that secret knowledge is the hallmark of Brown's gospel.

Don't Cast Stones at Glass Fortresses

In his novels, Brown loves to shroud an elite, all-knowing few under a cloak of secrecy, and in order to survive, his protagonists must uncover the secret. In *Digital Fortress,* the NSA leaders leak the news that the powerful code-breaking computer TRANSLTR doesn't work—the whole operation was a great failure. This, of course, is a lie to cover up the fact that TRANSLTR works very well and is intercepting and reading e-mails at will. Only those with special access and knowledge know the truth.

The race is on to decipher a coded message threatening to destroy TRANSLTR. The NSA, a very secretive arm of the government intelligence community, must not allow the outside world to learn of the existence of TRANSLTR and its ability to decipher e-mail.

As Strathmore, Susan, and David attempt to uncover the message that's causing TRANSLTR to self-destruct, they're simultaneously concerned with covering up their own secrets. They each must also decide who is telling the truth and who isn't. The plot has so many twists and turns that by the end we're left wondering whether there really is any objective fact, let alone "truth."

In a world where good and evil are ambiguous, uncertain, and perhaps even mutually dependent, fighting secretive fire with secretive fire doesn't need to be so distasteful, even for our protagonists. Yet it should at least be troubling. While we don't need to be offended that the protagonists might keep their own secrets, it's hard to deny the general impression that the bad guys' guilt is more so only by degree.

Christians certainly understand that we all have flawed characters. In fact, Christian theology doesn't at all agree with the argument that humans are basically good. Rather, the Bible clearly teaches that every human being makes a regular practice of doing evil: "For all have sinned; all fall short of God's glorious standard" (Rom. 3:23 NLT).

The reason for this natural propensity to sin? We're separated from God, and that's why despite popular culture's mantras we can't trust our hearts: "The heart is deceitful above all things and beyond cure. Who can understand it?" (Jer. 17:9). Based on the Bible's appraisal, the protagonists in Brown's novels really can't trust their own motives, because we all sin and our hearts are suspiciously unknowable.

While we all in degrees hide truths and secret away facts for our own benefit, we know that's not the ideal. We know the world would be a much better place if we never had to make a choice between the lesser of two evils, because, ideally, circumstances would not dictate evil choices.

In that light we really shouldn't feel so good about applauding our protagonists' hypocrisy. That's not to say we should condemn a novel as evil when the good guys aren't always so good. As we've explored in earlier chapters, the job of story is to imitate life. And in life (by the Bible's accounting, anyway), good people aren't always so good. (See Rom. 3:23.)

However, we need to make an important distinction here. We acknowledge the protagonists' tendency to keep secrets and perhaps concede that it isn't necessarily a good thing, and yet we still try to justify their efforts as nobler than that bad guy's cover-up of some national secret. Maybe as we follow our fictional good guys' search for truth (remembering that they represent us), we also need to be cautious about casting stones at the evil conspirators who hide the truth—at least if we don't want to be hypocritical. Maybe we need to ask why it is that a secret can be a virtue for some and a vice for others. Could it be the bottom line of our twisted logic is that when the other guy holds the secret it's evil, but when we hold it for ourselves it's good?

All this confusion of motives and power plays makes the prophet Jeremiah's appraisal of the human heart more convincing. Who can really know it for sure?

Scaling the Walls

The human heart is hard to know or judge, as evidenced by *Digital Fortress*'s character Ensei Tankado, a brilliant computer programmer with a huge chip on his shoulder. His mother died during childbirth due to complications from her exposure to radiation when the nuclear bomb was dropped on Hiroshima. Tankado harbors a deep resentment toward the United States for robbing him of his mother and toward his father, who put Tankado up for adoption because the boy was born with severe physical deformities.

As a boy, Tankado learns the basics of computer programming and is soon considered a top young programmer. He is hired to work with the NSA to develop TRANSLTR. Told that the machine would only intercept and decode e-mail messages flagged by the U.S. Department of Justice, Tankado becomes enraged when he learns the NSA intends to read any and all e-mails. This, Tankado says, is a violation of basic human rights, and he quits his job with the NSA on the spot. As he is escorted out of the building, he looks at Trevor Strathmore and makes this prophetic statement: "We all have a right to keep secrets. Someday I'll see to it we can" (37).

When Susan Fletcher is called in to work on a Saturday, she knows something big is happening. Strathmore tells her that Tankado has sent a message, intercepted by TRANSLTR, that has bogged down the machine for more than fifteen hours when most messages, even ones with heavy encryption, take an average of six minutes to decode. Tankado's message is acting like a computer virus, taking TRANSLTR to the edge of self-destruction. Susan's fiancé, David Becker, must discover Tankado's secret passkey to stop the virus from destroying TRANSLTR.

Can we altogether blame Tankado's motives for attempting to destroy TRANSLTR? Isn't there something to his declaration "We all have a right to keep secrets" that seems reasonable? Whose is the nobler secret? What makes a secret good or evil?

Those standards of truth may not be so clearly defined—except by degree. But the balance of power most definitely resides in the secret. In *Digital Fortress*, secret knowledge and the search for a deeper knowledge is salvation for Susan, David, and the NSA.

The Point of a Deception

Chasing after the main characters in *Deception Point*, we find ourselves taking many of the same roads we find in *Digital Fortress*. President Zach Herney's administration leaks the news that NASA has suffered yet another setback, when the truth is that NASA has made a remarkable discovery it wants to keep secret. Only a few select people have knowledge of this discovery.

Rachel Sexton works for the National Reconnaissance Office, the government agency that in real life is in charge of building and operating spy satellites, or, as it proudly announces on its Web site, "The nation's eyes and ears in space" (www.nro.gov).

When Director Pickering asks Rachel to meet with the president, she assumes he wants to see her about an intelligence brief she had prepared. In actuality the president wants Rachel to go on a top-secret mission to brief his staff on a startling find. NASA discovered a meteorite that contains a fossil of a type of lice, which proves there is in fact life on other planets.

But not all is as it seems. Those who find clues that may bring the authenticity of the fossil into question meet with violent ends. Rachel and marine biologist Michael Tolland race to find the truth and to save their lives.

Then there's also the small matter of the presidential race. Rachel's father, Senator Sedgewick Sexton, is challenging Herney for the nation's highest-elected office. Rachel knows the secrets her father has kept hidden in his closet, and she despises the way he treated her late mother. Rachel does not want to purposely hurt her father's election chances, but neither does she want to see his lies hurt others. As it turns out, one of the targets of Sexton's campaign is NASA, which he believes has outlived its usefulness.

Again, twists and turns abound. One minute you think you know whom you can trust, and the next you're shocked to find out this person may be the one behind the mischief. This major theme of Brown's novels—the search for the truth—is transferred to the reader as well. We're also searching for truth—and it's not until the very end of Brown's stories that we learn whom we can trust to be telling the truth—or can we?

That, ironically, is the point of a deception—to win another's trust through falsehood. And while there might be some distinction between keeping a secret and telling an outright lie, in the end the point of it all is really the same: to hide the truth from some (or many) people.

Deception Point Plot Summary—the Beginning

1. Thirty-four-year-old Rachel Sexton works as an intelligence coordinator with the National Reconnaissance Office (NRO) under President Zach Herney's administration. Rachel's father is Senator Sedgewick Sexton, Herney's opponent in the upcoming presidential election. Over breakfast Senator Sexton tries to persuade his daughter to leave her current job to work for his campaign, an offer she refuses.

2. Rachel receives a page to report immediately to the office of NRO director William Pickering. Pickering tells Rachel that the president wants to see her. Rachel is then flown by helicopter to a secure landing strip where the president is waiting aboard Air Force One. Herney asks Rachel to go on a mission to observe and then update his staff on an important scientific discovery. Rachel then boards an F-14 and is flown to an ice shelf above the Arctic Circle.

3. Senator Sexton prepares for a debate on CNN with the help of his campaign aid Gabrielle Ashe. He seduced Gabrielle in his office when they first met, but now she keeps their relationship strictly business. She has counseled the senator to make the NASA budget one of his main campaign issues, which he has with great success. Gabrielle says she has a contact in the White House who informed her that the president recently received bad news from NASA—news that could seriously harm his re-election campaign.

4. Upon landing on the Milne Ice Shelf, Rachel meets Lawrence Eckstrom, NASA administrator. He introduces Rachel to Mike Tolland, a marine biologist who hosts a TV show called *Amazing Seas*. Rachel also meets Corky Marlinson, a well-known astrophysicist, as well as other scientists who have come to the Arctic because of this great discovery. The big news is that NASA satellites recently found evidence of a meteorite buried deep below the ice shelf. A drill reached the meteorite and returned a sample that contained fossils of a type of insect—proof that there is life beyond the earth. This news will validate NASA for good, no matter what the budget.

5. During the CNN debate, the president's senior advisor, Marjorie Tench, engages Senator Sexton on the topic of NASA and space exploration. Sexton says that NASA is a dinosaur and the money would be better spent on education. Sexton refutes the idea that NASA might find proof of life on other planets. Tench, while appearing stunned by this remark, is secretly thrilled at Sexton's on-camera put-down of NASA.

6. As the meteorite is brought up through the ice, Rachel talks with the president to find

out just why he sent her to this remote location. Herney says he wants Rachel to prepare a tele-vised briefing—not to the nation, but over closed-circuit television to his staff. He wants Rachel to validate this incredible find by NASA. At the same time, another scientist notices something strange in the water pit the meteorite came through. As he bends over to get a sam-ple of the water, he's stung by a tiny flying object and plunges into the icy water.

7. Gabrielle's secret source at the White House, whom she's never met, requests a meeting. Gabrielle goes warily, only to be shocked to learn that the person who has been covertly feeding her sensitive information useful to Senator Sexton's campaign is Marjorie Tench. Tench shows Gabrielle proof that Sexton has been accepting illegal campaign contributions from businessmen who want to privatize space exploration, as well as compromising pictures taken of Sexton and Gabrielle. Tench wants Gabrielle to publicly admit her affair with the senator, or the president will go public with Sexton's illegal contributions.

8. On the ice shelf, Rachel, Mike, Corky, and Norah Mangor prepare to go outside to take readings on the ice to see if there is any salt-water detectable. Norah insists that the ice is pure freshwater, but tests on the water in the pit where the meteorite was extracted show some saltwater, which casts a shadow on the veracity of the discovery. They need to conduct the test quickly because a press conference is sched-uled in less than two hours.

9. Gabrielle leaves the White House and goes to Senator Sexton's private apartment, hoping to learn that what Tench told her was all lies. But when she arrives, she overhears Sexton meeting with men who represent private space firms. She quietly leaves without letting the sen-ator know she was there.

10. Outside in the howling wind at the Arctic Circle, Norah takes readings that show salt is in the ice, invalidating NASA's discovery. She prints out the proof and gives it to Rachel, who tucks it in an outer pocket of her suit. But before she and the others can get back to the shelter, they are ambushed by men firing ice bullets at them. Norah is killed and Corky is knocked uncon-scious. Mike and Rachel open up a Mylar balloon that acts as a sail in the gale-force winds, taking them and Corky, who is still teth-ered to them, away from the assailants but toward the cliff of the ice shelf and the Arctic Ocean.

Continued on page 121

A Master Deceiver

Niccolò Machiavelli, fifteenth-century politician and diplomat to the city state of Florence, Italy, is best known for his treatise *The Prince,* which is the classic argument for the ends justifying any means, including those that compromise traditional moral values. Machiavelli had no qualms insisting that people in leadership need to be willing to deceive in order to retain power: "Men are so simple and so ready to obey present necessities, that one who deceives will always find those who allow themselves to be deceived" (ch. 18).

Machiavelli

Niccolò Machiavelli (3 May 1469–21 June 1527) [was a] Florentine political philosopher, musician, poet, and romantic comedic playwright.... The best known work of Machiavelli is his political treatise *Il Principe (The Prince).* It was written in an attempt to return to politics as an advisor to Lorenzo di Piero de' Medici. It has been argued that *The Prince* is not representative of Machiavelli's beliefs, as his advocacy of tyranny seems to contradict his earlier works. However, Machiavelli seems to have been in earnest when he argued the advantages of cruelty and fraudulence.... Since its publication, *Il Principe* has become a legendary handbook on how to become and remain a ruler.

Modern appreciations:
- Machiavelli was ranked #79 on Michael H. Hart's list of the most influential figures in history.
- In his book *Warrior Politics,* author and journalist Robert D. Kaplan cites Machiavelli as a proponent of a "pagan ethos," which Kaplan feels is preferable to Judeo-Christian morality in decision-making by politicians and businessmen.
- The late Tupac Shakur took on the alias of "Makaveli," a modified form of Machiavelli's name, shortly before he was murdered in 1996. Later, an album was released under the alias "Makaveli," *Makaveli: The Don Killuminati: 7 Day Theory,* which sold over 5 million copies.
- In the satirical *The Daily Show with Jon Stewart Presents America (The Book): A Citizen's Guide to Democracy Inaction,* Machiavelli is listed as having "No Impact" on American democracy.

—"Niccolò Machiavelli," Wikipedia

It might be easy to reject Machiavelli's utilitarian pragmatism, but every leader faces tough choices at one time or another in his or her career about whether to be forthright or to cover up and conspire. When your survival is on the line, it can be hard to be idealistic about things like truth.

Deception Point Plot Summary—the Conclusion
(**Spoiler Warning**—ending of the novel is revealed on this page.)

11. The wind takes Rachel, Mike, and Corky over the edge of the cliff but onto a small block of ice still attached to the shelf. The assailants come to the edge and decide to drop a "flash-bang" between the main ice shelf and the block of ice instead of shooting the three, thus sending them out to sea to die. The plan works. The ice block drops into the sea. Death is minutes away.

12. Gabrielle takes a cab to ABC News headquarters in D.C. She visits with her friend Yolanda Cole, who tells Gabrielle not to expose her affair with Senator Sexton. She assures Gabrielle that all this talk of illegal contributions and leaking pictures is just political smoke. Then the president's press conference begins, during which he reveals the great discovery of life on other planets to the world.

13. On the ice floe, Rachel pulls out an ice pick and begins to pound on the ice. A nearby U.S. submarine picks up the sound and rescues the three just in time. Rachel calls the White House from the submarine to stop the president from giving his press conference until she can show him the evidence that the meteorite was planted under the ice shelf. But Tench intercepts the call and accuses Rachel of a cheap trick to help her father in his campaign. The president proceeds with his speech.

14. Rachel calls NRO director Pickering on a videophone from the submarine. Mike and Corky are on the line with her. She shares the proof with Pickering that the meteorite was inserted in the ice. Pickering agrees that something is wrong. At the same time, Tench is informed that Rachel's call to the White House was placed from a sub in the Arctic Ocean.

15. Senator Sexton, taken aback by the announcement of NASA's incredible discovery, learns that the satellite system used to make this discovery—PODS—may not be working as NASA claims it is. And if it doesn't work, then how did NASA find the meteorite? Sexton sends Gabrielle to NASA to investigate. Gabrielle finds the PODS manager and gets him to confess that the satellite system is not operating properly. Gabrielle and Sexton now have proof that NASA—and the president—are lying. But Gabrielle wants nothing more to do with Sexton. She plots with Yolanda a way to get out of the relationship.

16. Pickering and Tench agree to meet to discuss the mess that's developing around NASA's discovery. The meeting is set for late at night at the FDR Memorial. But before Pickering can get there, a black helicopter swoops down and fires a missile that blows up Tench's car, killing her immediately. Meanwhile, Rachel, Mike, and Corky have been picked up from the submarine and are being transported back to the States, where they will board Mike's ship to conduct further tests on the meteorite. Pickering makes arrangements for their transportation.

17. Once on board Mike's ship, the three conclusively prove that the meteorite is actually an altered terrestrial rock. But before they can let anyone know, they are attacked by the same assailants who tried to kill them on the ice shelf. Leading the attack is Pickering himself, who confesses to planting the meteorite to save NASA. They overpower Pickering and escape.

18. Senator Sexton holds a press conference to reveal that the PODS system doesn't work, and thus, the meteorite must be fake. But instead of giving the press the handouts he had prepared to expose PODS as an inoperative system, the senator unknowingly gives the press a substitute handout that Yolanda Cole prepared—a handout containing pictures of the senator and Gabrielle in an intimate moment. Gabrielle and Rachel arrive at the press conference just as the truth hits Sexton. His political career is ruined.

19. Rachel, Mike, and Corky are invited to the White House and learn the president had nothing to do with the meteorite hoax. Afterward, Rachel and Mike reveal their love for each other.

It's All about Power

The reason for this struggle with truth is reasonable enough: survival. It's one of our basic instincts. As we saw in the previous chapter, utilitarian self-preservation can make sense in an amoral kind of way. And this is the instinct that is behind any deception and secrecy. By whatever means, the deceiver wants to acquire or maintain control and power. Countless forces are at work trying to rule your life, one way or the other. And as much as you would like to think you're the master of your own destiny, the Machiavellis of the world stand ready to pat you on the shoulder and patronizingly say, "You just keep telling yourself that."

That's what is so satisfying about conspiracy thrillers. Readers are allowed to vicariously experience the fear, the insecurity, the paranoia of the stories' protagonists, and still walk away reasonably sane. We experience a kind of catharsis when people we trusted in a story betray us by betraying the hero. We might even admire their Machiavellian cunning while remaining sufficiently detached so our morality remains conveniently intact.

Dan Brown has learned the formula for keeping readers turning his novels' pages. Conspiracies lurk around every corner. Someone is hiding the truth, and your life—and the protagonist's life—is in danger if you try to expose it. And Brown's gospel? Those who are really in control hide their identities. We can never know for certain whom the real power is that is actually pulling the strings. All we know is "they" are out to get us.

The Gnostic Way—Secret Knowledge

Gnosticism is something of a spiritual worldview for the Machiavellian rationale, since a core value is truth that is hidden from the generally ignorant masses. And in an increasingly Machiavellian world, gnostics and gnosticism have gained a lot of ground, especially since the release of *The Da Vinci Code*. Gnostic voices—such as those of Elaine Pagels, *The Gospel of Thomas,* and *The Gospel of Mary Magdalene*—are all mentioned in *The Da Vinci Code* as sources of the "truth" about Jesus. But *The Da Vinci Code* wasn't the first time Brown wrote about gnosticism. We actually see hints and characteristics of gnostic faith in *Digital Fortress* and *Deception Point*.

So what exactly is gnosticism? Even professed gnostics disagree as to what comprises gnostic faith, just as Christian denominations have differences about what makes up the peripheral components of the Christian faith. But most gnostics embrace several core values that define their religious worldview and distinguish them from Christians. (We'll explore many of these distinct core values in chapter 9.) However, one key gnostic value that is especially relevant to Brown's earlier novels is secret knowledge. Predictably, therefore, the gnostic's "true god" is mysterious and unknowable.

Gnostics believe that there is one true God, but this god did not create our world—or anything, for that matter—for everything created is flawed, and the one true God is perfect. Dr. Peter Jones explains this clearly in his book *Stolen Identity*:

> Gnosticism affirms that it is easy to know "the Creator of all creatures," but it is impossible to know the true God. The Creator is an imposter. The true God stands behind the false, clothed in mystery. Such is the mystery of God that the Gnostics end up saying only what he is not. "He is neither divinity nor blessedness nor perfection" (*Allogenes* 63). He is better than that. (18)

Unknowable as their God is, gnostics do see in created things bits and pieces of this truly perfect essence. In the gnostic faith, all is God and God is in everything. Sound familiar? It should. Gnosticism is a form of monism.

The Early Church and the Gnostics

Irenaeus (ca. AD 130–202) was bishop of Lugdunum in Gaul (now Lyon, France). Almost all of his writings were directed against gnosticism but affirmed orthodox Christian theology. He was a disciple of Polycarp, who was a disciple of Jesus' beloved disciple John (the Evangelist). One of his works, *Against Heresies* (AD 175–185), is ironically an invaluable resource to modern scholarship in understanding second-century gnostic teachings. (Irenaeus also provided the first explicit witness to a fourfold gospel canon: Matthew, Mark, Luke, and John.)

In book 3 (2.2) of his treatise, he wrote,

> But, again, when we [Christians] refer them [the Gnostics] to that tradition which originates from the apostles, [and] which is preserved by means of the succession of presbyters in the Churches, they object to tradition, saying that they themselves are wiser not merely than the presbyters, but even than the apostles, because they have discovered the unadulterated truth. For [they maintain] that the apostles intermingled the things of the law with the words of the Saviour; and that not the apostles alone, but even the Lord Himself, spoke as at one time from the Demiurge, at another from the intermediate place, and yet again from the Pleroma; but that they themselves, indubitably, unsulliedly, and purely, have knowledge of the hidden mystery: this is, indeed, to blaspheme their Creator after a most impudent manner! It comes to this, therefore, that these men do now consent neither to Scripture nor to tradition.

In addition to this "perfect God," many other lesser and more knowable gods exist. Gnosticism is therefore pantheistic. One of the most important "other gods" is Sophia, the representation of wisdom. The feminine aspect of the divine is a significant part of gnostic faith.

Salvation for gnostics is not freedom from sin but freedom from ignorance. Salvation comes from discovering hidden knowledge. For humans to reach this *gnosis,* or perfected knowledge, we need divinely ordained help. Messengers have come to reveal this knowledge through their words and lives.

One such messenger was Jesus, who, according to gnostics, is a "savior" not by his death and resurrection but by his words of wisdom and life of peace. The gnostic *Gospel of Thomas* portrays Jesus as just such an imparter of secret knowledge:

> Jesus said, "I am not your master. Because you have drunk, you have become intoxicated from the bubbling spring which I have measured out....
>
> "He who will drink from my mouth will become like me. I myself shall become he, and the things that are hidden will be revealed to him." (qtd. in Lambdin, vv. 13, 108)

Gnostics believe that Jesus was a god who put on human flesh for a while in order to teach us the way out of ignorance. On the cross Jesus "shed his skin" and ascended to heaven—not really dying, but leaving his fleshly costume to regain his heavenly one.

To gnostics, each individual must pursue the secret knowledge that will allow him or her to shed the skin of ignorance and, upon death, to free the divine spark we all have.

The Christ Way—Open Truth

The gnostics' Jesus may have bought into this Machiavellian worldview, but the Jesus of the Bible didn't. And while you wouldn't call Jesus cynical by any means, the label "idealist" doesn't quite fit either—certainly not in the sense of naïveté, anyway. This man who said he was the Son of God knew from the beginning of his story that he'd come into the world to die for humankind. Jesus wasn't whistling in the dark while trying to peer into it through rose-colored glasses. He saw death, horrific suffering, and sickness, and he knew what Judas was up to as well (Mark 14:17–21).

In Mark's gospel, when Jesus told his parable about the seeds that were sown in various types of soil (some fertile for growth, some dead and unyielding), he specified one scenario in which the seeds fall among thorns—a scenario that goes against the common Machiavellian and gnostic wisdom of the world.

> Still [other people], like seed sown among thorns, hear the word; but the worries of this life, the deceitfulness of wealth and the desires for other things come in and choke the word, making it unfruitful. (4:18–19)

Comment on Mark 4:18–20

In Jesus' parable of the seeds planted in various soils, he describes a type of soil that represents some people who "hear the word" but are preoccupied with the cares and riches of this life. In this passage, he describes three concerns that compete against his gospel message for a person's soul: distracting "worries of this life"; the "deceitfulness [deceptive lure] of wealth"; and the "desires for [all sorts of] other things" in place of God's Word. These unbelieving audiences have heard Jesus' truth, but because of the thriving, distracting thorns in their lives, the truth is choked to death. No new life will grow and produce in them.

But by contrast, others "hear the word" and "accept it" (the Greek word literally means "welcome it for themselves"). These are genuine disciples, who bear fruit in their lives (v. 20).

—Quoted from John Walvoord and Roy Zuck, *The Bible Knowledge Commentary*

The worries of this life, the deceitfulness of wealth, and the desire for things: All of these so-called thorns drive not only Machiavellians but most of the rest of us. Our motivations are fundamentally based on the desire for power and control over our lives. And yet Jesus used exactly the opposite kind of language, characterizing these desires in terms of death.

Machiavelli would have taken issue with Jesus on this point, at least as it relates to those called into leadership. From a Machiavellian viewpoint, Jesus did come to a tragic end. He failed to look out for number one. He didn't take up the mantle of leadership and play ball with the power brokers. You have to wonder how Jesus would measure up to the tough pressures of today's Machiavellian world.

Then again, he did claim to be God himself—the Creator and ultimate Leader of the universe. And his leadership method is no secret.

Out in the Open

In Mark 4, Jesus was speaking to a large crowd on the beach by the Sea of Galilee. That was the setting for Jesus' parable of the seeds falling among choking thorns. A huge crowd was pushing in to listen to him. If you've ever been caught up in a large crowd, you can probably appreciate the irony of God the Son finding himself crowded from all directions. So Jesus got into a boat and pushed a little way out into the water; then he turned and spoke to those on the shore (v. 1).

What Jesus had to say wasn't premised by a secret handshake, arcane symbology, or cryptic words spoken to a select few. Jesus' gospel isn't a we-versus-they proposition. He speaks plainly to anyone "who has ears to hear" (v. 9):

> Does anyone bring a lamp home and put it under a washtub or beneath the bed? Don't you put it up on a table or on the mantel? We're not keeping secrets, we're telling them; we're not hiding things, we're bringing them out into the open. (Mark 4:21–22 MSG)

As we saw in the previous chapter, Jesus did want to keep his identity secret until the time was right to reveal to his followers who he really was. But this was more like a closely guarded secret kept until the right moment, like when your friend walks through a door and into a surprise party. Timing matters, and when the right time had come, Jesus' message that he was God in the flesh was not to be kept secret any longer.

This message was to be openly proclaimed throughout the world to both Jews and Gentiles. The key point in Mark's gospel is that we don't need to acquire any secret knowledge to enter into a relationship with Jesus. The gates have been thrown wide open, and all are welcome. We don't have to guess who can be trusted. Jesus himself is Truth.

The readers of Brown's novels must constantly try to decipher whom to trust; the readers of Jesus' message in Mark don't have to break any code—Jesus made it clear that his message is not to be kept hidden.

In contrast, the world says there literally is a secret to success that's measured by keeping the secret and making sure to keep everyone else in the dark—or at least as many as possible. The fewer there are to share success, the more there is for you. In contrast, the Christian gospel, in its true form, welcomes all. That's what Jesus preached, and that's what his church practices. If it doesn't, then it's apparently operating by the opposing worldview and needs to examine whether it's indeed a truly Christian church.

The Power of Humility

God's truth is available to everyone, but in order to experience that truth, each of us must receive it. The growth of faith's seed is dependent on the soil's fertility.

As the apostle Peter wrote several years after Jesus' death and resurrection, God is actually willing to wait for every single person to turn to him: "He is being patient for your sake. He does not want anyone to perish, so he is giving more time for everyone to repent" (2 Peter 3:9 NLT). But while God isn't in a hurry, he also knows that many people will not believe. Many throughout history wouldn't— and won't—buy in to giving up power and control; they didn't see the thorns or care about fruitfulness.

On one side of the scale are humans, who operate in secrecy and deception, clawing their way to the top as best they can, trying to be the fittest so they will survive for just a little longer. Is there any question about their self-deception when it comes to having any real control over their own lives—or when they try to impose it on others?

And then on the other side is this all-powerful and all-controlling God, who operates with full disclosure and personifies truth. He doesn't even worry about grasping at glory or power, because this all-everything God is humble. He puts the needs of others before his own well-being.

The Humble God

Your attitude should be the same that Christ Jesus had. Though he was God, he did not demand and cling to his rights as God. He made himself nothing; he took the humble position of a slave and appeared in human form. And in human form he obediently humbled himself even further by dying a criminal's death on a cross.
—Philippians 2:5–8 NLT

That's why Jesus lowered himself to the point of being crowded and forced offshore, where he preached stories from a fishing boat, with gospel messages of total inclusiveness to anyone who would believe. He reduced himself for their sake, giving them the power to choose. He left it to every man, woman, and child to decide whether to reject him.

All of Jesus' human life was characterized by giving over power and control. The Bible's gospel story presents Jesus as the omnipotent and omniscient God the Son, who became finite flesh. For his thirty-plus years on this earth, he set aside his divine power and control for the sake of human beings past, present, and future.

So here you have the Creator of the universe growing up as a human "in wisdom and stature, and in favor with God and men" (Luke 2:52). It seems preposterous, certainly by the world's standards, but it's not so preposterous if you've studied the rest of the Bible's account of God leading up to the New Testament gospels. God has always been remarkably patient and long-suffering, repeatedly meeting people where they are at, even at the risk of being misunderstood and misrepresented. God condescends in grace, never to disgrace.

That naturally is the character of the Bible's Jesus as well. You can see it consistently … a humble Jesus, the Son of God, constantly about the business of serving others and glorifying God the Father, and never grasping after power.

So it's no wonder that this same Jesus was able to resist Satan's temptations in the wilderness.

The Ploys of the Great Deceiver

Mark's gospel gives only a quick, short nod to this fascinating scene in Jesus' life: "At once the Spirit sent him out into the desert, and he was in the desert forty days, being tempted by Satan. He was with the wild animals, and angels attended him" (Mark 1:12–13). Matthew's gospel actually goes into more detail, filling out the same story. In it we see two starkly contrasting images—one of truth personified and proclaimed, the other of deception and hidden agendas.

What's interesting about Satan's temptations of Jesus is the premise, "If you are the Son of God ..." (Matt. 4:3, 6). It's the same premise used today in the debate over the historical Jesus. Those who question Jesus' deity demand proof that he truly was God—"If Jesus really is the Son of God, then prove it!" But according to the Bible, Jesus was open and forthright about being the Son of God—in fact, that's what got him killed.

A better conspiracy gospel story would have had only a select few knowing this about Jesus as he worked in secrecy to build his power base. And maybe Judas could have been conspiring with Jesus. Together they might have pretended to build an allegiance with the power brokers in the Jewish government and conspired to overthrow the Roman oppressors.

Then they would have betrayed the Jewish leaders as well and set Jesus up as the true Messiah who could lead the Jewish people to a new era of self-rule and perhaps even world domination. It could have been an epic story of shifting power and control.

But the version of "God the Son" that Jesus clung to wasn't going to take the story anywhere except to defeat an apparent death.

That's where Satan's proposition could have made a lot more sense, at least by the world's standards. Because Satan offered Jesus a way to glorious victory in a world Satan controlled, if only Jesus would play by the world's rules.

The first temptation of Jesus was simple enough: to take just a short break from his intense spiritual preparation time. It was certainly understandable that he would be hungry after fasting forty days and forty nights (Matt. 4:2). But Jesus knew how easy it is to become distracted by the physical worries of the world, and he wouldn't give in to the temptation to take control by simply turning stones into bread (vv. 3–4).

Same Tactics, Different Response

The Bible's account of Satan's tempting Jesus shows him using very similar tactics to those used he employed through the serpent with Eve in the garden of Eden:
- He appealed to physical appetite. He tempted Jesus to make bread from stones (see Matt. 4:3), and he tempted Eve to eat the forbidden fruit (see Gen. 3:1–3).
- He appealed to personal gain while denying the consequences. When tempting Jesus, there was the implication of the Messiah's gaining fame and idolizing followers without any personal sacrifice, when he said, "You will not strike your foot" (Matt. 4:6); and he likewise told Eve that with the benefits of eating the fruit, "You will not surely die" (Gen. 3:4).
- He appealed to power and glory. He promised Jesus the world's kingdoms (see Matt. 4:8–9), and he promised Eve, "You will be like God" (Gen. 3:5).

In Genesis the serpent questioned whether God really said what Eve recalled. In Matthew, it's particularly significant and ironic that Jesus quoted God's Word when he was being tempted, especially since he is God the Son:
- In response to the first temptation, Jesus quoted Deuteronomy 8:3: "Man does not live on bread alone but on every word that comes from the mouth of the LORD."
- To the second temptation (an out-of-context misrepresentation of Psalm 91:11–12), Jesus quoted Deuteronomy 6:16: "Do not test the LORD your God."
- To the third temptation, Jesus affirmed Deuteronomy 10:20: "Fear the LORD your God and serve him."

The Tempter then became a little more overt in his challenge for Jesus to take control and prove to Satan, the world, and to himself that he was God the Son. He called God's bluff by challenging him to perform a miracle—to test God by throwing himself off the highest point of the temple so that the world would see he was God's Son, and everyone would have to believe. But Jesus still would have none of it (vv. 5–7).

Finally, Satan laid all of his cards on the table. He offered Jesus the very thing a messiah should have been looking for. Satan guaranteed Jesus power and control and dominion over the world. All Jesus had to do was bow down to Satan. In exchange for allegiance to Satan, Jesus could rule the world and lead it into a new era under his benevolent dictatorship. Jesus wouldn't have to spend the rest of his days progressively losing power and control of his own life, only to die a horrible death on a cross. He could live and rule as he was meant to. Wasn't that his Father's will, after all?

But Jesus couldn't seriously entertain thinking that way, because as the God of the Bible, he was characterized by humble selflessness—by his willingness to give over power and control to people so they could choose to accept or reject him.

Ironically, it was by *not* grasping power and control that Jesus proved he was literally made of the same stuff as his Father. Can't you just picture Satan walking away after Jesus told him to get lost: "Away from me, Satan! For it is written, 'Worship the Lord your God, and serve him only'" (Matt. 4:10)? The Devil must have been furiously muttering, "Typical. He's just like his Father."

The tactics of any deceiver are subterfuge, cover-up, and misdirection, all in order to grasp control. The Machiavellians of the world—even the well-intentioned gnostics—insist that is the only way to maintain power. And we can only hope that the good guys who employ the world's methods are at least reasonably good. That's all we can rely upon, according to the world's gospel.

But the God of the Bible's gospel is about humility—about lowering himself to the point of sacrifice for the sake of others who may very well reject him. The humble God Jesus is far removed from the alleged conspiracy of *The Da Vinci Code,* which would have Christ followers hijacking a gnostic faith and changing a rabbi named Jesus into a god. So bent on control are these conspirators, that with godlike foresight, they somehow know their kind will one day take control of civilization.

Yet the Christian gospel portrays God as releasing control that is rightfully his and giving himself into the hands of those he created. It's all about power; but according to the Bible's gospel, that's only because the all-powerful God has given us the power to accept or reject the gift of his Son.

Dan Brown's gospel is about survival by any means of power obtainable; the Bible's gospel is about absolute power given away for death on a cross. Ask yourself the same question we posed earlier regarding self-sacrifice: Which gospel resonates with your soul? Which do you want to be true? Is God the unknowable, mysterious, and covert God who has nothing to do with this corrupt creation? Is he the God of the gnostic and Machiavellian world, the *Digital Fortress* and *Deception Point* world that dictates that he who holds the secret holds all the cards?

Or is he the God of revelation and accessibility, of open humility, inclusiveness, and sacrifice, who lays down his life for a people who can choose to accept or reject him?

Don't we all want the God who conquered sin and death and offers the same to anyone—without exception—who will follow him? Covert, exclusive, and secretive; or open, inclusive, and revelatory. It's your choice.

7

The Yin & Yang of
Angels & Demons

John sat across from his daughter, Sharon. She'd just returned from college, and he was trying his best to make conversation with her. But it was hard. "I'm sorry, honey. I don't see this yin-and-yang stuff relating to the real world."

Sharon smiled patiently at him and tried once more. "It's daylight now. But it will be dark in about six hours."

"Seven."

"Fine, seven. The point is, day always gives way to evening, and evening to night, and night to morning, and morning to noon. So light and darkness are always in a balanced cycle in nature."

"Did your all-knowing professor happen to point out to you the very long days that take place on the sun?"

"Yin-and-yang philosophy says that there is balance out there somewhere in the universe for everything—a black hole, for instance. Day and night are just one example. For water there's fire, for cold there's hot, for south there's north, and for left there's right."

"And for your mom, there's me." John eyed his empty glass on the table, then looked over his shoulder for a waitress.

"Well, yeah. For male, there's female too. It really makes a lot of sense to me. It explains a lot about the way things are, especially evil and good. I mean, I learned in church that there is God and there is the Devil, and for angels there are demons. They both exist and they both need each other, though they'll never admit it."

"Neither would your mother or me."

"Right, and just like in marriage, it's when they get out of balance that things go so wrong."

John suddenly grew serious. "So this ying-yang god of yours created evil? And that's a good thing?"

"Yin, Dad. And … not really created. See, this only works if you understand that God isn't just some separate being out there who snapped his fingers and things came into existence. God is everything. And God has always existed. Everything has always existed, just in different forms. God is always evolving, changing, growing into something new and better."

"And always in balance?" John picked up his empty glass and eyed it even more intently.

Yin and Yang

The concept of yin and yang—the belief that everything in the universe is composed of these opposing but complementary elements—has its origin in ancient Chinese philosophy and metaphysics. Yin, the feminine element, is passive, dark, cold, wet, downward seeking, and corresponds to the night; yang, the masculine element, is active, light, warm, dry, upward seeking, and corresponds to the day. Water often symbolizes yin, and fire is often a symbol of yang.

—"Yin and Yang," Wikipedia

"Right! Always in balance."

"Well, I have an imbalance, here." He pointed his empty cup at Sharon. "My cup is empty, and yours is full. How about helping me out by balancing things out a bit?" He smiled mischievously. "See— then mine'll be half empty, and yours'll be half full."

Brown's Balance of Powers

Much of what Brown's world of *Angels & Demons* means to you depends on how you look at the world and reality. One thing's for sure, though—it's not the world of the supernatural, suspense novels depicting a spiritual warfare between angelic and demonic hosts—at least, not in the traditional sense that many Christians might have been thinking when they first encountered the title of his second novel.

Angels & Demons Plot Summary—the Beginning

1. Harvard professor of symbology and Illuminati expert Robert Langdon is contacted by Max Kohler, the director of CERN, the world's largest nuclear-research facility. Langdon is flown from Boston to Switzerland on a Boeing X-33 superjet in order to help decipher the murder of CERN physicist Leonardo Vetra, who died with *Illuminati* branded on his chest. Meanwhile, the murderer "Hassassin" plots his next move with the mysterious mastermind who has employed him: Janus.

2. At CERN headquarters Langdon meets crippled Kohler, who explains the purpose of CERN, Vetra's duality as a Catholic priest and a scientist, and Kohler's own abhorrence of religion. Langdon explains that the Illuminati was a sixteenth-century secret society of enlightened scientists who opposed the Catholic Church's teachings about science and were severely persecuted as a consequence.

3. Vittoria Vetra, daughter of Leonardo and herself a CERN physicist, joins Langdon and Kohler. They discover that the murderer has stolen antimatter for terrorist purposes against the Vatican, where a new pope is being elected. The antimatter will detonate in twenty-four hours. Kohler sends Vittoria and Langdon to Rome.

4. Langdon and Vittoria meet a skeptical Commander Olivetti and then the more receptive camerlengo priest, Carlo Ventresca, who is in control of the Vatican until a new pope is elected. While Langdon and Vittoria explain the situation to Olivetti and Ventresca, a phone call is put through from the Illuminati Hassassin who gloats as he tells them that he's holding four cardinals captive and will kill one cardinal each hour until the final culmination at midnight when Vatican City will be destroyed.

5. Langdon and Vittoria go to the Vatican archives in search of clues to the locations of the impending assassinations. They discover and decipher the symbolic Illuminati map, hidden in a secret "third book" written by Galileo, that contains clues invoking the ancient four elements: earth, air, fire, and water. They identify the first marker as the Pantheon, enlist the help of Olivetti and his guards, and rush to the site.

6. At the Pantheon, Langdon and Vittoria realize they're in the wrong place. After

regrouping, they realize the correct site is Chigi Chapel. They speed off in a taxi, followed by Olivetti and his guards and, unbeknownst to all, two BBC reporters. At the church they find a crypt, but they're too late: The first cardinal is dead, suffocated with dirt and branded on the chest with the word *Earth*.

7. Langdon and Vittoria determine that the next site is Saint Peter's Square. There they discover the second cardinal dead, with his lungs punctured and *AIR* branded on his chest. BBC reporters broadcast the event worldwide, soon followed by Illuminati claims to have poisoned the late pope.

8. Langdon, Vittoria, and Olivetti rush to the third site, the Church of Santa Maria della Vittoria, and discover the cardinal suspended from cables and being burned to death. The cardinal's chest has been branded with the word *fire*. Before they can intervene, the Hassassin attacks them: Vittoria is knocked unconscious, Olivetti is killed, and Langdon barely escapes by hiding in a sarcophagus.

9. When firemen rescue him, Langdon realizes the Hassassin has taken Vittoria. He determines the fourth site—Bernini's Fountain at the Piazza Navona—and rushes there, where he confronts the Hassassin, who attacks and overcomes him. Langdon feigns death underwater, and the Hassassin leaves. Langdon recovers too late to save the fourth cardinal but deciphers the last clue to the Illuminati lair and rushes to save Vittoria.

10. Langdon arrives just in time, fights the Hassassin, and, with Vittoria's help, the Hassassin falls to his death. Looking over at the nearby Vatican, they see a helicopter arrive. Vittoria realizes that the person descending the gangplank is Max Kohler. She and Langdon conclude that Kohler must be Janus, and they rush down to a secret tunnel connecting the castle to the Vatican.

Continued on page 139

You won't find a literal angel or demon in Brown's complex and fascinating plot. While the subject matter is very spiritual, it's rooted in the physical reality we know. Brown's spirituality is very "down to Mother Earth."

Angels & Demons, written after *Digital Fortress,* has as its driving theme and purpose a struggle that's as familiar as the grand battle between good and evil: the battle between science and religion. Brown witnessed this conflict firsthand:

> My parents' opposing views (my father an agnostic mathematician and my mother a religious church musician) made for an interesting childhood. I grew up surrounded by the paradoxical philosophies of science and religion, and though I wanted to believe in Christianity, as I got older and studied more science, I had a hard time reconciling the two.... This was how I ended up writing *Angels & Demons*—a science vs. religion thriller set within a Swiss physics laboratory and Vatican City. ("Dan Brown Witness," pars. 39, 41)

Angels & Demons is Brown's sincere attempt to reconcile these two forces—science and religion—that in today's culture are seen as diametrically opposed. We might be tempted to leap to a conclusion as to which force is the "angel" and which is the "demon," but it isn't that simple. Brown's solution to the conflict is a mind shift, a completely different worldview from Judeo-Christian sensibilities. In Brown's world the battle can't be understood in terms of good triumphing over evil, or vice versa; rather, salvation is to be found in the balance of yin and yang, the two opposite but complementary elements in the universe.

This symmetry between yin and yang is at the heart of *Angels & Demons*. In the next two chapters, we'll compare and contrast Brown's gospel story with two of the Bible's gospel stories, Luke and John. We selected Luke because he was a doctor with a keen analytical mind, and he recounts in his gospel several encounters with both angels and demons. We chose John because he was the most abstract, philosophical thinker of the four gospel writers.

Dan Brown would no doubt like both of these gospel writers; perhaps he would even appreciate the duality of these two different approaches to the same gospel story.

A Beautiful Symmetry

Early in the novel, Vittoria Vetra reveals to CERN director Max Kohler and protagonist hero Robert Langdon the remarkable discovery that she and her just-murdered father had recently made:

> [Antimatter is] a fact of nature. Everything has an opposite. Protons have electrons. Up-quarks have down-quarks. There is a cosmic symmetry at the subatomic level. Antimatter is *yin* to matter's *yang*. It balances the physical equation. (75)

It's true that much about our existence can be seen in terms of duality: light and dark, heat and cold, masculine and feminine, life and death. These facts characterize, and to some extent even define, our lives. But how do we interpret the facts? As we've seen, that's always going to be the big question of truth.

We enter into *Angels & Demons'* complex labyrinth of intrigue and conspiracy by way of a horrific and bizarre murder. Leonardo Vetra's murderer had cruelly branded the word *Illuminati* on his victim's chest. When Langdon first sees this evidence in a fax, he is astounded. "'Illuminati,' he stammered, his heart pounding. 'It can't be ...'" (6). His worst fear is confirmed when he turns the fax upside down and discovers that the word is still legible. The symbols used to form the word are symmetrical; they can be read both ways. Langdon isn't sure why or how the Illuminati symbols have reemerged, but it can't be good. Later, at the crime scene, Langdon further reflects, "Ancient documents described the symbol as an *ambigram—ambi* meaning 'both'—signifying it was legible *both* ways" (31).

Langdon knows the use of ambigrams to be the legendary Illuminati's modus operandi because symmetry was one of their core

Character Sketch: ROBERT LANGDON

The forty-year-old Harvard professor of religious symbology has "what his female colleagues referred to as an 'erudite' appeal—wisps of gray in his thick brown hair, probing blue eyes, an arrestingly deep voice, and the strong, carefree smile of a collegiate athlete." He also has "the body of a swimmer, a toned, six-foot physique that he vigilantly maintained with fifty laps a day in the university pool" (5). From the start of the novel, Langdon is preoccupied with aging and loneliness. He wears a Mickey Mouse watch "as a daily reminder to stay young at heart" (114). A self-described "callow romantic" (192), Langdon nevertheless sustains an intellectual agnosticism toward Christianity, science, and even Vittoria's neo-pagan overtures.

values. In fact, Langdon says that Galileo was something of a charter member of the Illuminati, and his alleged philosophy explains the deeper significance of symmetry.

> Galileo was an Illuminatus. And he was also a devout Catholic.... He held that sci-
> ence and religion were not enemies, but rather *allies*—two different languages
> telling the same story, a story of symmetry and balance ... heaven and hell, night
> and day, hot and cold, God and Satan. Both science and religion rejoiced in God's
> symmetry ... the endless contest of light and dark. (32–33)

Heaven and hell, God and Satan. That perhaps best sums up what this philosophy of duality means to us, because the premise behind the worldview in *Angels & Demons*—that opposites, such as God and Satan, are really two sides of the same coin—can make all the difference in how we view our existence. It also impacts the choices we make, because it necessarily determines our understanding of good and evil, or right and wrong, and whether there even is such a thing as morality.

The Rhythm of Pure Symmetry

Robert Langdon, while deciphering the ancient Illuminati map, realizes the significance of four lines of poetry written by poet John Milton (also an alleged member of the Illuminati):

> Iambic pentameter was a symmetrical meter based on the sacred Illuminati numbers of
> 5 and 2!... Five ... for Pythagoras and the pentagram. Two ... for the duality of all
> things.... Iambic pentameter, on account of its simplicity, was often called "pure verse"
> or "pure meter." (218)

A Monist Balancing Act

The yin-and-yang philosophy of symmetry fits perfectly with a monist worldview. While it embraces the duality and symmetry of all things in nature, it also asserts that all opposite forces are interdependent and bound together into a unified whole. But that's not to say the unified whole can't sometimes be a bit lopsided.

This, the yin-yang monists will explain, is why all of nature is continually in flux, always trying to achieve balance. If you shake a

Angels & Demons Plot Summary—the Conclusion
(Spoiler Warning—ending of the novel is revealed on this page.)

11. Kohler is ushered in to see camerlengo Ventresca. Meanwhile, a guard lets Langdon and Vittoria into the Vatican. They hear a scream coming from the pope's office. Kohler is aiming a gun at the camerlengo, and Ventresca is writhing in pain with *Illuminati* branded on his chest. Guards shoot Kohler and the apparent infiltrator, Swiss guard Rocher. The dying Kohler hands Langdon a video-recorded message.

12. With minutes to spare before the antimatter detonation, guards escort the group out of the Vatican to the helicopter, carrying the injured Ventresca. But Ventresca breaks free, displaying before horrified spectators and media his branded chest. Seeming to experience an ecstatic message from God, he rushes back into the Vatican and down into the catacombs, where he finds the antimatter canister on Saint Peter's tomb. He rushes back outside with the canister and commandeers the helicopter. Langdon joins the camerlengo to help get rid of the antimatter before it detonates.

13. All watch the helicopter take flight. A couple of minutes later, the detonation lights up the sky. Langdon and Ventresca are believed dead. But Ventresca miraculously appears on the basilica's roof. Meanwhile, Langdon plunges into the Tiber River and is rescued.

14. While fading in and out of consciousness, Langdon pieces together what happened: Ventresca locked the canister in a cargo box and threw away the key. Then he jumped out of the helicopter with a parachute strapped around him, leaving Langdon to die. Langdon jumped without a parachute but used a windshield tarp to slow and steer himself toward the river.

15. After being pulled from the river, Langdon is taken to a local hospital and treated by a medical team. When he recovers consciousness, he listens to Kohler's message and realizes the truth.

16. In a frenzy after the clearly miraculous circumstances, the cardinals of the conclave gather in the Sistine Chapel, ready to elect Ventresca as the new pope. But Langdon arrives with the mini-camcorder and plays the video on a television screen for the conclave. On it Kohler confronts Ventresca as being Janus. Ventresca also admitted his conspiracy and then branded his own chest.

17. When Ventresca enters the conclave, expecting to be greeted as candidate for pope, he instead sees Robert Langdon playing a video. Confronted with the truth, he confesses to the cardinals that there were no Illuminati and that he conspired to lift up faith above science again, while also bringing retribution to the pope, who Ventresca believed had betrayed his vow.

18. Ventresca slips away from the conclave and in his madness douses himself with lamp oil. He appears on the papal balcony before the still ignorant, adoring masses and lights himself on fire. Without screaming, the camerlengo succumbs to the flames and dies.

19. The details of Ventresca's crimes are not revealed to the public, which perpetuates myths of his miraculous ascension to heaven. Langdon and Vittoria retreat together to some well-earned peace.

tub of water, it will slosh back and forth, with greater volume favoring one side and then the other. So it goes with so-called evil; if one side gains power, then the pendulum swings back to the other side, until finally everything settles down into balance.

Even the generally agnostic Langdon seems to have such an appreciation—perhaps even a yearning—for this balance. When flying in a helicopter over Rome on his way to the Vatican, he sees the convoluted traffic below. *"Koyaanis-qatsi*, he thought, recalling the Hopi term for 'life out of balance'" (118).

And who doesn't long for balance? It's a good thing to have in life, after all. Too much work and no play make Johnny a very dull boy—and eventually a dead boy, if he doesn't learn his personal balancing act. Christians should endorse such an approach to life as well. The biblical Jesus knew when to take time out from his busy ministry to pray and be still before God. (See Luke 5:15–16.)

Perhaps the Illuminati hit the mark, at least originally, before they went and got all imbalanced themselves. Were their aspirations so sinister? Why wouldn't we have at least as an ideal this "New World Order" in which society, politics, and religion could be in perfect balance (39)?

Janus the Two-Faced

Behind the brutal machinations of the Hassassin is the Illuminati's modern incarnation, Janus. Though his face isn't revealed until the end, his name captures our imagination, as it does the Hassassin's: "Janus ...Was it a reference, he wondered, to the Roman two-faced god ... or to the moon of Saturn?" (14).

The pagan god Janus is a perfect avatar for the terrible duality that the *Angels & Demons* Janus is living. The classic Roman two-faced god represents the idealistic symmetry of looking forward and backward. In true yin-yang fashion, he symbolized change and transition, as in the progression of past to future or the middle ground between barbarity and civilization (or as in *Angels & Demons*, religion and science).

But Brown's Janus has a disturbing side. He isn't who he seems to be. He's two-faced, living a lie. And he is carrying out horrific atrocities in the name of what he believes to be right and good. To call him a hypocrite would be an understatement. And yet there is a kind of symmetry and balance in Janus, isn't there?

Balancing Good with Evil

The problem is, monists pretty much have to justify everything—no matter how "evil" our gut says something might be—in their allegiance to wholeness and balance. That can be very difficult to buy in to when you start poring over the great tragedies and evils that have occurred throughout history. When you're holding the empty glass, it's hard to appreciate your neighbor who has the full one.

That's because thoughts like *That's wrong!* or *How can anyone accept such injustice?* go through your head. In *Angels & Demons* it may be argued in yin-yang fashion that the horrific works of the Hassassin are the consequences of imbalance that need to be countered, and yet the brutality of each cardinal's murder is portrayed as nothing less than evil. Ironically, Brown clearly intends it to be. And the bitter realization of who Janus is at the end of the story multiplies the evil tenfold.

When terrorists flew two planes into the sides of the twin World Trade Center towers in Manhattan, killing nearly three thousand civilians, it would seem unreasonable and even outrageous for someone to explain away the tragedy by claiming that it happened to correct some cosmic imbalance, wouldn't it? There was something deep inside each soul that looked on in horror at the television on Tuesday, September 11—something that universally cried out in so many words, "No! Please no!" No matter the ensuing speeches, the politics, or the conspiracy theories, every human knows the attack was viciously wrong.[†]

So it's all the more outrageous when, at the climax of *Angels & Demons,* Ventresca the camerlengo priest—the one spiritual character who shines as a beacon of hope and sanity throughout most of the novel—reveals himself to be anything but. Stranger still, he reveals himself to be more monist than Christian in his rationale. The reasoning he uses to justify his actions has strikingly yin-yang overtones:

> Show them the old demons. Remind them of their fear. Apathy is death. Without darkness, there is no light. Without evil, there is no good. (533)

This statement from the same man who had earlier preached pleadingly to the worldwide masses a more virtuous, spiritual balance:

[†] If you haven't read the *Angels & Demons* and don't want to know a major plot twist, skip the next five paragraphs.

> Our resources are drying up from our campaign to be the voice of balance as you
> plow blindly on in your quest for smaller chips and larger profits. (381)

Perhaps this balance of hypocrisy makes good sense, in a yin-and-yang kind of way. You have to take the good with the bad. Or, into every balanced life, a little evil (at least) must fall.

The Imbalanced Christian God

The God of Christianity is decidedly imbalanced, at least by yin-yang standards. But what we might perceive as imbalance is in God's view a complete wholeness and unity that we can't begin to imagine. It's all just a matter of which scales you're using. And as we've been saying throughout this book, you will have to choose which gospel to believe—or, in this case, which scale you'll live by.

Think back to the premise established in chapter 3: God is a person, and we can't presume to define him according to our personal standards or preferences. The God of Christianity won't force you into a mold against your will, and you certainly can't hope to get away with doing that to God. As he makes repeatedly clear throughout the Bible, he is who he is. Who he is exactly, well, that's the fun of theology, of discovering what he has revealed about himself in the Bible. But whether or not you decide to get to know him for who he is, he is, regardless.

And if you study what God has revealed about himself in the Bible, you'll quickly learn one thing about Christianity's God: He's not at all what yin-yang followers might wish him to be. Even so, Vittoria Vetra, Brown's most articulate and sincere pagan apologist and evangelist, is very interested in putting God in her little yin-yang box:

> "Mr. Langdon, what does the Bible say about the Creation? What did God create?"
>
> Langdon felt awkward, not sure what this had to do with anything. "Um, God created … light and dark, heaven and hell—"
>
> "Exactly," Vittoria said. "He created everything in opposites. Symmetry. Perfect balance." (72–73)

Langdon and Vittoria are, of course, basing their own interpretation of truth according to their particular spin on Genesis 1:

And God said, "Let there be light," and there was light. God saw that the light was good, and he separated the light from the darkness. God called the light "day," and the darkness he called "night." And there was evening, and there was morning— the first day. (vv. 3–5)

Brown's dualistic view of creation certainly raises some interesting philosophical questions that we could no doubt debate in a manner reminiscent of philosophers arguing whether trees actually make a sound when they fall in forests if no one can hear them. Can God create the absence of something? No more than logic dictates you can't prove a negative. Regardless, nowhere does the text in Genesis say that God created darkness. It does say he created light, which he deemed a "good thing." And it says that he *separated* light *from* darkness—energy from the absence of energy.

Character Sketch: VITTORIA VETRA

Langdon's first impression of Vittoria is that she's "not overly beautiful" (56). (Before we're too hard on him, Langdon himself is likewise "not overly handsome" [5].) Still, he is attracted to Vittoria, who will inevitably become yin to his personal yang. She's a young Italian woman—tall, thin, lithe, and graceful, with long black hair and chestnut-colored skin. Max Kohler is quick to point out that "she is a strict vegetarian and CERN's resident guru of Hatha yoga" (49–50). She is the adopted daughter of Leonardo Vetra, the first Illuminati murder victim, and as senior researcher and Bio Entanglement Physicist for CERN, she works in dangerous ecological systems for months on end. Langdon finds himself drawn by "an aura of composure about her—an almost magnetic radiance of wholeness" (107). She's the novel's clarion call for monist paganism, with a "bewitching clarity in her eyes ... a purity in her voice" (110–11).

Moving Toward the Light

This is consistent with the metaphors used throughout the Bible, and by Jesus himself, of light representing goodness and darkness representing evil (see John 1:5–9; 3:19–21; 8:12). These physical states of light and darkness are themselves amoral—they serve only as analogies for moral realities. So when we put our kids to bed at night, we needn't worry them about darkness itself being evil.

It's also clear from the repeated duality themes in *Angels & Demons* that the characters who speak of material duality in nature also apply it to spiritual questions of morality. We're not just talking about light and darkness, up-quarks and down-quarks, matter and antimatter—we're talking about the yin-and-yang balance of good and evil.

The Christian's biblical worldview is not at all a matter of duality, achieving a balance between light and darkness (good and evil); rather, it's about imbalance, tipping the scale toward the light, because darkness is a vacuum without light. In God's economy, there's no balance of power. He has it all. You could no more belong to God and retain some balance of evil than you could cling to darkness if you lived on the sun. It's all light—no darkness.

God did not create evil, nor did he create any person to be evil. He only gave human beings the option of separating from his goodness. Sin and evil are the consequences of this choice, but God didn't create them. They are only the corrupt result of separation from what is good.

Mixing Messages

Many well-intentioned Christ followers have adopted dualistic ideas into their faith and, consequently, have their gospel stories mixed up. (In theological circles this is called *syncretism*.) These mixed-up Christians tend to believe that Satan and demons are on an equal footing with God and angels in the battle between good and evil. It's as if Satan and his team and God and his team are two warring forces, and it might very well be a toss-up as to who's going to win in the end—at least if you don't do your part. Some Christians even believe that God created evil just to keep things in balance.

Not only is this strange rationalization nowhere to be found in the Bible, but it doesn't make any sense. If God is a person (not a human being, mind you, but all that makes a human a person and all that Christians mean by being "made in God's image"), then he couldn't be a good person if he created evil. He would be either prone to evil like the rest of us or inept, which begs the question, "So who or what out there does define what is supremely good?"

If evil were a created thing, the pagan-monist worldview would be the only approach that would make sense. It would be conceivable that matter and antimatter, light and darkness, and good and evil have always coexisted in various evolving forms. But then, you cannot have your cake of moral ambiguity and eat it too. We're back to "evil" being kind of a good thing in the overall balance.

An example of this same moral ambivalence, but between life and death, is presented in two significant scenes in *Angels & Demons* involving Robert Langdon. In the first scene, while fading into unconsciousness, Langdon dreams about a formative event that took place during his childhood. He had fallen into an abandoned well and struggled to survive for nearly five hours before being rescued. "Exhausted, he wanted to give up. And yet he felt the water buoy him, cooling his burning fears until he was numb" (390).

In the second scene, Langdon has miraculously survived a fall from a helicopter into the Tiber River, and he is again slipping into unconsciousness: "The lapping that lulled in him a far-off sense of peace was also pulling him back. It was trying to awaken him from a dream" (503).

The yin-yang god of nature, personified in water, will both drown as well as buoy and cool; it will lull him into a peaceful oblivion while also "trying to awaken him" to a redeemed life. Whatever the outcome, the novel shows no apparent moral value or preference either way—not for light over darkness or life over death or angels over demons.

Angels

Dan Brown's gospel story has no literal angels. Most are the stone variety, as in the countless sculptures that populate Rome. Robert Langdon's entire clue hunt is guided by these statues, from Bernini's *Habakkuk and the Angel*—in Chigi Chapel, pointing the way to the second Illuminati clue (285)—to the mammoth bronze angel that crowns Castel S. Angelo, entered by way of the famous Bridge of

Angels, itself flanked by twelve towering Bernini seraphs (425). In Brown's world they prominently stand as contrasting the Christian yin with the equally prominent yang—pagan images and sculptures (Rome's demons), also all over the city, as well as within the Vatican itself. (Ironically, there actually is a Roman bust of the yin-yangesque god Janus in the Vatican.)

Brown's Angel of Justice

Angels & Demons also contains a few other telling angelic allusions. For instance, the Hassassin boasts to himself that he is something of an angel:

> Now they [the Illuminati] had bestowed on him the ultimate honor. He would be
> their hands and their voice. Their assassin and their messenger. The one his
> people knew as *Malak al-haq*—the Angel of Truth. (66)

Considering the depraved reward he has just reaped for himself at a brothel and the vicious brutality upon which he is about to embark, the Hassassin's association with anything angelic is clearly ironic. But there's also the yin-yang angle. The pagan-monist needs to remember, after all, the hard-line question of Pilate: "What is truth?" (John 18:38). To this Muslim assassin, of a people long abused by so-called Christians, vengeance is truth. He is the angel of justice. Maybe we shouldn't be so quick to judge his dehumanizing abuse of women or his torturous murders of the four cardinals and Leonardo Vetra. What is demonic to us might well be angelic to others. Yin and yang.

Brown's Angel of Mercy

In another scene an angelic image is presented from the perspective of a tragically suffering victim. Max Kohler, the bitterly atheistic physicist and CERN director, remembers the horrific pain of a childhood sickness that resulted in his lifelong paralysis. It was all brought on by the folly and false faith of his parents, who refused him medical care. His only salvation in the end was a doctor who secreted the cure behind his parents' backs:

> It was then that Max sensed the figure hovering over him. *An angel?* ... Max recognized it as one of the doctors ... the one who had sat in the corner for two days,

never leaving, begging Max's parents to let him administer some new drug from
England. (453–54)

With a twist on childlike faith, this angel-of-mercy experience is
ironically what drives Kohler to his imbalanced passion for science.
His parents' Christianity (in error as it was) destroyed him body and
soul. But science was his savior and deliverer, and he committed his
life to its pursuits with an evangelistic fervor. His life had been
forged by angels and demons, science and religion.

Special Delivery from God

Angels, who figure prominently throughout the Bible, appear
and are referred to many times in both the Old and New
Testaments. They're a fascinating study in theological circles, and
predictably, the discipline that focuses on their existence is called
angelology. Even so, this has always been something of a dicey subject in orthodox Christian studies:

> One has only to peruse the amount of space devoted to angelology in standard
> theologies to demonstrate this. This disregard for the doctrine may simply be neg-
> lect or it may indicate a tacit rejection of this area of biblical teaching. Even Calvin
> was cautious in discussing this subject. [*Institutes*, I, xiv, 3] (Ryrie, ch. 17)

Perhaps the reasons for such caution are evident in the vast array
of popular, nonbiblical teachings one might find on the Internet. A
simple Web search for angelology brings up countless sites, the vast
majority actually representing pagan-monist slants on—or perhaps
even a *Da Vinci Code*-style hijacking of—the Bible's ancient teachings and representations of angels.

Taken at face value, the Bible always presents angels as nothing
less than literal, created beings who sometimes appear as humans
but are decidedly other than human. In the New Testament, they
are described as "ministering spirits sent to serve those who will
inherit salvation" (Heb. 1:14). Even so, a great deal of fable, lore,
and figurative symbolism have developed around them, fostering a
kind of stereotype that clouds our understanding of who these
uniquely created spiritual beings are. For instance, nowhere does the
Bible even hint at the common image of dead loved ones in robes
strumming harps in the sky. Neither does it say anywhere that

angels have wings or halos (although the separate beings called "cherubim" and "seraphim" are sometimes described as winged).

Too often, though, well-meaning parents and even religious leaders can foster mythical beliefs about angels, some of which ironically convey messages contrary to that which angels themselves were sent to communicate. Vittoria remembers receiving just such a message from a nun when she was a child. She recalls telling her soon-to-be adoptive father, Leonardo,

> Sister Francisca says raindrops are angels' tears coming down to wash away our sins.... Raindrops fall because *everything* falls! *Everything* falls! Not just rain! (60)

Sister Francisca's explanation has a nostalgic warmth and simplistic beauty about it on the order of Santa Claus, but there's nonetheless a false message in the little gospel image the sister (presumably a Christian teacher) communicated—that sins can be washed away by a natural means.

Enter Gabriel

In Luke's gospel we witness an angelic intervention in human affairs, but the gospel writer gives us no sense that we should take the story or the angelic image figuratively or symbolically. As Dr. Luke establishes in the premise to his gospel,

> Since I myself have carefully investigated everything from the beginning, it seemed good also to me to write an orderly account for you ... so that you may know the certainty of the things you have been taught. (1:3–4)

Then, remarkably, Luke proceeds to recount as historical fact the appearance of angels to humans:

> In the sixth month, God sent the angel Gabriel to Nazareth, a town in Galilee, to a virgin pledged to be married to a man named Joseph, a descendant of David. The virgin's name was Mary. The angel went to her and said, "Greetings, you who are highly favored! The Lord is with you." (1:26–28)

Mary was surprised, but she never doubted what she was experiencing. (See v. 29.) Gabriel tells her not to be afraid and that she's going to give birth to a son, whom God by his power would cause to grow in her, even though she would remain a virgin. (See vv. 30–35.)

Seems fantastical by a materialist's standards, but no more so than the proposition that God created everything out of nothing in the first place. That's the idea of his being supernatural—he's above nature. He made it; he can do as he pleases with it. So arranging a virgin birth really shouldn't be any trouble for the Creator of the universe. In fact, it might be said to be a comparably minor thing.

But the real zinger comes when Gabriel concludes his announcement with the truly radical declaration that this virgin-born baby, brought into human existence by the Holy Spirit, "will be called the Son of God" (v. 35).

This is a large part of what angels did in the Bible: They communicated particularly significant messages directly from God, especially at a time when people didn't have God's written Word, the Bible. God also used select humans, known as prophets, to communicate his messages.

In Mary's case, the Bible says she accepted, with a remarkable and humble faith, this angel-delivered message from God. (See v. 38.) But the gospel of Matthew recounts that her husband-to-be, Joseph, still needed to be persuaded. When it was discovered that Mary, who was already betrothed to Joseph, was "with child" (Matt. 1:18)—albeit through the Holy Spirit—Joseph was going to "divorce her quietly" (v. 19). So God sent an angel to Joseph, this time in a dream, explaining that the child had been conceived by the power of God's Spirit and that "he will save his people from their sins" (v. 21).

This gospel account of angels' dealings with humans is opposite from Sister Francisca's children's fable in which sins are washed away by angel tears. The Christmas gospel stories of both Matthew and Luke are about angels announcing to humans that God himself was going to supernaturally intervene in their lives. While angels in the Bible communicate God's sacrificial work of bridging the gap between him and sinful humans, the angels in Brown's novels are figurative beings, personified in the mundane and natural, who bring perhaps a momentary warm fuzzy—a temporary, yet always fleeting, consolation.

Clothed in Lightning

Angels figure prominently not only in Jesus' birth into this world but also in his resurrection. Luke recounts how several women, who had followed Jesus from the beginning of his ministry in Galilee, followed Joseph of Arimathea after the crucifixion to see where he laid Jesus' body. Among the group of women were Mary Magdalene (the very same woman *The Da Vinci Code* portrays as Jesus' wife), Joanna, Mary the mother of James, and others. (See 24:10.)

The women didn't have time to properly prepare the body before the Jewish Sabbath began, so they left his corpse lying in the tomb, and the Roman soldiers sealed the entrance with a large stone. The women would return to the tomb after the Sabbath to prepare the body with spices. (See 23:55–56.) When they came back early Sunday morning, they were astonished to find the massive stone rolled away from the tomb's entrance. But more surprising were the beings who greeted them:

> While they were wondering [what happened to Jesus' body], suddenly two men in clothes that gleamed like lightning stood beside them. In their fright the women bowed down with their faces to the ground, but the men said to them, "Why do you look for the living among the dead? He is not here; he has risen!" (24:4–6)

The women ran to tell the disciples what they had witnessed, but the disciples thought they were nuts. (Clearly this would *not* be the last time women would try to explain a truth to a bunch of men who don't get it.) Peter at least went to see for himself, and sure enough, the tomb was empty.

John's gospel picks up the story at this point and describes a specific scene after the disciples returned home. Mary Magdalene is left alone at the tomb, weeping. She bends over to look again into the tomb, and through her tears she sees two angels, this time sitting inside the tomb "where Jesus' body had been, one at the head and the other at the foot" (20:10–12). The angels ask her, "Woman, why are you crying?" (v. 13).

There's a significant difference between the angelic accounts Luke and John present in their gospel stories and those of Dan Brown. It's the same as the difference between the Christian God and the god of pagan monism. In the Bible neither the Creator God nor his angels are figurative objects or forces to be balanced or molded into our own images. Like God, the Bible's angels are uncompromisingly absolute, unalterable in nature, because, like God, they too are persons.

You can give and take from a metaphor, a force, or a theory—but neither Christians nor anyone else can alter the core identity of a sentient person. As we said earlier, you are who you are, God is who he is, and therefore, angels are who they are. Wanting to make them into our own personal metaphors, symbols, or attendants won't change the reality of these existential persons.

The angels described by Luke and John were sent by a personal God to communicate his personal messages to human beings—and they did it personally. They assured the still-virgin Mary that she didn't need to be afraid (see Luke 1:30), and they asked Mary Magdalene why she was crying (see John 20:13). These real persons engage with humans with compassion and empathy.

The Bible won't let us reduce these noble, powerful servants of the living, personal God to mere yins to some oppositional yet complementary demon yangs. For the same reasons that it is outrageously wrong and unreasonable to reduce the evil of September 11 to merely a cosmic yin-yang balancing act, it is also unreasonable to consider angels as counterpoints to demons.

Angels are persons of the light—there is no darkness in them. They belong to the light not because they must be opposites, but because they're connected to and serve God, who is the infinite light.

The few humans who have encountered these real persons have seen that light radiating from them like lightning.

8

Angels of Science and Religious Demons

(ANGELS & DEMONS)

Albert Einstein had become an international celebrity, a rising star who offered the hope of human progress through science. And the world needed hope. Society was slogging through the Great Depression, fascism and Nazism were on the rise, and people were still grappling with horrific memories of a war that was supposed to end all wars.

It was 1930, and the popular press was abuzz: If the new priesthood of modernism was comprised of scientists, then fifty-one-year-old Einstein was its pope. And yet, this quintessential man of science had a philosophical bent. In a *New York Times* magazine article titled "Religion and Science," dated November 9, 1930, Einstein provocatively asserted that science must be driven by religious experience: "The cosmic religious experience is the strongest force and the noblest driving force behind scientific research."

Two decades after this article was published, America was upbeat and optimistic. Science was building at a remarkable pace upon the foundations laid by early pioneers. Yet ironically, Einstein came back to his questions of science and religion, this time with a more negative tone.

The revered father of relativity published *Out of My Later Years*, a book that reflected back on his life. In the chapter "Science and Religion," he included his writings from 1941 on the same topic, plucked from the time when America would finally enter World War II: "Science without religion is lame; religion without science is blind" (19–28). Einstein knew the schism between science and religion was growing. The line in the sand between the two had solidified, cracked, and a fissure had formed.

In the ensuing decades, this fissure became a chasm that in the last third of the twentieth century looked impassable. It is also the philosophical setting for Dan Brown's *Angels & Demons*. And remarkably, his hope echoes that of Einstein's—he wants to unite the canyon walls, to fill the gap and join together the yin-yang landscapes.

However, Brown's main protagonist, Robert Langdon, has no such grand delusions. To his way of thinking, traditional religion is the problem that needs to finally be put to rest. That's at least the gist of his thoughts as he reflects on the gruesome murder of Leonardo Vetra. With language that suggests Brown's own decided sympathies for the Illuminati, he shows his colors when it comes to Christian myth:

> The brotherhood held that the superstitious dogma spewed forth by the church was mankind's greatest enemy. They feared that if religion continued to promote pious myth as absolute fact, scientific progress would halt, and mankind would be doomed to an ignorant future of senseless holy wars. (38)

Langdon credits this view to the Illuminati, but it's safe to say he agrees with it. He would probably say that the problems of ignorance and "senseless holy wars" are attributable to "superstitious dogma" and "pious myth"—more specifically, to religion's propensity to cling to as fact what others would know to be merely abstractions of truth.

In short, the world's problems are largely a result of all those religious folk taking things way too literally.

Giving the Devil His Due

If we applied this same viewpoint to the Nazi bid for world domination, would we characterize Hitler's actions as a holy war begotten out of a misguided enthusiasm for pious myth?

As much as we'd like to relegate the evil policies of Nazi Germany to ignorance, a brief study of the Nazis shows that they were not uneducated, superstitious people. In fact, some of the greatest and best scientific minds of that era were wholeheartedly engaged in Nazism.

So, perhaps the greatest enemy of humanity during that not-so-holy war was Hitler himself? It's easy to talk abstractly about evil, but what about the people doing the evil? During Nazi rule many Germans seemed to have no difficulty embracing the abstract ideology of racial supremacy while ignoring Adolf Hitler and the atrocities his regime was committing.

Hitler was a real person. The extermination camps were real places. And the individuals in the Nazi Party were also real people who not only did great evil but were personally evil as well.

Brown's Problem with Evil

However, *Angels and Demons'* yin-yang-leaning priest, Ventresca, would probably prefer to consign Hitler himself to an abstraction—perhaps to Ventresca's own abstract understanding of evil as merely a bad case of apathy:

> Nothing unites hearts like the presence of evil. Burn a church and the community rises up, holding hands, singing hymns of defiance as they rebuild.... Forge modern demons for modern man. Apathy is dead. (536)

Character Sketch: CARLO VENTRESCA

The camerlengo, *il camerlengo*—chamberlain to the late pope—was "dressed ... in a simple black cassock that seemed to amplify the solidity of his substantial frame. He looked to be in his late-thirties" and was "surprisingly handsome" with "a swirl of coarse brown hair, and almost radiant green eyes." He also speaks in perfect English (144). "The priest had the air of some mythical hero—radiating charisma and authority" (145).

Perhaps Hitler's problem was merely that he didn't care enough, if at all. How much easier it is to see evil through the colored glasses of impersonal abstractions.

Brown's gospel deals with the problem of evil in a way that's very similar to how it deals with God. Because yin-yang concepts have it that God is not a person but an abstract unifying wholeness or force, Brown's evil is also found in abstractions, such as ignorance and unenlightened worldviews.

Christianity's Problem of Evil

Christianity teaches that evil is found in those people who are separated from the person of God. In the Christian worldview, evil is also a very personal thing. But it exists not because there arbitrarily must be some ignorance to balance out intelligence or Hitlers to balance out Jesuses or demons to balance out angels. Rather, the ignorant, the Hitlers, and the demons are the way they are because they are separated from their Creator.

Christians call this state *sin,* and the reason it's such a big deal to the Christian God is precisely because it perpetually spawns people like us who are separated from him. Some may be deeper into darkness than others, but we're all people basically in the same boat, floating in the pitch-black night, sitting uncomfortably close to Hitler and demons.

In this chapter we will examine the other half of the yin-yang *Angels & Demons* equation: demons. Talking about demons can be much more awkward than discussing angels because the folklore, myths, and clichéd cartoon imagery of demons are even more pervasive in our culture. Yet, cutting through the red suits, pitchforks, and horns, both Brown and the Bible present a much more serious perspective on the spiritual world's darker side.

The demons of Brown's fictional world are strictly of the human variety—they aren't fallen angels. Instead, they predictably symbolize abstractions of evil. Two particular characters who reflect demonic imagery represent extremes on the yin-yang continuum: the wholly evil Hassassin and the epic hero Robert Langdon.

The Inhuman Demon—the Hassassin

The nameless Hassassin is as close as anyone might come in the novel to wearing a red suit and horns and clenching a pitchfork in his fist. His lust for violence is matched only by his desire for sexual conquest, and in both pursuits, he reduces human beings to mere objects of pleasure.

Character Sketch: THE HASSASSIN

The notorious Muslim assassin ("his people did not celebrate Christmas" [35]) has a voice "metallic and cold, laced with arrogance … [and an] accent. Middle Eastern, perhaps?" (151). He has a well-earned reputation for secretiveness and deadliness. "He [is] a powerful man. Dark and potent. Deceptively agile" (12). And he has an assassin pedigree of which he is very proud. His ancestors "were renowned not only for their brutal killings, but also for celebrating their slayings by plunging themselves into drug-induced stupors. Their drug of choice was a potent intoxicant they called hashish"—hence the name *Hassassin:* "the followers of hashish" (14).

Early in the novel, the Hassassin's objectifying dehumanization of his victims is disturbingly apparent. When he enters a brothel chamber, his first reaction to the prostitute who awaits him is, *"I killed last night. You are my reward"* (36). Whether his intention is violence or sexual conquest, he doesn't equivocate or rationalize:

> Running his palm across [the woman's] neck, he felt aroused with the knowledge that he could end her life in an instant. What would it matter. She was subhuman. (65)

Yet as loathsome as we must find the Hassassin, within him is a strange yang to his sinister yin. As we saw in the previous chapter, he views himself as an "Angel of Truth," serving a higher cause (66).

Such a glimmer of light in an otherwise pitch-black character is reflective of Christian reality. All beings created in God's image have within them a moral compass that, in spite of being marred because of separation from the Source of spiritual life, can still occasionally waver toward true north, at least by way of a conscience. That's why good storytelling will reflect even in its most evil characters at least an occasional hint of potential good, even if that meager hint is ironic or cynical.

Simplistic, clichéd villains in stories fall generally flat as characters because we know that real people, no matter how evil, are not simplistic. Brown's Hassassin displays an occasional glimmer of sophistication, but he is otherwise very close to a paper-thin stereotype of evil. What is striking about him, however, is that in his proximity to pure evil on the yin-yang continuum, he himself becomes an anonymous, impersonal abstraction. He is more a symbol than a human—ironically, an objectified demon that we can safely hate.

The Heroic Fallen Angel—Langdon

Brown's world also contains demons that are much further along on the "enlightened" side of the yin-yang scale. You may be surprised to learn that Robert Langdon also reflects demonic imagery, but the symbolism and mythological allusions are of a far different nature than those of the Hassassin.

The most telling image associating Langdon with demons is the sympathetic allusion to the classic pagan Greek myth of Daedalus. The first reference to this famous classical figure occurs as Langdon warily enters a dark passage to the Chigi Chapel, the location of the first clue and the first murder:

> For an instant Langdon recalled the ancient myth of Daedalus, how the boy kept one hand on the wall as he moved through the Minotaur's labyrinth, knowing he was guaranteed to find the end if he never broke contact with the wall. (262)

There's a similar allusion when Langdon enters the dark passageway leading up to the Hassassin's lair: "He ascended into the total darkness, keeping one hand on the wall" (435).

According to Greek legend, Daedalus was the most skillful, if not the father, of all artificers and was even said to have invented images. One of his greatest inventions was a massive labyrinth, built

The Myth of Daedalus and Icarus

Daedalus was shut up in a tower to prevent his knowledge of the labyrinth [he had built] from spreading to the public.... Since [King] Minos controlled the land and sea routes, Daedalus set to work to fabricate wings for himself and his young son Icarus.... When both [of them] were prepared for flight, Daedalus warned Icarus not to fly too high, because the heat of the sun would melt the wax, nor too low because the sea foam would make the wings wet and they would no longer fly. Then the father and son flew away. They had passed Samos, Delos, and Lebynthos when the boy began to soar upward as if to reach heaven. The blazing sun softened the wax which held the feathers together, and they came off. Icarus fell into the sea. His father cried and, bitterly lamenting his own arts, called the land near the place where Icarus fell into the ocean Icaria in memory of his child.

—"Daedalus," Wikipedia

to imprison the Minotaur. But another of his mythological inventions is more commonly associated with his name: He created wings of feathers and wax so that both he and his son, Icarus, could escape imprisonment. As the story goes, Icarus flew too close to the sun despite his father's warning; the wax on the wings melted, and Icarus plunged tragically to his death. The story has come to represent a classic mythological motif: heroic people who aspire to godlike heights and consequently bring about their own destruction.

A natural comparison to fallen angels comes to mind. Langdon himself would probably point to this comparison as yet more evidence that "Christianity is filled with examples of sun worship" (242). Because, as the Christian story goes, one of the great angels, Satan, strove to become like God along with a third of the angelic population, and consequently they were cast down by God as rebel demons.

Langdon seems to be similarly aspiring to godlike heights, and it's nearly his undoing. The image of a falling angel is hard to miss in chapter 125 when Langdon miraculously escapes the antimatter explosion by leaping from the helicopter.

The antimatter explosion itself is a direct revelation of the pantheist god. (Vittoria had earlier prophesied as much: "Pure *energy* is the father of creation" [72]). The explosion also becomes a sun unto itself: "Night had become day" (500). And Langdon would certainly have been destroyed after casting himself into the Tiber River, had it not been for the fortunate coincidence of a Dr. Jacobus and his medical staff being nearby:

> If it had not been for Jacobus and his crew standing out on the shore watching the spectacle in the sky, this falling soul would surely have gone unnoticed and drowned. (512)

Langdon literally found himself a little too close to the pagan god of creation and antimatter, and it was nearly his undoing—and humanity apparently faces the same threat. For if the power of creation exists in the yin-yang worldview, there also must exist the power of annihilation.

What's rather remarkable, though, is Langdon's momentary flirtation with an apparently theistic God, even as he is facing destruction at the hands of the pantheistic god of antimatter (neither of which the agnostic Langdon can believe in). Falling through the night toward the Tiber River, Langdon resigns himself to his fate:

> He pulled with all his might and accepted somehow that it was now in the hands of God. He focused hard on the widest part of the serpent [the river] and ... for the first time in his life, prayed for a miracle. (508)

Christians would find it sadly typical that somehow it never registers with Langdon that his prayer might have been answered by Someone much more personal than an antimatter force.

Demons Are People Too

Many people, including some Christians, say they don't believe in literal demons or Satan because we don't need them; we humans are plenty capable of accomplishing evil on our own. That's evil-as-abstraction talking again, preferring to keep demons strictly symbolic.

One might just as well insist, "I don't believe in terrorists"—and yet tragically they exist just the same. We can whistle in the dark and deny terrorists a place in our own personal reality, but that worldview has no bearing on whether or not they are actually real. The same holds true for demons.

According to the biblical Christian's understanding of reality, no one (angel or human) exists as a weight on a scale of good and evil. God is absolutely good, or to use the figurative language of Scripture, he's absolute light. So God didn't create demons as evil. He created spiritual beings, which we call angels, and to them—as with humans—he granted the choice to be with him or to live independent of him.

The Bible alludes to an angelic rebellion and fall. (See Isa. 14:12–14 and Ezek. 28:15–17, references to the kings of Babylon and Tyre that also allude to Satan and his demons.) Today a great spiritual war continues, as Paul described in his letter to the Ephesians: "Our struggle is not [merely] against flesh and blood, but ... against the spiritual forces of evil in the heavenly realms" (6:12). And this angelic civil war will apparently rage until the last days of human history, as John described in Revelation 12:7–9.

The God of the Bible did not make darkness, he did not make evil, and he did not make angels fallen. Death—physical as well as spiritual—is simply the all-too-real consequence of being cut off from life. Lies are simply the consequence of being disconnected from truth. And all evil is a result of being cut off from absolute goodness.

In his classic *The Screwtape Letters,* C. S. Lewis prefaces his fictional correspondence between a senior demon and a novice with the following ironic caution:

> There are two equal and opposite errors into which our race can fall about the devils. One is to disbelieve in their existence. The other is to believe, and to feel an excessive and unhealthy interest in them. They themselves are equally pleased by both errors and hail a materialist or a magician with the same delight. (3)

The Luciferian-Shaitan Myth

By Lewis's measure of reality, Langdon would definitely have erred on the side of the materialist. And his error leads him (and Brown, apparently) into something of a prejudicial error of fact as well. While explaining to Kohler—with great admiration—the noble roots of the Illuminati, Langdon seems to laud their aspirations for a secular New World Order:

> "A New World Order," Langdon repeated, "based on scientific enlightenment. They called it their Luciferian Doctrine. The church claimed Lucifer was a reference to the devil, but the brotherhood insisted Lucifer was intended in its literal Latin meaning—*bringer of light.* Or *Illuminator.*" (39)

Despite Langdon's innuendo of Christian conspiracy, the reference to Lucifer actually predates the Illuminati by about two-and-a-half millennia. The Christian tradition of associating Satan with the alias Lucifer ("bringer of light") had nothing to do with the church's demonization of supposedly enlightened Illuminati. Any etymology dictionary will confirm that it's taken from a reference in Isaiah: "How art thou fallen from heaven, O Lucifer, son of the morning! [Some translations say "O morning star."] How art thou cut down to the ground, which didst weaken the nations!" (Isa. 14:12 KJV).

Whether or not the traditional pseudonym for Satan—Lucifer—has a legitimate double meaning in Isaiah's prophecy, the premise that Satan was originally an angel of light who rebelled against God has biblical merit. Langdon's simplistic word association may be a convenient rationalization for pagans and gnostics, who like to think of themselves as truly enlightened. But it's far from historical fact, let alone truth.

In his conversation with Kohler, Langdon similarly suggests that the name Satan was contrived by a conspiratorial church that would smear its enlightened adversaries:

> Satanists historically were educated men who stood as adversaries to the church. *Shaitan.* The rumors of satanic black-magic animal sacrifices and the pentagram ritual were nothing but lies spread by the church as a smear campaign against their adversaries. (37)

The word *satan* actually has a much clearer origin. The contemporary word is in fact a direct derivative of the original ancient language, in this case the New Testament Greek word *Satan/Satanas.* (Direct derivatives are an extremely rare phenomenon.) And the Greek word is a direct transliteration from the ancient Hebrew word *s-t-n* (commonly pronounced "satan," since ancient biblical Hebrew had no written vowels).

Since its earliest recorded usage (in Job 1—2, as much as three millennia before the Illuminati), the word *satan* has consistently meant "adversary—one who plots against another." As with the name "Lucifer," "adversary" and "accuser" have long been understood by Jews and Christians alike as the biblically derived descriptions of the great fallen angel who rebelled against God and who battles for human souls to join in his rebellion.

The early church would have understood the word *satan* in its Greek context alone, long before the existence of the Islamic word *shaitan,* which Langdon oddly enough associates with the enlightened Illuminati. (Ironically, the literal meaning of *shaitan* is "astray" or "distant" or "illusionist" [Wikipedia]).

More confounding still is Langdon's statement that satanists "historically were educated men who stood as adversaries to the church" (37). Langdon's logic here is circular, since it's clear that anyone who follows Satan (in the Christian and Jewish sense of the word) would literally be an "adversary" of the Christian church. (Remember, that's the definition of *satan,* and it would likewise be the sense of *satanist.*)

As for Langdon's appraisal that satanists were educated men, this is beside the point, if not a straw man. No one is arguing that satanists are who they are because they're uneducated.

Brown (via Langdon) assumes that members of "satanic cults" are *not* of a "devil-worshipping" nature, but this is something that should be proven rather than assumed (37). If you presume that a personified Satan and devils are merely symbolic abstractions, then it probably seems laughable to believe there are literal devil worshippers.

But wait. If a personal God created nonhuman, spiritual persons (angels), and if some of them rebelled (and thus became fallen angels or demons), is it so laughable to believe that some rebel human beings would choose to ally themselves with these fallen spirits? And would it be so unreasonable to describe these human cohorts as satanists or even devil worshippers?

Theists and monists might differ as to who or what Satan and devils are, but they cannot help but agree that these beings are by definition the adversaries of the Christian God. Likewise, despite Langdon's simplistic appraisal that "modern Satanism was born" out of relatively contemporary Christian conspiracy (37), it's really as old as the ancient struggle between pagan monism and Judeo-Christian theism. In fact, from a Judeo-Christian perspective, it's as old as the fall of humanity.

Set aside the "black-magic animal sacrifices and the pentagram ritual" (37). Set aside the allegation that the church conspired to use these "rumors" as a smear campaign against its adversaries. The question still remains: Are these spirit beings merely Dan Brown's mythological symbols representing facets of a monistic whole? Or are there really spiritual beings out there other than humans? What if the Bible's spiritual beings—God, angels, Satan, and demons—do exist as self-aware, sentient persons? What would that mean to you?

The ramifications aren't so laughable; in fact, they're kind of disturbing. After all, abstractions are much easier to control—much safer than people, much safer than God, angels, and demons.

The Science of God

It's out of this context of depersonalized abstractions that Langdon describes science as the basis of a New World Order (39). To the neo-pagan monist, this makes good sense, because if the impersonal, natural universe comprises God, and if science is dedicated to the study of that natural universe, then science is the theology of this New World Order.

The neo-pagan theology has embraced science as its perfect discipline to educate the masses in a newer, truer doctrine. The foundation of this new doctrine is evolution, though not merely that of fish from amoeba or humans from apes, but of sectarian religions into a unified, monistic whole and a higher form of spiritual consciousness.

And what better means do we have of evolving from individual truths into abstractions than science? As James Herrick surmises in his excellent critique *The Making of the New Spirituality,*

> Under the New Religious Synthesis, evolution is the principle animating the cosmos. Human beings, evolution's conscious products, can now achieve even-higher levels of consciousness by directing their own evolution. (149)

No longer do the spiritually evolved worship the ancient pagan personifications such as Poseidon (Greek god of the sea and earthquakes); instead, they pay homage to the ocean—the ecological face of God—with worship led by high-priest scientists, such as Vittoria Vetra, a "Bio Entanglement Physicist" doing "biological research in the Balearic Sea" (49).

Savior Science

"I believe science will save us ... although I tend to be an optimist. Obviously, science has wonderful potential to control disease, create new fuel supplies, engineer efficient food sources, and even allow us to migrate to new worlds. The problem, of course, is that every technology is a double-edged sword. The rocket engine that carries the space shuttle can also carry warheads. The medical breakthroughs that can eradicate disease—genetic research, for example—if misused, can bring about the end of the human race. The question is not whether or not science will expand to meet man's growing needs, but whether man's philosophy will mature [i.e., "evolve"] fast enough that we can truly comprehend our new power and the responsibility that comes with it" (Brown, "Conversation," par. 53).

The Imbalanced Scientist and the Balanced

Famed American astronomer Carl Sagan went so far as to laud a grander beauty in this evolved spirituality, as compared to banal Christianity that fails to "take sufficient account of the grandeur, magnificence, subtlety and intricacy of the Universe revealed by science" (35).

In *Angels & Demons*, Max Kohler, the atheistic director of CERN, won't go so far as to revel in the aesthetics of neo-pagan spirituality—not like the young zealot Vittoria Vetra, anyway. He's of an older, modernist, reductionist generation that despises anything religious because it stands in the way of progress.

Character Sketch: MAX KOHLER

Kohler is a "discrete particle physicist" (3) and the director of CERN, a nuclear research facility in Switzerland. When Langdon meets the wheelchair-bound man, he notes that Kohler "looked to be in his early sixties. Gaunt and totally bald with a sternly set jaw, he wore a white lab coat and dress shoes propped firmly on the wheelchair's footrest. Even at a distance his eyes looked lifeless—like two gray stones" (18). Kohler is known "behind his back as König—King ... a title more of fear than reverence for the figure who ruled over his dominion from a wheelchair throne" (19). Kohler's rage at Christianity stems from the childhood disease that crippled him—and the fact his parents insisted on prayer in lieu of medical intervention (452–55). Reflective of Kohler's nature as a scientific reductionist, his name in German means "burner"—something that chars to a coal state. When you burn away all that is organic, you're left with dead coal—carbon, the base of life but without life.

Yet Kohler also longs for a New World Order utopia in which humanity has evolved beyond the clutches of religion. He tells Langdon,

> All questions were once spiritual. Since the beginning of time, spirituality and religion have been called on to fill in the gaps that science did not understand....
> Soon *all* Gods will be proven to be false idols. (25)

By contrast, the spiritual patriarch of *Angels & Demons* is the catalyst for the entire novel: Leonardo Vetra, adoptive father of Vittoria and the first Illuminati murder victim. Ironically, it's the atheist

Kohler who must painstakingly explain Vetra's theology—an anomaly to Kohler's tidy modernist worldview, since Vetra was both a priest and a world-class physicist.

The name *Vetra* has an interesting meaning in the Lithuanian language: "powerful wind." The Vetras (both father and daughter) represent a powerful wind of change in both the scientific and religious communities, and for the same reasons Leonardo Vetra had called himself a "theo-physicist" (44). With an evangelistic fervor, he was bent on proving to the "doubting masses" that God exists. Kohler's commentary to Langdon is telling:

> "Leonardo believed his research had the potential to convert millions to a more spiritual life. Last year he categorically proved the existence of an energy force that unites us all.... There is a single force moving within all of us.... A recent *Scientific American* article hailed *New Physics* as a surer path to God than religion itself."
>
> Langdon felt disconcerted. *And the power of God shall unite us all.* (45)

To the uninitiated, this worldview is disconcerting. Science and religion were perceived by modernists as opposites, and yet the pagan monist would bring together these centuries-old yin-yang rivals.

The Gospel of Science

But a new generation of neo-pagan Vittoria Vetras is coming into its own, and to their way of thinking, science itself is the stuff and meaning of life—true spirituality. Vittoria shares and even surpasses her father's religious zeal with a passion that wants to be holy: "As Vittoria listened to [Ventresca's] words, an unexpected grief surfaced as tears ... tears for her own mentor ... her own holy father" (341).

Passionate faith is not all in the *Angels & Demons'* New World Order that mimics the trappings and traditions of the Christian church. The Glass Cathedral at CERN is like a house of worship with physics as the religion (18) and where the CERN scientists perform miraculous signs daily (21, 452). And by Langdon's estimation, science appears to be much more providential than God (*"God does not protect you. Intelligence protects you. Enlightenment.... Who needs God? No! Science is God"* [174]).

But even more overt is the unique version of Christ offered up through repeated imagery in the *Angels & Demons'* neo-pagan gospel of science, represented by none other than Carlo Ventresca. In him we have a scientific answer to the Christian virgin birth. As Cardinal Mortati explains in the presence of Ventresca, Langdon, Vittoria Vetra, and the entire conclave in the Sistine Chapel that His Holiness (the Pope) fathered a child—Carlo Ventresca—without breaking his vow. His love remained chaste (543):

> "[It was] a new miracle of science—a process by which two people, without ever having sexual relations, could have a child.... A year later she had a child through the miracle of artificial insemination ...

> "Carlo ...?" Mortati crumbled. "His Holiness's child ... is *you*." (544)

Character Sketch: CARDINAL MORTATI

As overseer of the conclave to elect the new pope, Mortati is the most senior cardinal present (122). He is of a more liberal, enlightened group in the Catholic Church: "Mortati, many believed, could have been Pope in his younger days had he not been so broad-minded" (161). He's also "a modern man in an ancient faith. Miracles had never played a part in his belief.... Mortati's rational mind had always justified [miraculous] accounts as part of the myth" (501). After the conclusion of the remarkable events at the Vatican, the conclave elects Mortati as the next pope: "The College of Cardinals had obviously chosen a noble and munificent leader" (565). Interestingly, his name evokes the same Latin root as the word *mortal*—death, perhaps representing an end to the old church ways.

The "Holy Father" and "Mother's" only begotten son (553), Carlo Ventresca, imitates many of the features supposedly attributed to Jesus Christ. From chapters 124 to 134 we witness a transformation from an apparently calmly and humble Christian priest to a fanatical monist zealot who would begin a newly transformed pantheistic Christianity. From the moment of his apparent death at the hands of God through the antimatter explosion, Ventresca follows a path that alludes to Jesus' resurrection and, ultimately, his ascension:

- To the amazement of Mortati and the masses, a living Ventresca appears resurrected after the antimatter blast: "There, on the right of Jesus [the statue], arms outstretched to the world ... stood Camerlengo Carlo Ventresca" (502).
- From his vantage point on the rooftop terrace of Saint Peter's Basilica, Ventresca senses a type of resurrection power: "He looked different somehow. Divine.... He felt transformed, otherworldly.... He felt as light as a ghost.... [The people] were chanting his name.... They were experiencing ... a substantiation of the power of the Creator.... He wanted to cry out to them. *Your God is a living God! Behold the miracles all around you!*" (510–11).
- Ventresca sees the prospect of his death as sacrificial for the sake of humanity: "'Yes!' he shouted into the madness. 'I would die for man! Like your son, I would die for them!'" (530).
- And more specifically, he would presume to die for the sins of humankind: "Most Holy Trinity, I offer Thee the most precious Body, Blood, Soul ... in reparation for the outrages, sacrileges, and indifferences" (554).

But the God of Dan Brown's gospel is nothing resembling the God of the Bible. Carlo Ventresca's God is ironically the same neo-pagan-monist entity as Vittoria's, even though he doesn't realize it.

The Neo-Pagan Evangelist

Toward the beginning of the novel, Vittoria bears witness to her pagan theology, compellingly responding to Langdon's questions while en route to Vatican City. Langdon aptly replies by summing up her philosophy in true gnostic fashion:

"So you believe God is fact, but we will never understand Him."

"*Her,*" she said with a smile. "Your Native Americans had it right.... *Gaea.* The planet is an organism. All of us are cells with different purposes. And yet we are intertwined. Serving each other. Serving the whole." (110)

Likewise, when Vittoria confronts Ventresca near the end, she has the opportunity to preach her gospel:

> Religions evolve! The mind finds answers, the heart grapples with new truths.... God is not some omnipotent authority looking down from above, threatening to throw us into a pit of fire if we disobey. God is the energy that flows through the synapses of our nervous system and the chambers of our hearts! God is in all things! (535)

Something that's easy to miss is the fact that Carlo Ventresca is actually a monist pantheist—undoubtedly of the gnostic variety. Lest we assume otherwise, consider his response to Vittoria. Significantly, he doesn't object to any of Vittoria's impassioned pagan message of monistic universalism or to any of her characterizations of an impersonal God-force that binds all and evolves all. But when Vittoria states that "God is in all things!" the camerlengo fires back, with pity in his eyes, "*Except* science" (535).

Ventresca can never incorporate science into his own neo-pagan theology because of the crime it inflicted upon him in childhood— the death of his mother from a bomb, the technological spawn of science. And therein is the bitter irony: Ventresca is yin to Kohler's yang. Both flee to opposite ends of the continuum: one to the imbalanced extreme of antiscience, and the other to atheism. And all because of the personal demons that afflicted them in childhood: For Ventresca it was demon science; for Kohler, demon Christianity.

Carlo Ventresca's only heresy as a monist is simply that he cannot include science in the otherwise wholeness that is the neo-pagan god. Perhaps Carlo might need to evolve on this point. Then again, maybe his ignorance is a necessary yin-yang balance to all the enlightenment (minus the spirituality) that Kohler possessed. But regardless of his incomplete neo-pagan theology, Ventresca is clearly a monist to the very end. In his final moment, his vision echoes Vittoria's sermon:

> He could feel [the world watching him] in his soul. Even in his anguish, the unity of the moment was intoxicating. It was as if a connective web had shot out in all directions around the globe. In front of televisions, at home, and in cars, the world prayed as one. Like synapses of a giant heart all firing in tandem, the people reached for God, in dozens of languages, in hundreds of countries. (553)

And then Ventresca's crucifixion and ascension: *"My work here is done,"* he reflects, echoing Jesus' "It is finished" on the cross. Like the women who prepared Jesus' crucified body for burial, Ventresca has "anointed his body" with the "sacred, vitreous oils from the lamps." And finally, he whispers his last words from a verse in *Judgments*† "And when the flame went up toward heaven, the angel of the Lord ascended in the flame." He ignites himself in all-consuming fire before an awestruck world (554).

Behold the man, who would take away the apathy—and the science—of the world.

The God of Science

Ironically, we're hard-pressed to find any truly Christian theist characters in *Angels & Demons*. We don't have much to go on in terms of the former pope, but then again, he's dead. Perhaps the only truly Christian moment is at the death of Cardinal Baggia, sacrificially murdered at the pagan Piazza Navona. Chained and weighted down beneath the water, his final thoughts are still selflessly sublime:

> His physical shell was in agony … burned, bruised, and held underwater by an immovable weight. He reminded himself that this suffering was nothing compared to what Jesus had endured.
>
> *He died for my sins …* (417)

It's hard to imagine that he is contemplating an abstraction of a symbolic Jesus who somehow figuratively died for Baggia's theoretical sins. We're not given much more than a glimpse into this man's mind, but his God and his Jesus seem personal.

And so does his death.

In the context of the overwhelmingly neo-pagan gospel throughout *Angels & Demons*, it seems strange that Brown would allow this moment. But perhaps in this scene at least is a momentary yearning for more than a universal God-force that binds and comprises all.

---

† An Islamic text from the *Sahih Bukhari*, which is one of the Sunni six major hadith collections.

We want Jesus to be God, the Creator who made us and who himself died for Baggia's sins and ours. We want the personal myth, in the end, to be true.

John's Jesus, the Word

What Baggia confessed in his dying thoughts—that Jesus died for his sins—is the essence of John's gospel. And when we're considering monist and neo-pagan abstractions about truth, the gospel of John is the best source for comparison, because John himself was about the most abstract thinker of all the gospel writers. But his abstractions always point to a very personal Jesus and God.

In the prologue to his gospel, John describes Jesus in very theistic-Creator terms. Yet John intriguingly names him "the Word," combining both the essence of personhood and the communication of thought:

> In the beginning the Word already existed. He was with God, and he was God. He was in the beginning with God. He created everything there is. Nothing exists that he didn't make. (1:1–3 NLT)

It soon becomes evident who exactly is this Word John is writing about—it's Jesus. (See v. 17.) John clearly proclaims that Jesus existed before that "in the beginning" moment. He is, of course, alluding to the first words of the Bible, which recount God's creation of the universe. (See Gen. 1:1) John insists that it was Jesus himself, the alleged God-the-Son, who was with God before the beginning, and Jesus himself who created. John further insists that Jesus the Word made everything in existence—all forms of matter and energy.

So despite Ventresca's insistence to the contrary, the "everything" that both John and Genesis 1:1 say God made has to include science. The Christian God couldn't be opposed to science because he's the Originator of it. The Christian theist's God is above nature because he created it.

It's interesting that Vittoria Vetra recalls a fond childhood memory of her father artfully describing an apparently personal God in the act of creating: "The laws of physics are the canvas God laid down on which to paint his masterpiece" (61). Knowing both Vittoria's and Leonardo's monist bent, we could say that this is

Leonardo's simplified personification of an otherwise monist god, made accessible to a young girl. But then again, it's just plain hard to discuss creation in terms other than a Creator. It takes a great deal of faith to believe that everything has always existed without anyone creating it.

This is why thousands of Christian scientists practicing their particular disciplines in colleges and universities worldwide don't have a problem affirming their love for science through their love for a personal Creator-God and a personal Jesus Christ. But they might be harder pressed to persuade an overwhelmingly antagonistic higher-education population. Still, they press on, little lights shining in an otherwise oppressive darkness. They are the enlightened ones, not because they possess special knowledge, but because they know personally the origin of light and the Creator of what they study.

That's the sense of John's further description of Jesus the Word in verses 4 and 5: "In him was life, and that life was the light of men. The light shines in the darkness, but the darkness has not understood it." Those who are cut off from the Source—the Creator of all life and light must logically be living in death and darkness. It's a matter of relationship with a person, not the acquisition of secret knowledge.

For that reason, God the Word, "the true light," determined to give "light to every man" by "coming into the world" (v. 9). But the problem was that "though the world was made through him, the world did not recognize him" (v. 10). Like people who have perpetually lived in a dark cave, they can't recognize light when they see it. Even so, the Word, God the Creator, "became flesh and made his dwelling among us" (v. 14).

And as John's gospel bears out, many Christ followers did eventually get it—they saw the light and became truly enlightened. "Yet to all who received him, to those who believed in his name, he gave the right to become children of God" (v. 12).

The rest of John's gospel recounts Jesus' remarkable ministry in which he defied many natural laws by performing miracles. Theists who believe a personal God created these natural laws won't have a hard time believing that such a Creator would not be bound by them. They also wouldn't have a hard time fathoming that the

Source of all "life" (v. 4) could conquer death and be resurrected (John 20).

But most significantly, they know that if the personal Creator of all that exists, including them, became a flesh-and-blood human, well, that Word-made-flesh would definitely be qualified to die for the sins of humanity. If there is a Creator, he could do it—definitely.

Cardinal Baggia believed that Jesus died for his sins. And Christ followers believe it too. We believe that all who have placed their faith in Jesus, like Baggia, will one day be face-to-face with their Creator—the Creator of all science, Jesus, who also died for their sins.

9

Turning On the Light

(THE DA VINCI CODE)

Following are just a few of the many rave reviews of *The Da Vinci Code* that Dan Brown has posted on his Web site:

> WOW … Blockbuster perfection. An exhilaratingly brainy thriller. Not since the advent of Harry Potter has an author so flagrantly delighted in leading readers on a breathless chase and coaxing them through hoops. (Janet Maslin, *New York Times*)

> This masterpiece should be mandatory reading. Brown solidifies his reputation as one of the most skilled thriller writers on the planet with his best book yet, a compelling blend of history and page-turning suspense. Highly recommended. *(Library Journal)*

> A heart-racing thriller. This story has so many twists—all satisfying, most unexpected—that it would be a sin to reveal too much of the plot in advance. Let's just say that if this novel doesn't get your pulse racing, you need to check your meds. *(San Francisco Chronicle)*

> A thundering, tantalizing, extremely smart fun ride. Brown doesn't slow down his tremendously powerful narrative engine despite transmitting several doctorates' worth of fascinating history and learned speculation, *The Da Vinci Code* is brain candy of the highest quality—which is a reviewer's code meaning, "Put this on top of your pile." *(Chicago Tribune)*

This is high praise coming from some of the top popular critics in the United States. And it's probably not surprising to them that *The Da Vinci Code* has not only remained a top seller but has also become an international phenomenon.

According to George Barna's research, *The Da Vinci Code* has been read "cover to cover" by roughly 45 million adults in the United States—that's one out of every five adults (20 percent). That makes it the most widely read book with a spiritual theme, other than the Bible, to have penetrated American homes. The research goes on to note that while only 5 percent of readers had their religious beliefs changed by the book, that percentage represents two million Americans alone. "Any book that alters one or more theological views among two million people is not to be dismissed lightly. That's more people than will change any of their beliefs as a result of exposure to the teaching offered at all of the nation's Christian churches combined during a typical week." There's no question that *The Da Vinci Code*'s success is due primarily to its remarkable capacity to blend story with historical and religious information in order to give readers "a compelling blend of history and page-turning suspense," as one reviewer put it. It's also rather remarkable that Brown manages to give readers both history and theology lessons while making them much more palatable with a spoonful of adventure.

Laurie Goodstein, in her May 21, 2006, *New York Times* "Week in Review" article, identifies the theological signs of our times, just within the movie:

> *The Da Vinci Code* is, in the sweep of Christian history, a historical marker—encapsulating in one muddled movie an era in which many Christian believers have assimilated a whole lot of new and unorthodox ideas, as well as half-truths and conspiracy thinking, into their faith, while still seeing it as Christianity. Call it Da Vinci Christianity. [*It's Not Just a Movie, It's a Revelation (About the Audience)*]

That's the power of Brown's method: We get to savor the suspense, intrigue, and a good whodunit at the same time we're looking through the eyes, minds, and hearts of Robert Langdon, Sophie Neveu, Bishop Manuel Aringarosa, or even Silas. As characters face moral choices and struggle with ambiguity in an untrustworthy world, we struggle too—and even experience some catharsis through their suffering.

Clearly the depth of artistic expression in *The Da Vinci Code* doesn't even begin to approximate the likes of Shakespeare or Milton, but that wasn't Dan Brown's purpose. Even so, Brown crafted an engaging story populated by characters we can care about, who have some degree of emotional sophistication that allows us to believe in them, and whom we can observe as they grow and learn.

The Da Vinci Code Plot Summary—the Beginning

1. Renowned Louvre curator Jacques Saunière is murdered by an albino monk, Silas. Visiting lecturer Robert Langdon, a Harvard professor of religious symbology, is asked to decipher the symbols at the murder scene.

2. Silas recounts over the phone to his mysterious Teacher his success in killing three Priory of Sion sénéchaux (officers) and the Grand Master. He also tells the Teacher that all four of the victims confirmed the existence of a legendary keystone. This engraved tablet supposedly contained "the brotherhood's greatest secret" (13). The Teacher then calls Bishop Manuel Aringarosa, who is on a plane bound for Rome, and tells him that the keystone has been located.

3. Langdon meets Bezu Fache, captain of the French Judicial Police (DCPJ), at the Louvre. Analyzing the body and the crime scene, he explains to Fache the pagan symbol—a pentacle—and the message Saunière demarked in his final moments of life. Agent Sophie Neveu (DCPJ cryptography) arrives to report that she's deciphered the numeric portion of the code Saunière left and to inform Langdon that he is to call the U.S. Embassy. Langdon calls, but the voice message is from Sophie, warning that he's in danger. She leaves Fache's office, and Langdon excuses himself to use the restroom.

4. At the Saint-Sulpice church, Sister Bieil is instructed to allow an Opus Dei numerary late-night access to the church. Waiting outside the church, Silas remembers his tragic and violent childhood and how he was taken in and converted by Aringarosa. When Silas enters the church, the sister leaves him in the sanctuary to pray. Silas thinks he's discovered the keystone but soon realizes that the sénéchaux lied. He then kills the sister.

5. Sophie corners Langdon in the restroom and informs him that he's Fache's prime suspect and that Langdon has a GPS (global positioning system) dot planted on him. She explains that she's Saunière's estranged granddaughter and that the clues he left were for her. Langdon and Sophie must escape the Louvre and get Langdon to the U.S. Embassy.

6. Through Sophie's clever diversion, the police leave the Louvre. Before escaping, Langdon deciphers another of Saunière's clues. It leads them to the *Mona Lisa*, where Langdon explains that the combination of clues indicates Saunière was a member of the Priory of Sion, a secret society.

7. Langdon and Sophie discover Saunière's next clue: "So dark the con of man," a Priory maxim against the church. Just then a security guard confronts Langdon at gunpoint. Meanwhile Sophie realizes that Saunière's clue is an anagram for Leonardo's *Madonna of the Rocks*. She retrieves a key on the back of the painting and convinces the guard to relinquish his gun. Then she and Langdon escape to her car.

8. While driving, Sophie remembers the traumatizing and alienating discovery of her grandfather's *Hieros Gamos*, a pagan spiritual ceremony that involved sex rites. Then she and Langdon come upon a police blockade and are cut off from the embassy. Managing to lose the police, they make their way to a train station, ditch her car, and catch a cab. Langdon notices an address written on the key, and they tell the cabbie to take them there.

9. In the taxi Langdon explains the history of the Priory of Sion, the Knights Templar, and the *Sangreal*—the Holy Grail. Sophie hears the taxi driver speaking to the police on his radio, grabs the Louvre security guard's gun from Langdon's pocket, and commandeers the cab. She and Langdon make their way to the address—a Swiss bank—and realize the key is to a safe deposit box.

10. Bishop Aringarosa's plane arrives in Rome. He's driven to Castel Gandolfo, where high-ranking Catholic officials give him a briefcase full of large-denomination Vatican bearer bonds.

11. Captain Fache has put out an Interpol APB on Langdon and Sophie. When they enter the bank, a guard recognizes them and calls Interpol. André Vernet, president of the Paris branch of the Bank of Zurich, is a close friend of Saunière. He warns them that the police are coming. Sophie and Langdon use the key and a deciphered code to access a container from which they remove what appears to be a large wooden jewelry box. Vernet helps them escape in the back of an armored car, which he drives himself.

Continued on page 179

Learning is an especially strong motive in Brown's writing, and it's the key to his success. The gospel story of *The Da Vinci Code* has some significant messages that Brown as teacher wants the world to learn. In his witness statement, submitted in his plagiarism defense, Brown affirmed his educational motives:

> [My] characters help decipher clues and teach the reader.... I tried to write a book that I would love to read. The kind[s] of books I enjoy are those in which you learn. My hope was that readers would be entertained and also learn enough to want to use the book as a point of departure for more reading. When I was researching the book, I would learn things that fascinated readers. ("Dan Brown Witness," pars. 47, 52)

To that end, Brown's main protagonists are either teachers or researchers—people who seek knowledge and truth, always inquiring and digging deeper. Much of the unique appeal of both *The Da Vinci Code* and *Angels & Demons* is in fact how readers are allowed to vicariously experience the positing and theorizing of academics in a far less stuffy atmosphere than a typical classroom.

Also in his witness statement, Brown insists, "While it is my belief that some of the theories discussed by these characters may have merit, each individual reader must explore these characters' viewpoints and come to his or her own interpretations" (par. 217). And that perhaps is the honest assessment each reader must come to grips with and be continually reminded of whenever he or she engages controversial elements of fiction. After all, as the novel reminds us, not all that's taught is reliable or the gospel truth.

The Zealot's Fable

This caution against assuming that all pedagogical material in a book is reliable or entirely truthful is particularly applicable when it comes to the history lessons in *The Da Vinci Code*. As we said earlier, we're not going to argue the theological or art-history details in the novel. Rather, we want to look at some of the big-picture themes.

The Da Vinci Code Plot Summary—Continued

12. In the back of the armored car, Langdon and Sophie open the box to discover a lettered cylinder—a cryptex—created by her father. Sophie explains how a combination will open it, but if forced, the contents will be destroyed. Langdon realizes the cryptex is the legendary keystone, which must hold a map to the great Priory secret.

13. After some exposition by Langdon on Masonic secrecy and keystones, the truck pulls over, and Vernet opens the door pointing a gun at them. Langdon overcomes Vernet, and he and Sophie speed away in the truck. Later, Vernet calls the bank and instructs the manager to activate the truck's homing transponder, alerting police to the couple's location.

14. Langdon and Sophie go to the home of retired British Royal Historian Leigh Teabing. Langdon asks Teabing to fill Sophie in on the Grail legend.

15. Chapters 55–61 (pages 229–62) contain the core of the controversy surrounding *The Da Vinci Code*, for the most part posited by Teabing. His theoretical pagan history is as follows:

- The pagan Roman emperor Constantine allegedly conspired at the Council of Nicea to establish Jesus as divine—"the Son of God"—and to selectively "collate" the Bible we have today.

- In Leonardo's painting of *The Last Supper,* he supposedly represented the teachings in gnostic texts by portraying Mary Magdalene (instead of John) as the Grail: as Jesus' closest disciple, and his pregnant wife.

- In the early church's move to recast Jesus as God, they scandalized Mary Magdalene, who bore Jesus' child.

- The Holy Grail *(Sang Real)* is represented by three legends:

  i. Chests of documents proving the gnostic version of history.

  ii. Jesus' and Mary's royal bloodlines, the *sang real*, that continued through French history to this day.

  iii. The entombed body of Mary Magdalene, "the wronged Queen."

- The Priory's mission is to protect all three legends from a church that would destroy evidence against Jesus' deity.

16. The police prepare to storm Teabing's Château Villette, but Silas has already entered the grounds, having been redirected by the Teacher. Just as Langdon is figuring out the clue in the wooden box, Silas attacks, knocking him out. Teabing feigns giving over the keystone and strikes Silas with his crutch, incapacitating him; but Silas's gun discharges into the floor, alerting the police.

17. Langdon and Sophie tie up Silas and then realize the police are coming. They flee in Teabing's Range Rover, with Teabing's butler, Rémy, driving, and Silas tied up in the back. They go to a private airfield where Teabing has a plane ready to take them to England.

18. In the jet Teabing makes the case to Sophie that she is responsible to reveal the Priory truth to the world, once it's discovered. They try to decipher the script on the box. Sophie recognizes it as mirrored script in English, mimicking Leonardo da Vinci's style. They realize from the iambic-pentameter clue that they must identify a word of wisdom.

19. Fache chases after the fugitives. He learns they'll be landing in Kent and advises local police to have the plane surrounded and wait for him to get there.

20. Meanwhile Bishop Aringarosa, having been contacted by Fache, learns of what's transpired and changes his flight destination to London.

21. While alone for a moment, Langdon explains to Sophie the pagan sex rite, Hieros Gamos. She acknowledges this was what she'd witnessed, causing her to be alienated from her grandfather. Langdon and Teabing decipher the clue and come up with SOFIA. But when Sophie dials the cryptex and opens it, there is a smaller cryptex inside with a new clue.

22. Through Teabing's clever diversion, Langdon and Sophie elude capture and escape in his limo. Teabing insists the next clue to the keystone will be solved at the Temple Church. They make their way there and explore the Templar crypt, only to realize Teabing was wrong.

Continued on page 196

One of those broader themes is decidedly history. But, as we discussed in chapters 1 and 2, how factual or certain is anybody's history? Brown's character Teabing is fond of quoting Napoleon's cynical appraisal, "What is history, but a fable agreed upon?" And, smiling, Teabing further explains to the rather docile Sophie, "By its very nature, history is always a one-sided account" (256).

So it would seem logically consistent and even tolerant of Teabing to then conclude, "In the end, which side of the story [the gnostic's or the Bible's] you believe becomes a matter of faith and personal exploration, but at least the information has survived" (256). That seems reasonable enough—even consistent with the ambiguity in Brown's statement at his plagiarism trial.

Practicing What We Preach

The problem is, Teabing doesn't appear to believe much in what he preaches. Despite the occasionally generous tipping of historical hats to his Christian opposition, Teabing is very inflexible when it comes to his own take on the past. He rattles off assertion after assertion as if each were fact, leaving no room apparently for reasonable doubt.

Libraries of rigorous, academically sound publications flatly refute many of Teabing's "facts," such as the royal bloodline of Jesus Christ. For all the chronicling "in exhaustive detail by scores of historians" (253), hundreds more have at least as convincingly shown these "facts" to have no more historical basis than fairy tales.

Likewise, Teabing's supposed proof of the existence of the *sang real* in the end relies upon legends and rumors, similarly refuted by experts who will readily point out the evidence is about as certain as that of King Arthur's sword in the stone. Ironically, even in the novel itself, we never get so much as a glimpse of the legendary tomb of Queen Mary Magdalene. And, notoriously, the likes of her "Purist Documents," which just might prove the truth once and for all, are at best *reputed* to exist (256).

On one hand we have Teabing with his dossier of research and experts, and on the other hand we have a decidedly larger body of both Christian and secular research that supports the Bible's historical account. Obviously we don't want to be so simplistic as to defer to the majority ruling here, but the point remains that we cannot ignore it either.

Still, what upsets many Christians is that in this novel Teabing's voice is a lot louder than any dissenter's. Actually, it's pretty much the only voice in the room.

Character Sketch: SIR LEIGH TEABING

Teabing is a former British Royal Historian, knighted, and is now living in Versailles, France. He suffered from polio during his childhood and now wears leg braces and uses crutches (221). "Portly and ruby-faced, Sir Leigh Teabing had bushy red hair and jovial hazel eyes that seemed to twinkle as he spoke." He wears "pleated pants and a roomy silk shirt under a paisley vest. Despite the aluminum braces on his legs, he [carries] himself with a resilient, vertical dignity that [seems] more a by-product of noble ancestry than any kind of conscious effort" (227–28). He's an eccentric character with a love for riddles and solving mysteries.

His life passion is the Grail, and when "whisperings of the Priory keystone surfaced about fifteen years earlier, he moved to France to search churches in hopes of finding it" (216). Teabing and Langdon met when Teabing and the BBC produced a controversial program revealing his theory about the Grail. Langdon appeared on the program as a corroborating historian. As Brown acknowledges, ironically in his courtroom testimony, "Sir Leigh Teabing is, of course, an anagram of the claimants, Messrs. Baigent and Leigh" ("Dan Brown Witness," par. 203).

Sophie seems to see Teabing's earlier claims of evenhandedness as disingenuous. She objects, "But what good is a [reputed] documented genealogy of Christ's bloodline? ... It's not proof. Historians could not possibly confirm its authenticity." And to this, Teabing's best reply is merely a chuckle: "No more so than they can confirm the authenticity of the Bible" (256). So the sum total of all his counterintelligence is that the other side's truth is just as questionable.

Consider the Source

But there is another factor that must be weighed when we give Teabing our ear. Is he a trustworthy source?[†]

[†] If you haven't read the novel and don't want to know its final outcome, skip over the next paragraph.

Although we don't know it at the time of his sermonizing on pagan history, Teabing himself is of course Silas's Teacher. So zealous is he for his version of truth and history that he's willing to have several people killed to reveal it, and he very nearly would have murdered his friend Langdon as well as Sophie. Ironically, when all is said and done, the only conspiracy that really does exist was contrived and implemented by Teabing.

Teabing demonstrates a monomaniacal streak that will justify any means to accomplish his end. That should at least bring into question all other means he employs to accomplish that same end, including his means of persuasion. It certainly would if a fundamentalist Christian zealot were the one claiming, "I serve a far greater master than my own pride. The Truth. Mankind deserves to know that truth" (410).

It's also telling when Langdon finally expresses some doubt over Teabing's connecting the dots of the murders to the Roman Catholic Church, especially when the church believes the evidence to be false in the first place. Teabing's ironic, impassioned retort hints at protesting just a bit too much:

> What happens to *those* people [uncertain in their faith], Robert, if persuasive scientific evidence comes out that the Church's version of the Christ story is inaccurate, and that the greatest story ever told is, in fact, the greatest story ever *sold.* (266–67)

Nice textual sound bite. But this, you'll recall, is in spite of Teabing's earlier insistence that "which side of the story you believe becomes a matter of faith and personal exploration" (256). Apparently, the faith option is only viable so long as science doesn't get in the way with its facts—as if the discovery of other ancient documents will inevitably disprove the Bible let alone be considered "scientific" evidence. Even if other gospels that contradict the Bible's Gospels could be shown to be comparably old, is it really going to come down to who holds the oldest?

The Softer Sell

Langdon isn't the zealot Teabing is, but he's of the same mind. He believes a pagan truth is out there that could somehow disprove

Christianity's history. But what is really at the heart of Langdon's zeal is not the search for who has the most authentic ancient texts; rather it's a desperate need to find anything that might be an alternative to the Christian Bible's alleged history.

To the Teabings and Langdons of the world, the historicity of the Christian myth is just plain unacceptable. Why? Because the Bible's gospel accounts present the story of a personal Creator becoming a human way too literally while insisting that this historical person actually performed miracles. But worse yet, the Bible's Gospels recount them in a way that measures up by all standards to any other historical document. The gospel accounts would be accepted as authentic historical documents outright if it weren't for the magical stuff. Within academe especially there is a kind of intellectual bigotry against the supernatural.

That's why when Langdon waxes philosophical about all faiths being based on fabrications, his comparison between Jesus' and Buddha's births is not only patronizing, it's a cheap shot. "Should we wave a flag to tell the Buddhists that we have proof the Buddha did not come from a lotus blossom? Or that Jesus was not born of a *literal* virgin birth? Those who truly understand their faiths understand the stories are metaphorical" (342).

For some of us dullards who don't understand, it still seems ironic that the Langdon of *The Da Vinci Code* has forgotten the Langdon of *Angels & Demons,* who had to come to grips with a scientific approximation of a virgin birth: artificial insemination. Bottom line, what's really implausible to him isn't the question of a virgin birth but the question of a supernatural Creator creating the seed. In fact, it's the question of a supernatural Creator existing at all.

The only point of comparison between the stories of Buddha and Jesus is the motif of a supernatural birth. But the Buddhist myth doesn't even attempt to approximate the criteria for historical reality; Christianity's myth does. Langdon just refuses to acknowledge it, because a virgin birth just has to be a myth. Doesn't it?

Langdon—as well as many of the rest of us—needs to be careful of denying too quickly the unanswered elephant in the room. Indeed, many Christians would press the issue: "Yeah, but what if the myth actually happened? What if the Christian gospel was not only true but *fact?* Can you prove the negative—that it wasn't?"

So with all the posturing on both sides of the religious aisle over whose history is fact, we would do better to accept Teabing's original, saner proposition: History has to be taken on faith. We must choose which story to believe. To build arguments on the shaky foundation of presumed historical facts, even in this era of technologically recorded history, is self-delusion at best. We can't know for certain, at least in this existence. We can only have good reasons for what we believe.

For instance, it's plausible that all the history surrounding Abraham Lincoln's assassination is a grand conspiracy initiated by a beleaguered president who'd just plain had it and ran off to live quietly in Bermuda. Perhaps all the documents were contrived and forged, the pictures staged, the witnesses complicit or bribed, and the assassin a dupe.

Can you even say that Abraham Lincoln's assassination is a fact, even if you had been there? It's very reasonable to believe it really did happen—even to a 99.99 percent certainty—but there's still that remote .01 percent chance it didn't.

History Is a Matter of Faith

Christians are ironically as disingenuous as Teabing when they insist that the Bible's gospel stories are facts, because one thing the biblical Jesus was very clear about was that his message must be accepted by faith. As reasonable and reasoned a faith as Christianity is, and as good a case as we can make for its factual historicity, in the end it's *more* than reason or fact. It still remains a choice whether to believe it's all true.

And that's a good thing too. Because if we were to find that Christianity is as factually quantitative as $2 + 2 = 4$, then the elite and the intelligent would be the most holy of Christians, salvation would be an earned degree, and children and the foolish would be the damned or at least relegated to the slums of heaven.

That, ironically, probably best draws the distinction between biblical Christianity and the gnostic gospel. The historical Jesus of the Bible consistently preached unconditional, relational grace, while the gnostic gospel consistently hinges on merit.

The Old Gnostic Story

In chapter 6 we looked at one important distinction between the biblical Jesus and the gnostic Jesus: Gnostic theology hinges on secret knowledge all the while acknowledging that its supreme god is unknowable. As *The Da Vinci Code* bears out, this theology is radically different from and in many regards necessarily opposed to the biblical worldview.

Gnosticism was actually one of the earliest deviations from orthodox Christianity, and no wonder; its pagan roots are as old as Christianity's Jewish roots. Gnosticism came into its own in the second century AD:

The Proto-Gnostic

Forms of Gnosticism were already emerging when the apostle Peter [a first-hand witness and disciple of Jesus] wrote of cleverly devised myths (2 Peter 1:16) that would threaten Christian faithfulness to historic, divine revelation. Historians call Marcion [from Pontus, AD 90–160] a proto-Gnostic because his system was not nearly as developed as those that appeared in the second century and produced the kind of literature discovered in Nag Hammadi. (Garlow and Jones 162)

The gnostics were so named because of their belief in personal revelations of a special knowledge. And just as Dan Brown calls himself a Christian—although, as we pointed out earlier, there's some confusion over his definition of the word—many gnostics would also claim to be Bible-believing Christians. After all, they don't outright reject the Bible; rather, they simply add to the Scriptures another source of knowledge or insight that supersedes the Bible. That source is the *gnostikoi,* a select few (to this day) who receive special, private revelations that carry all the divine authority Christians would attribute only to Scripture.

Back to Those Pagan Roots

Gnosticism's pagan roots go back at least two millennia before Christ, plainly evident in the competing religious worldviews against the monotheistic Jews, an out-of-place minority in a pervasively poly- and pantheistic world. As Langdon points out to Sophie in *The Da Vinci Code,* "When Christianity came along, the old pagan religions did not die easily" (238). Though his intentional meaning is true enough, he's literally incorrect: Paganism didn't die at all. It simply morphed with the times into gnosticism.

Brown actually makes this same gnostic connection to ancient paganism through Langdon's frequent expositions. While searching for a clue from Jacques Saunière in the *Mona Lisa,* Langdon reflects on the famous painting's history by recalling a lecture he gave before a remarkably engaged classroom of prison inmates participating in a Harvard outreach program.

In his analysis of the painting, Langdon interprets Leonardo's apparently pagan sexual themes that undoubtedly contribute to her famed smile. Then he breaks down the painting's very name as conclusive proof:

> So we have the [Egyptian] male god, Amon.... And the female goddess, Isis, whose ancient pictogram was once called L'ISA.... AMON L'ISA.... Gentlemen, not only does the face of Mona Lisa look androgynous, but her name is an anagram of the divine union of male and female. And *that,* my friends, is Da Vinci's little secret, and the reason for Mona Lisa's knowing smile. (120–21)

Gnostic texts affirm this pagan heritage, invoking for their own goddess Sophia the same identity as the ancient Egyptian goddess Isis. In the recently discovered gnostic text *The Thunder, the Perfect Mind,* the goddess proclaims in consciously self-contradicting terms that she is "the one whose image is great in Egypt and the one who has no image among the barbarians" (Peel, par. 7).

Earlier in the same text, she proudly characterizes herself in similarly dualistic terms (reminiscent of the *Angels & Demons'* yin and yang we discussed in chapter 7):

> I am the whore and the holy one. I am the wife and the virgin.... I am the barren one and many are her sons.... I am the bride and the bridegroom.... You who deny

me, confess me, and you, who confess me, deny me. You who tell the truth about me, lie about me, and you, who have lied about me, tell the truth about me.... I am war and peace. Give heed to me. (par. 2)

The Making of Robert Langdon

Robert Langdon views "the world as a web of profoundly intertwined histories and events" (15). In Dan Brown's witness statement at his plagiarism trial, he describes Langdon as an amalgam of many people he admires. In the early 1990s, Brown first saw the artwork of John Langdon, an artist and philosopher and a close friend of his father. The real Langdon is "most famous for his ability to create ambigrams" ("Dan Brown Witness," par. 43). Brown named the protagonist Robert Langdon not only as a tribute to John but because the name sounded "very 'New England,'" and he simply likes "last names with two syllables" (see par. 45).

Brown says that with Langdon he wanted to create a teacher: "Many of the people I admire most are teachers—my father is the obvious figure from my own life" (par. 45).

Another teacher Brown greatly admires is Joseph Campbell, a religious historian and symbologist who partially informs Langdon's character. He recalls when first seeing Campbell on a TV program being impressed by "Campbell's open-minded and unthreatening delivery, especially when he spoke about controversial topics like myths and untruths in religion." Brown wanted Langdon "to have this same open-minded tone" (par. 46). Brown also makes clear that he intends to make Langdon his primary character for years to come. "His expertise in symbology and iconography affords him the luxury of potentially limitless adventures in exotic locales" (par. 49).

In *The Da Vinci Code,* when Langdon later tries to explain to Sophie the spirituality of the pagan sex rite Hieros Gamos, he again invokes the gnostic heritage in Isis: "Since the days of Isis, sex rites had been considered man's only bridge from earth to heaven" (308). It's a critical link because the gnostic influences on Christianity throughout history are very much "pagan to the core," as Langdon asserts when referring to church architecture (339). And the pantheistic pagan worldview requires gods and goddesses, the yins and the yangs that bring balance to nature. Somehow, though, there always seems to be greater balance in the pagan world when the goddesses are in control of things. In good mea-culpa form on behalf of the masculine gender, Langdon grows nostalgic: "The days of the goddess were over. The pendulum had swung. Mother Earth had become a *man's* world, and the gods of destruction and war were taking their toll" (125).

Apparently, in those good old pre-Christian pagan days, there wasn't much in the way of war and destruction. But Langdon's right when he recollects that there was a time when paganism ruled the majority of human minds. But the question is, did the pendulum really swing at the time of the Nicene Council, if ever?

An Ancient Conflict

As we saw in chapter 7, the pagan worldview cannot abide an imbalanced, monotheistic, Judeo-Christian God of the universe. Ironically, within their unity, monists must have pluralism, in spite of what the word denotes. All is one, but within that oneness is the diversity that gods and goddesses bring to the table.

For monotheists, there's only one God, but that one God is also characterized by a kind of duality. Although he's sovereign over all he created, he also created in such a way that people can exist in opposition to his will. His children can rebel.

Since the earliest records, monotheists and monists have stood in opposition to one another. The Isis-worshipping polytheists of Egypt enslaved and oppressed ancient Israel. (See Ex. 1—14.) And pretty much the entire Old Testament is about one struggle after another between the monotheistic Israelites and the vast majority of their polytheist and pantheist neighbors.

It's remarkable that the Israelites survived: With the Egyptians, Babylonians, Assyrians, Philistines, Canaanites, Ammonites, Midianites, and dozens of other "ites," and, by the New Testament era, the Romans, it makes no natural sense that an insignificant little nation believing in one true God should have endured.

Yet some three-and-a-half-millennia later, the *Shema* is proclaimed today in Jewish homes and synagogues all over the world: "Hear, O Israel: The LORD our God, the LORD is one. Love the LORD your God with all your heart and with all your soul and with all your strength" (Deut. 6:4–5). And Christians, whose roots are in monotheistic Judaism, affirm the same belief: There is only one God, and he is a person to be loved with all of one's heart, soul, and strength. (Note the decidedly monotheistic affirmation of the *Shema* that Jesus gave in Mark 12:29–30.)

Even so, ancient Israel continually struggled against the pressures to assimilate into the surrounding pagan cultures, much the same as Christianity does today in the face of pervasive neo-paganism. Ironically, what Robert Langdon wants to see as signs of pagan roots in early Jewish theology, the ancient texts of the Bible represent as infiltrations by an enemy, analogous to Nazism infiltrating a democracy. They may proselytize natives and win them over to their ideology, but the ideology is fundamentally opposed to the people of the land's beliefs.

The Infiltrators

But Robert Langdon (and, by inference, Dan Brown) doesn't get this. Langdon pauses after his awkward explanation of Hieros Gamos to Sophie and recalls past lectures that flabbergasted his Jewish students: "Early Jews believed that the Holy of Holies in Solomon's Temple housed not only God but also His powerful female equal, Shekinah" (309).

The word *shekinah,* though not found anywhere in the Bible, derives from a Hebrew word meaning "the dwelling or abiding glory of God"—that's still the *Shema*-affirming, one true God. (See sidebar on the following page for more information on Shekinah.) The description of the brilliant manifestation of God's glory is quite clear—it was a powerful light from God himself, not another god along for the ride.

However, although Langdon is unclear about the source for his decidedly pagan spin on Shekinah, there's plenty of precedent in the Bible for pagan infiltrations into the otherwise very monotheistic religion of the Jewish people. The Jews who embraced pagan idolatry in the Old Testament may well have seen the Shekinah or the supernatural manifestation of God's glory as a second deity, perhaps on the order of Isis. But this was by no means representative of the Jewish religion itself. If it had been, the Jews by definition would have been pagan monists.

As we mentioned earlier, this mixing or combining of fundamentally different beliefs is called *syncretism.* It was such a common

Shekinah

[The Jewish epithet, "the shekinah glory"—"the dwelling or abiding glory"—is derived from the Hebrew verb וַיִּשְׁכֹּן (*vayyishkon*, "dwelt, abode").]

The Hebrew verb is וַיִּשְׁכֹּן (*vayyishkon*, and dwelt, abode), from which the Jews derived the epithet "the Shekinah Glory," the dwelling or abiding glory. The glory of Yahweh was a display visible at a distance, clearly in view of the Israelites on Mount Sinai where Moses went up to receive the ten commandments (*Net Bible*, notes on Exodus 24:15–16).

When the people of Israel finished constructing the tabernacle [during their Exodus period with Moses], an amazing thing happened. "Then the cloud covered the Tent of Meeting, and the glory of the Lord filled the tabernacle. And Moses was not able to enter the Tent of Meeting because the cloud had settled upon it, and the glory of the Lord filled the tabernacle" (Ex. 40:34–35). That cloud of glory seems to have been brilliant light, so bright that Moses could not look at it or stand before it. It was called by the Jews the *Shekinah*, a non-Biblical term derived from a Hebrew verb meaning to dwell, emphasizing God's presence among His people in that shining cloud of glory. The same *Shekinah* glory filled Solomon's temple years later when it was completed (1 Kings 8:10–11). When Ezekiel saw a vision of the glory of the Lord, he too described it in terms of brightness: "As the appearance of the rainbow in the clouds on a rainy day, so was the appearance of the surrounding radiance. Such was the appearance of the likeness of the glory of the Lord" (Ezek. 1:28 NASB).

—Richard L. Strauss

problem for the Israelites that the God of the Bible addressed it twice in his Ten Commandments: "You shall have no other gods before me" and "You shall not make for yourself an idol in the form of anything in heaven above or on the earth beneath or in the waters below" (Ex. 20:3–4).

But anyone who has read the Old Testament knows that the penchant for integrating beliefs was the Israelites' fatal flaw, and, by the Bible's account, it was fundamentally their undoing. God would lift his protection from the nation of Israel, leaving them to their own devices and their enslaving love affairs with other gods.

The struggle to remain monogamously committed to the one God was also an issue in the earliest years of the Christian church and well into the following two centuries with the rise of gnosticism. And since—as Langdon reminds us—old paganism does not "die easily," the gnostic appeal to the Christian mind continues to this day. This worldview is very much alive and well not only among its own followers but also within elements of both mainline and emerging-church Christianity.

This is why discerning Christians aren't really surprised by Langdon's sensational revelations of pagan influences upon Christianity. It's really no wonder that "pagan symbolism [is] hidden in the stones of Chartres Cathedral" (7) or that there could be any number of churches like Saint-Sulpice, with its "pagan astronomical device like a sundial" (105). They wouldn't even find it particularly surprising, if true, that a political Constantine, supposedly a life-long pagan, was brilliantly successful at "fusing pagan symbols, dates, and rituals into the growing Christian tradition," thereby creating "a kind of hybrid religion that was acceptable to both parties" (232).

Most Christians will likewise collectively shrug their shoulders when Teabing insists, "Nothing in Christianity is original" (232). As we explored in chapters 1 and 2, Christians believe there is nothing new or original under God's sun; he is the Creator of all myths. Even the supposed original myths that Teabing or Langdon might cite only mimic or echo God's original story.

Ironically, this gets to the core reason Christians are very aware but generally ambivalent about pagan assimilations within many of their practices. And it really rubs gnostics the wrong way. A key premise of Christianity is God's incarnation: that God the Son took on flesh, became a man, and lived among us. He met people where they were.

That's why Christianity has never really had a problem with taking on the cultural trappings of even a pagan religion and Christianizing them. That's been its modus operandi for millennia. Christians don't have a problem remembering Jesus' birth (Christmas) on a pagan holiday (especially since there's no time of the year specified in Scripture), or tying Easter to pagan holidays and traditions (though the precedent time of the year for Jesus' resurrection is specified in the Bible), or even worshipping on Sunday instead of the traditionally Jewish Saturday Sabbath. (Perhaps there are convenient pagan connections to Sunday worship, but the primary reason the early church moved to Sunday was because it was the day of the week Jesus was resurrected.)

But while the surface appearances of the Christian faith—the incarnational flesh; the bodily physical appearance—would be adapted to better reach various cultures, the gospel message of the one true God becoming a man, dying, being resurrected, and offering salvation to all who believe is a universal and unchanging truth.

Christians are about winning people over to the Christian worldview. To that end, they might agree in a sense with Langdon's assessment of "the Vatican's campaign to eradicate pagan religions and convert the masses to Christianity," and even with the church launching "a smear campaign against the pagan gods and goddesses, recasting their divine symbols as evil" (37). But words like "eradicate" and "smear campaign" carry some heavy-duty negative connotations.

Christianity in its truest form has always been about winning the hearts and minds of people through persuasion, not coercion. Granted, many times in history so-called supposed Christians have employed un-Christlike methods to make converts. Just as great evil has been carried out in the name of science, patriotism, and atheism, so have evil malpractices been committed by self-proclaimed Christians.

But if these people were Christians in any sense of the word, they certainly weren't acting according to the will of the Bible's God. No immoral means can justify a truly godly end. No mind can be forced into the kind of authentic faith Jesus preached. If the Christian God won't force people to believe, how could any authentic Christian think he or she might pull it off?

But Christians shouldn't have to apologize for believing that there are evil practices, beliefs, and symbols that advocate a be-your-own-god existence of rebellion against God. After all, according to the Christian's worldview, if something isn't connected to the light, it's darkness. If it's not redeemed and in relationship to God, it's evil—whether that evil might be a Hieros Gamos worship service or fudging on your taxes. Either way, it's still a practice that's independent of and in rebellion against God.

That doesn't mean Christians should think they're better than pagans simply because they're connected to the light. It just means that being in the light enables Christians to see the darkness for what it is.

Sadly, some of us might be prone at times to confuse being in the light with being the light ourselves, and we misrepresent God in the process. But perhaps some of the Langdons and Teabings of the world can forgive us for wanting so much for others to be in the light.

The Light of the World

More than six centuries before Jesus Christ was born, the Jewish prophet Isaiah foretold of the Messiah, who would come to Israel, specifically to the regions of Galilee, by way of the sea along the Jordan: "The people walking in darkness have seen a great light; on those living in the land of the shadow of death a light has dawned" (Isa. 9:2). In Matthew's gospel, Jesus fulfilled that prophecy as he passed through those regions preaching his message of repentance. (See Matt. 4:13–17.)

All of the gospels build on this image of light in a dark world. Often in Jesus' teachings he would build on the same metaphor, declaring that he himself was the light in an otherwise hopelessly dark world. The key to this light was always a relationship with Jesus himself: "I am the light of the world. Whoever follows me will never walk in darkness, but will have the light of life" (John 8:12).

But Jesus was about more than personal enlightenment for a select few. He taught that those who followed him and who had become connected to the "light of life" were to reflect that light in a darkened world. Those who would fault Christians for shining Jesus' light and trying to call people out of the darkness really have a problem with the biblical Jesus himself:

> You are the light of the world. A city on a hill cannot be hidden. Neither do people light a lamp and put it under a bowl. Instead they put it on its stand, and it gives light to everyone in the house. In the same way, let your light shine before men, that they may see your good deeds and praise your Father in heaven.
> (Matt. 5:14–16)

But there's another remarkable reference to Jesus as the light, and it isn't figurative language. It's *transfigurative.* True to how God operates time and time again, he gives us a glimpse of the metaphor becoming literal. We realize that when Jesus said he was the light of the world, he wasn't just talking philosophical theory or esoteric *gnosis*—he was talking real-life light:

> After six days Jesus took with him Peter, James and John the brother of James, and led them up a high mountain by themselves. There he was transfigured before them. His face shone like the sun, and his clothes became as white as the light. Just then there appeared before them Moses and Elijah, talking with Jesus.
>
> Peter said to Jesus, "Lord, it is good for us to be here. If you wish, I will put up three shelters—one for you, one for Moses and one for Elijah."
>
> While he was still speaking, a bright cloud enveloped them, and a voice from the cloud said, "This is my Son, whom I love; with him I am well pleased. Listen to him!" (Matt. 17:1–5)

The kind of enlightenment Jesus taught was not speculative theorizing. And it was more than Langdon's enlightening outreach to prison inmates: "Da Vinci was in tune with the *balance* between male and female. He believed that a human soul could not be enlightened unless it had both male and female elements" (120). The Jesus of the Bible called people to personally reconnect with their Creator, the definition of light and knowledge.

And troublingly, provocatively, and unwaveringly, Jesus insists that the only way to do so is through him.

10

The Secret Spiritual Code to Life

(THE DA VINCI CODE)

The day after Christmas 2004, an earthquake deep in the Indian Ocean triggered a tsunami. It hit Asian islands and countries with such force that entire villages were swept away. Homes and buildings not anchored firmly tumbled as if in a washing machine. More than 275,000 people died that day, many who had been living their lives as normal or enjoying a sunny day at the beach.

They never knew what hit them.

As the tragedy unfolded in the media over the next week, a sickening, familiar ache settled into many of our hearts. *Why does this kind of thing happen? Why would God create a world with such cruelty?* Time and time again we will find ourselves asking the same question: Why would a supposedly good God allow such evil to happen?

Part of what makes *The Da Vinci Code* more compelling is not only its staccato story line but some degree of depth in its characters. And as the life of one particular character—Silas—unfolds, we can see evidence in him of at least a bit more sophistication to this gospel story. Silas's tragedy is in the evil that he has both suffered and inflicted ... and all ironically for a greater good. The reason this portrayal of evil works in this story is because we know it imitates life. There are people who become great powers of evil and destruction in our world. And when, for instance, they commit murders, we find ourselves asking (over and over again), *Why?*

The gnostic's answer is simple: The God who created the world was evil. The Bible, on the other hand, insists that a perfectly good God created everything good, but he allowed for the possibility of humans to rebel. As you might expect, the theist's and the monist's

The Da Vinci Code Plot Summary—the Conclusion
(Spoiler Warning—ending of the novel is revealed on this page.)

23. Meanwhile, in the back of the limo, Rémy frees Silas and gives him a loaded pistol. The Teacher has previously employed Rémy. Silas and Rémy both enter the church and confront the trio. They acquire the cryptex (the keystone) and then leave with Teabing as hostage. They return to the limo and place him in the back, bound and gagged.

24. The Teacher calls Silas in the limo and instructs him to get out at the Opus Dei residence in London while Rémy delivers the cryptex and Teabing to the Teacher. Later, the Teacher gets into the limo with Rémy, who gives him the cryptex. The Teacher poisons Rémy and then goes to the back of the limo to supposedly do away with Teabing. Then he makes his way to Westminster Abbey.

25. Langdon and Sophie go to the King's College Research Institute in Systematic Theology, where a librarian helps them find the final clue: Sir Isaac Newton's tomb at Westminster Abbey. They rush to the site.

26. Meanwhile, Aringarosa arrives in England. Getting into a police car, he hears the radio announce the ensuing pursuit of Silas. Aringarosa rushes to Opus Dei. Silas awakens and is alerted to police. He flees, acquiring one officer's gun. In the flurry he is accosted. He turns and shoots Aringarosa.

27. The Teacher is already at the tomb trying to decipher the final clue. He spots Sophie and Langdon and determines to use them. Langdon and Sophie find a message on the tomb, instructing them to go to the Chapter House to find Teabing. When they get there, they discover that Teabing is none other than the Teacher, gun in hand.

28. Teabing explains that Saunière had betrayed the Priory. Giving Langdon the cryptex, he challenges Langdon and Sophie to help him make known the Grail to the world. Teabing asks Langdon whether he's with Teabing or against him. Langdon steps away, as if considering. But then in an effort to save Sophie, he threatens to drop the cryptex. Teabing realizes he must kill both Sophie and Langdon, but he needs Langdon to put down the cryptex. Langdon feigns doing so, then tosses it up in the air. Teabing dives to save it, losing his gun. He catches the cryptex, but it breaks. Sophie holds the gun on Teabing, who realizes the cryptex has already been opened and the supposedly destroyed map is

not inside. Langdon had deciphered the password and, while turned away, removed the map. Fache rushes in with British police and arrests Teabing.

29. While Silas carries a wounded Aringarosa to the hospital, the bishop recalls the circumstances that led to the conspiracy. Opus Dei's affiliation with the Catholic Church was being severed, but soon after, the Teacher had contacted him with the conspiracy plan—all Teabing's deception. Silas delivers Aringarosa to the hospital, swearing vengeance, but Aringarosa pleads instead for Silas to forgive the one who betrayed them. Later, in the mist in Kensington Gardens, a lone Silas dies in a poignant scene from his gunshot wound.

30. Fache pieces together how Teabing planted bugs on artwork he had given to his key contacts and then won Aringarosa's trust as the Teacher. Fache visits a recovering Aringarosa in the hospital, who asks him to distribute the money from the Vatican to the families of those Silas had killed.

31. The cryptex map directs Langdon and Sophie to Rosslyn Chapel. Sophie has childhood memories of the place. At the nearby curator's house, she finds her grandmother, Marie Chauvel, and the young chapel docent is her brother, both of whom she thought were dead.

32. As the story unfolds, Sophie learns that the Priory suspected that Sophie's parents, the pure *Sangreal* descendants, had been murdered. The grandparents each took one child and raised them separately, hiding them from the church. Marie explains that Mary Magdalene's tomb had been at the church, but Saunière had finally moved her back to France, though she didn't know where. Sophie decides to stay with her grandmother while Langdon returns to Paris. But they agree to meet again soon.

33. Back in Paris, Langdon realizes that his own book manuscript contained a clue to the location of the Grail. Tracing the ancient meridian through Paris, he finds himself back at the Louvre. The inverse glass pyramid points down into the Louvre. Beneath it is a small, opposing pyramid—a tip of an iceberg submerged below the floor, where, awestruck, Langdon realizes Magdalene's tomb must reside.

accounts of the fall of humankind—what Langdon repeatedly refers to as "the original sin"—also varies significantly.

Langdon much prefers the gnostic spin on the story—a "fortunate" fall in which Eve's pursuit of the knowledge of good and evil was actually a good thing, even the will of the supreme gnostic god. What Langdon finds especially egregious about the church's account is that the church "demonized" (238) Eve and all her female descendants. By the pagan estimation of things, if any evil did come into the world through the garden-of-Eden myth, it would have been the scandalizing of the goddess Eve.

Scandalizing Eve

Dan Brown says in his witness statement that his wife, Blythe, helped him with much of his research for *The Da Vinci Code*. And she had a particular agenda that she hoped could become a strong message in her husband's gospel. Brown testifies, "In particular, she became passionate about the history of the Church's suppression of women, and she lobbied hard for me to make it a primary theme of the novel" ("Dan Brown Witness," par. 86).

Blythe apparently did influence the character development of Robert Langdon, who has come a long way since *Angels & Demons*, when he sat as a docile disciple at the feet of the pagan evangelist Vittoria. In *The Da Vinci Code*, his own pagan faith is strong as he preaches to Sophie: "It was *man*, not God, who created the concept of 'original sin,' whereby Eve tasted of the apple and caused the downfall of the human race." And, predictably, Teabing is quick to add, "Sadly, Christian philosophy decided to embezzle the female's creative power by ignoring biological truth and making *man* the Creator. Genesis tells us that Eve was created from Adam's rib. Woman became an offshoot of man. And a sinful one at that" (238).

No theistically Christian philosophy could claim that man is the creator; that belief would actually better fit a pagan worldview. Likewise, nothing in Christian theology argues that either Adam or Eve was created sinful. Traditional interpretations of God creating

Eve out of a rib from Adam's side affirm Eve's equality—she was bone of Adam's bone, flesh of his flesh. (See Gen. 2:21–23.)

However, Langdon disagrees. As he reflects on the significance of the "so dark the con of man" clue scrawled across the protective glass over the *Mona Lisa,* he knows the Priory of Sion rued the day the church had "conned" the entire world by converting it from matriarchal paganism to that "dark" patriarchal Christian worldview (124).

He recollects a holocaust in which "midwives also were killed for their heretical practice of using medical knowledge to ease the pain of childbirth—a suffering, the Church claimed, that was God's rightful punishment for Eve's partaking of the Apple of Knowledge, thus giving birth to the idea of Original Sin" (125). Never mind that such a concept of sin was by no means "original" to Christianity. The Genesis portion of the Torah itself gave birth to the concept, which predates Jesus' life on earth by centuries.

Nevertheless, this central theme of the scandalizing of Eve by attributing "original sin" to her is key to the novel's final clue, which Langdon deciphers at that critical moment in the Westminster Abbey Chapter House: "'APPLE. The orb from which Eve partook,' Langdon said coolly, 'incurring the Holy wrath of God. Original sin. The symbol of the fall of the sacred feminine'" (425).

Original Sin—Who's Really to Blame?

Langdon's interpretation of the Genesis story is ironically consistent with the gnostic interpretation of the Original Sin myth. By stating that "it was *man,* not God, who created the concept of 'original sin'" (238), he's basically saying that it was literally the male gender's handiwork. However, if pressed to explain where evil itself came from, the gnostic in Langdon might be forced to concede something to the effect of, "Well, God I suppose ... in a yin-yang kind of way." As Stephan A. Hoeller (a gnostic bishop, also known as Tau Stephanus) explains,

> Many religions advocate that humans are to be blamed for the imperfections of the world. Supporting this view, they interpret the Genesis myth as declaring that transgressions committed by the first human pair brought about a "fall" of creation

resulting in the present corrupt state of the world. Gnostics respond that this interpretation of the myth is false. The blame for the world's failings lies not with
humans, but with the creator. (par. 5)

Gnostics believe that the "fall" was actually caused by a flawed
creator called the Demiurge ("the craftsman"), who made our material world, including the physical attributes of humans. The
Demiurge was the son of the goddess Sophia, although not a son she
was particularly proud of. One of the most ancient Gnostic heretics
is Valentinus (AD 100–155), the proto-gnostic founder of a school of
"speculative Christian theology." He and his followers, who are
called Valentinians, equated this Demiurge with Jehovah, the God of
the Old Testament and Creator of the world.

Gnostics on Original Sin

According to [the] Valentinian myth of the fall, God held back perfect knowledge
(gnosis) of himself from his Aeons (including Sophia) so that they would search for
him. Until Christ manifested himself to them, the Aeons had not united in the "bridal
chamber," a metaphor for perfect knowledge of God. It was as a result of this with-
holding of gnosis that the fall occurred.

The separation of Sophia/Eve is described as the origin of our deficient relationship with God. In Valentinianism deficiency or ignorance is identical with spiritual
death. According to the Gospel of Philip, "When Eve was still in Adam, death did not
exist. When she was separated from him death came into being" (GP 63 cf. Genesis
3:19; see also Gospel of Philip 70).

—David Brons, "Sophia and Eve," The Gnostic Society Library

The Gnosis of Good and Evil

Both Jews and Christians would agree that the gnostic slant on
the Genesis story is a stretch from the biblical text's explicit intent.
The Genesis 3 story describes something more observably true in
human nature than the lack of some esoteric knowledge.

To the gnostic, this knowledge—the *gnosis*—is the ideal, the holy
purpose of any person's existence. Adam and Eve would have sinned
if they had *not* done whatever it took to obtain knowledge, be it
good or evil. But the unique premise of the Genesis story is that

there's a knowledge it's not good to have. It could never be good to understand firsthand hatred, fear, murder, rape, or war. In that light the serpent's temptation was fundamentally about breaching humans' trust of God, and therein becoming our own gods: "God knows that when you eat of it your eyes will be opened, and you will be like God" (Gen. 3:5).

Adam and Eve more or less decided God was hiding knowledge from them. So they ate the fruit, and now we have billions of little demigods throughout the world and history.

Setting the Record Straight

The idea that Eve is the original sinner who's to blame for all that's wrong with humanity is unbiblical. All theological references to original sin in the New Testament are consistently laid at Adam's feet; Eve is never even mentioned. Furthermore, a strong case can be made, based on Genesis 3, that Adam was present during the temptation of Eve. Eve may have been doing all the talking, and she did take the first bite of the fruit, but then she gave some to her husband, "who was with her" (v. 6). Most likely he looked her up and down after she took that first bite, confirming that she wasn't dead yet, and then "he ate it" (v. 6).

Christian theology unquestionably places the blame for human rebellion squarely on the shoulders of *both* Adam and Eve. They rebelled against God, were cursed, and were driven out of the garden. Then they had kids, who inherited their parents' state of separation from God. That's the story of the original sin according to the Bible. And that's how Christians can believe a perfectly good God creating everything, but everything ended up not so good.

And not to undo Jacques Saunière's clever final clue or anything, but nowhere in the Genesis account of Adam and Eve is an apple ever mentioned. Only "fruit" (3:3, 6).

Jesus Met a Girl

The gnostic misunderstandings about original sin lead to a related misunderstanding in *The Da Vinci Code*, though this one is a bit

harder for us to empathize with. According to Brown, the fundamental threat to Christianity, which will shake the very foundations
of the church, is that somehow the divinity of the Messiah will be
compromised by evidence of a Jesus who would "consort with
women or engage in sexual union" (257).

Jesus' alleged marriage to Mary Magdalene and his surviving
bloodline is a central plot device for the novel. Of course, we can't
prove history as absolute fact one way or the other (remember Abe
Lincoln in Bermuda?). Historical evidence stands as best as it can on
the side of the biblical gospels' account, but it's still a matter of faith
in the end. Those who want to believe the gnostic gospels' accounts
have enough evidence to satisfy their minds, no matter what the
preponderance of scholarship might show.

Interestingly, according to Brown's witness statement, his wife,
Blythe, apparently had some influence on this story element as well:

> Initially, I was reluctant to include the bloodline theory at all, finding it too
> incredible and inaccessible to readers—I thought it was a step too far. However,
> after much discussion and brainstorming with Blythe, I eventually became con-
> vinced that I could introduce the idea successfully. Blythe had suggested
> introducing it as a part of the Goddess worship theme—the lost sacred femi-
> nine being embodied by the Church of Magdalene that never was. The more I
> read on this topic—both in Blythe's notes and independently in the books and
> on the internet—the more plausible I found the storyline. ("Dan Brown
> Witness," par. 120)

The controversy surrounding the Jesus bloodline element single-
handedly established the novel's remarkable fame. By Teabing's
account, the stakes are profoundly high, not only within the fictional context, but perhaps in the real world as well:

> [The Church] could never have survived public knowledge of a bloodline. A
> child of Jesus would undermine the critical notion of Christ's divinity and
> therefore the Christian church, which declared itself the sole vessel through
> which humanity could access the divine and gain entrance to the kingdom of
> heaven. (254)

What's more, Teabing points out, though most of us have never
heard that Mary Magdalene is the Grail bearing the bloodline (the

baby) of Jesus, still "Christ Himself made that claim" (242). Of course, Teabing fails to distinguish which Jesus made the claim or where. He's obviously referring to the Jesus of the nonbiblical gospels, but which gospel? He never seems to mention.

What If Jesus Were Married?

But there's a more fundamental straw-man premise that goes largely ignored in *The Da Vinci Code:* How would Jesus' being a father somehow undermine his divinity and therein invalidate the church's reason for existing?

Character Sketch: SOPHIE NEVEU

Agent Sophie Neveu of the French Judicial Police studied cryptography at the Royal Holloway in England. "At thirty-two years old, she had a dogged determination that bordered on obstinate." An attractive woman, she walks with "long, fluid strides ... a haunting certainty to her gait." She is "dressed casually in a knee-length, cream-colored Irish sweater over black leggings.... Her thick burgundy hair [falls] unstyled to her shoulders, framing the warmth of her face." She's "healthy with an unembellished beauty and genuineness that radiates a striking personal confidence." And when she speaks, "her words [curve] richly around her muted Anglo-Franco accent." She has olive green eyes and a "strong gaze" (49–50). In chapter 13 it's revealed that she's Saunière's granddaughter. When she was four years old, she believes, her family was killed in a car accident, leaving only her grandfather to raise her (76). However, she learns otherwise by the end of the novel. (See the plot summary beginning on page 177.)

Sophie recalls a childhood conversation with her grandfather in which she asks, "Did Jesus have a girlfriend?" Her grandfather said nothing for a moment. Then he responded in a way that Christians should be able to resonate with at least a little: "Would it be so bad if He did?" (247). From a theological perspective, probably not.

The common expectation is that Christians would find repulsive and heretical the idea that Jesus could have had sexual relations. That's because the long-held gnostic tradition insists that anything of a physical nature is intrinsically evil. Being fully man, Jesus was not without sexuality, but he was without sin. Sex in and of itself isn't sin. The only condition the Bible places on sex is that it be practiced according to the way God designed it—a man and a woman becoming one flesh in the context of marriage.

In theory Jesus could have married Mary Magdalene, enjoyed sex without sin, and had a child by her. And that would have done nothing to deny his deity. However, the reliable texts of the Bible give no indication whatsoever that Jesus had anything more than a teacher-disciple relationship with Mary Magdalene, who was a close and committed disciple whom Jesus freed of demon possession.

A marriage relationship between Jesus and any woman most likely wouldn't have fit God's will, if for no other reason than what the novel illustrates: People would be distracted from Jesus' true mission, preferring to chase after and idolize his progeny as if they were pantheistic gods. They'd probably even venerate and worship Jesus' wife.

No eHarmonys in Bible Times

By biblical standards, it's entirely possible for a person to be single and celibate and remain in the will of God. After all, if Jesus was fully man and remained single and celibate, then he certainly remained in God's will, since he was also fully God. Matthew's gospel recounts Jesus' explanation of celibacy on one occasion:

> Some are eunuchs because they were born that way; others were made that way by men; and others have renounced marriage because of the kingdom of heaven. The one who can accept this should accept it. (19:12)

Celibacy flies in the face of Langdon's apparent common wisdom. "According to Jewish custom," he argues in *The Da Vinci Code*, "celibacy was condemned, and the obligation for a Jewish father was to find a suitable wife for his son" (245). Perhaps Brown extrapolated this theory from some obscure references to some Jewish sect way out in some corner of Jewish society. Regardless, celibacy clearly was practiced by some.

For instance the apostle Paul proudly acknowledged, "I am an Israelite myself, a descendant of Abraham, from the tribe of Benjamin" (Rom. 11:1). Yet in his first epistle to the Corinthian church he wrote, "I wish that all men were as I am" (7:7), specifying in verse 8 that he meant "unmarried."

Sex, Rites, and Manuscripts

By many gnostics' standards, it's not all right for Jesus to have remained single and, worse, celibate. Though the spiritual and the physical are necessarily separated in orthodox gnosticism, physical union through sex is for many gnostics the means by which humans can most closely accomplish *gnosis*. Dan Brown adapted the ancient pagan practice of sex rites to his story in the form of Hieros Gamos, as he explained in his witness testimony:

> While the history of Hieros Gamos is well documented, I made up the idea that it was practiced by the Priory [which is okay, as the Priory itself is made up]. The description of the ritual itself was inspired by Stanley Kubrick's film *Eyes Wide Shut*. ("Dan Brown Witness," par. 127)

It's in this spirit that Langdon attempts to explain the spiritual significance of the ancient pagan ceremony to Sophie, who had years earlier witnessed her grandfather in such a ritual. "'Hieros Gamos is Greek,' he continued. 'It means *sacred marriage*.... What you saw was not about sex, it was about spirituality. The Hieros Gamos ritual is not a perversion. It's a deeply sacrosanct ceremony'" (308–9).

Presumably, Langdon means that Hieros Gamos isn't about sex in the recreational or even the procreational sense. He alleges that this kind of pagan sex "had nothing to do with eroticism. It was a

Character Sketch: Jacques Saunière

Saunière is the renowned Louvre curator, but more significantly, he's "the sole guardian of one of the most powerful secrets ever kept" (5). For this secret, he is murdered by Silas in the novel's prologue (evoking the opening in *Angels & Demons*). He holds the secret because he is the Grand Master of the Priory of Sion.

Langdon reveres him professionally, admiring his books on the secret codes hidden in the paintings of Poussin and Teniers (15). Saunière had a "passion for relics relating to fertility, goddess cults, Wicca, and the sacred feminine." Over the span of twenty years, he'd "helped the Louvre amass the largest collection of goddess art on earth" (23). He's described as sharing "a lot of spiritual ideologies with da Vinci, including a concern over the Church's elimination of the sacred feminine" (46). Perhaps most significantly, he's also Sophie's grandfather (70).

In Brown's court testimony, he mentions that the name "Saunière ... is a playful reference aimed at conspiracy buffs, to the mystery at Rennes-le Château, which I did not include in *The Da Vinci Code*" ("Dan Brown Witness," par. 203).

spiritual act. Historically, intercourse was the act through which male and female experienced God" (308).

Sophie's doubts are understandable, and she looks skeptical as she responds, "Orgasm as prayer?" (309). Considering human nature—especially the masculine side of the gene pool—it's hard not to suspect some other-than-spiritual motives in this ritual.

In the Spirit of Sex

Christianity affirms that sex is a spiritual experience. God created sex in humans to be far more than procreative. That's because we have souls—the stuff of which sentient people are made; the stuff that defines our being created in God's image. This is what Langdon's pagan Hieros Gamos followers have tapped into: Human sex is spiritual.

However, for pagans who believe in *polytheistic* relationships with a multiplicity of gods, *polygamous* relationships with a multiplicity of humans also make perfect sense. With the pagan-monist sensibilities of all being one, and the physical universe itself comprising all that is God, then sex would be the height of spirituality. Any living thing about the business of procreating would be participating in a type of spiritual experience. Forget orgasm; cross-pollination would be prayer.

This gets to the core of why our understanding of God matters profoundly in terms of how we live our lives. Those of us who are Christians know we're in what is essentially a marriage relationship with God—it's not just about personal intimacy with him; it's about a permanent commitment to him alone.

Enlightened Sex

God designed sex as a beautiful gift to humans. But from the Christian perspective, the beauty is in how it mimics our intimacy with the one true God: It's a truly enlightened spiritual experience when it's monotheistic, and therein monogamous—one God, one spouse.

All sexual practices that the Christian Bible calls evil are not so simply because people believe God arbitrarily called some things good and some things bad. They're called evil for the same reason loving other gods would be equated with loving darkness. When we choose in favor of the many, and ultimately in favor of the self, we are denying our relationship with the One.

That's why in the Ten Commandments God not only calls his people into a committed relationship with him, uncompromised by worship of idols or other gods (see Ex. 20:3–4), but he also commands them not to commit adultery (v. 14) or covet another person's spouse (v. 17), since these behaviors are fundamentally opposed to an in-the-light relationship with him (vv. 5–6).

Celibacy in the City

How would intimacy with God be possible for Jesus or anyone else who commits to a lifestyle of sexual abstinence? Would Jesus' and Paul's nonexistent sex lives reflect a lack of intimacy with God? By pagan-gnostic standards, this actually would be the case. But not so with Christianity.

Consider an analogy. You're a lightbulb, and sex is a mirror. A lightbulb wouldn't burn brighter simply because a mirror is placed next to it to reflect the light. The bulb's brightness depends on its power source, not its reflection in a mirror. If the bulb is lit, the mirror will reflect the light. If the bulb isn't lit, the mirror itself can't lessen the darkness.

Our sexuality is a reflection of our relationship with God, not an indicator or source of relationship with God, as the gnostics would have it. Those who are in relationship with God (connected to the power source) and who practice monogamous sex (a mirror) within the context of marriage, reflect God (the source of light). But sex is a reflection of relationship with God, not the relationship itself. And so sexual abstinence doesn't lessen the power of relationship with God—the light of relationship of God just isn't reflected in that particular way.

The pagan will protest, "No, the mirror is itself the power source of spirituality." In fact, as Langdon affirms to his students, the pagan would insist that sex is the only means of authentic spirituality:

> The next time you find yourself with a woman, look in your heart and see if you cannot approach sex as a mystical, spiritual act. Challenge yourself to find that spark of divinity that man can only achieve through union with the sacred feminine. (310)

The Merit of Salvation

Of all *The Da Vinci Code*'s pagan themes, the most profound seems to have gone largely unnoticed, perhaps because it represents what makes Christianity unique from all other religions and philosophies—salvation by grace.

Monism, paganism, and gnosticism are consistent with the rest of the world when it comes to the salvation of a human soul. And so is the gospel message in Dan Brown's novel: Salvation and the hope of salvation are both acquired the very, very old-fashioned way: You have to earn them.

It's what drives *The Da Vinci Code*'s plot—the smart one who rises above the crowd and solves the mystery wins. Sophie's grandfather taught her this theology at a very young age. He would always give her birthday cards with a clue that started her on an elaborate treasure hunt around the house (a game that Brown fondly remembers from his childhood). With perhaps a little bit of well-earned pride, Sophie recollects, "Each treasure hunt was a test of character and merit, to ensure I earned my rewards. And the tests were never simple" (200).

A gift could never be given unconditionally; rather, it was always a prize to be won.

We all enjoy following clues to find a prize. And intrinsic to the thrill of the hunt is the question, "Will you be smart enough to measure up to the challenge?" This ethic is very much a core value of most secret societies, as Langdon explains to Sophie:

> Tests like this were extremely common in secret societies. The best known was the Masons', wherein members ascended to higher degrees by proving they could keep a secret and by performing rituals and various tests of merit over many years. The tasks became progressively harder until they culminated in a successful candidate's induction as thirty-second-degree Mason. (205)

All in good fun, Teabing similarly invokes the ethos of a bygone age of chivalry and honor in response to Langdon and Sophie's request to enter his villa: "First I must confirm your heart is true. A test of your honor. You will answer three questions" (221).

The virtue of earned favor is a powerful message in *The Da Vinci*

Code. The principle runs deep when the object of Langdon and Sophie's spiritual journey—the mother of all Holy Grails—can be found only by unraveling secret mysteries. The power and glory of merit earned promises truth and spiritual vitality for those who prove themselves.

Sophie states that the same principle exists within her profession: "In cryptology, that's called a 'self-authorizing language.' That is, if you're smart enough to read it, you're permitted to know what is being said" (205). And unfortunately, much of the debate surrounding *The Da Vinci Code* has been reduced to this question: "Are you smart enough?"

If you read the clues and get the message, you too might win more than the game—you just might win at life.

Matthew's Gospel:
Bad News and Good News

In his famous Sermon on the Mount, Jesus lays out example after example of how he would expect his followers to live if they are to be lights to the world. (See Matt. 5:14–16.) But then he goes on to describe moral standards that are humanly impossible to live by. For example, Jesus says it isn't enough to claim you've never murdered anyone. If you've just plain been angry with someone, you're

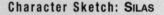

Character Sketch: SILAS

Silas is a complex and tragic antagonist who symbolizes the brutality of a religion that bases salvation on merit and good works. He's a "hulking" albino (12), "broad and tall with ghost-pale skin and thinning white hair" (3). He has "ghostly eyes," with pink irises and dark-red pupils (3). As a follower of The Way, he practices regular self-flagellation and wears a spiked *cilice* belt around his thigh that cuts into his flesh (14).

He's haunted and maddened by his past—his drunken father killed his mother, then young Silas killed his father (55). He grew up homeless and nameless on the streets of Marseilles and Toulon until he killed a man in a fight. He was imprisoned for twelve years. Then an earthquake freed him.

Taken in by the young Spanish priest Aringarosa, whom Silas saves from an attack, Silas takes the name of Paul's companion who was freed from prison by an earthquake. (See Acts 16:26.) Silas remained at Aringarosa's side until the Teacher took him into his temporary (and self-destructive) service (58–59).

asking for judgment. (See vv. 21–22.) And it isn't enough that you haven't committed adultery. If you look at someone lustfully, you've already committed adultery in your heart. (See v. 28.)

This is what the apostle Paul meant when he wrote, "For all have sinned; all fall short of God's glorious standard" (Rom. 3:23 NLT). To the church in the city of Ephesus he further explained, "Salvation is not a reward for the good things we have done, so none of us can boast about it" (Eph. 2:9 NLT). Nobody is ever going to live up to "God's glorious standard" because we have sinned, and no amount of good works is going to change that.

However, God offered us a solution. He loved the world so much that he sent his one and only Son to save it. (See John 3:16.) But the problem is that sin scenario Paul outlined: Humans are in darkness, and they don't *want* the light.

> Light has come into the world, but men loved darkness instead of light because their deeds were evil. Everyone who does evil hates the light, and will not come into the light for fear that his deeds will be exposed. (John 3:19–20)

But for each of the bad-news verses, good news is promised. It's grace—undeserved favor, unmerited love. For the Romans 3:23 blanket judgment that all have sinned, there's verse 24 (NLT): "Yet now God in his gracious kindness declares us not guilty. He has done this through Christ Jesus, who has freed us by taking away our sins." And for God's flat-out refusal to accept any of our good deeds as a way to earn his favor (Eph. 2:9), there's verse 8 (NLT): "God saved you by his special favor when you believed. And you can't take credit for this; it is a gift from God."

No hidden *gnosis* to figure out, no clue hunt on your birthday— the gift is free. The only condition is that we accept it. There are a lot of Teabings, Langdons, and Sophies described in John 3:19–20 who prefer to search in the darkness, bent on proving their worth. But then there are others who will claim Jesus' premise: "Everyone who believes in him will not perish but have eternal life" (John 3:16 NLT).

The Ultimate Gift

What's really amazing is that Jesus knew the response of most people to his gift would be to prefer living in darkness, searching for clues, proving their worthiness. Nevertheless, Jesus extends the gift with no strings or clues attached. "But God showed his great love for us by sending Christ to die for us while we were still sinners" (Rom. 5:8 NLT). Most of us sinners are going to laugh off God's gift or chase after a pagan god alternative. But Christ died for us anyway.

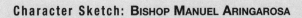

Character Sketch: BISHOP MANUEL ARINGAROSA

Aringarosa is president-general of Opus Dei ("God's Work"), where he has served for a decade (28). He's an "influential American bishop" (40), though originally from Spain (57). He's been enlisted in the conspiracy by "the Teacher," though he's never met him (30–31).

Aringarosa had taken in and renamed a fugitive albino Silas, who remained in his service. Aringarosa is decidedly conservative, distrusts the new liberal pope (148), and is impatient with the church's historic penchant for wasting resources to "dabble in science" (149). His attitudes are reminiscent of Carlo Ventresca in *Angels & Demons: "The Vatican has gone mad.* Like a lazy parent who found it easier to acquiesce to the whims of a spoiled child than to stand firm and teach values, the Church just kept softening at every turn, trying to reinvent itself to accommodate a culture gone astray" (150). Brown explains in his witness statement that Bishop Aringarosa's name is a play on words: This character looks like a villain; however, this turns out to be a red herring—*aringa* is Spanish for "herring" and *rosa* means "red" in Italian ("Dan Brown Witness," par. 203).

When you read Matthew's gospel account of how Jesus died for people who were still sinners, it's hard to believe that many would prefer trying to earn salvation by their own methods of merit:

> Pilate released Barabbas to [the Jews]. He ordered Jesus flogged with a lead-tipped whip, then turned him over to the Roman soldiers to crucify him.
>
> Some of the governor's soldiers took Jesus into their headquarters and called out the entire battalion. They stripped him and put a scarlet robe on him. They made a crown of long, sharp thorns and put it on his head, and they placed a stick in his right hand as a scepter. Then they knelt before him in mockery, yelling, "Hail! King of the Jews!" And they spit on him and grabbed the stick and beat him on the

head with it. When they were finally tired of mocking him, they took off the robe and put his own clothes on him again. Then they led him away to be crucified....

After they had nailed him to the cross, the soldiers gambled for his clothes by throwing dice. Then they sat around and kept guard as he hung there. A signboard was fastened to the cross above Jesus' head, announcing the charge against him. It read: "This is Jesus, the King of the Jews." (27:26–31, 35–37 NLT)

What about Mary?

It's sadly predictable that the gnostic and pagan reworkings of Jesus' gospel story would chase after a Mary Magdalene who amounts to the hidden clue—the one who would be specially loved by Jesus in a way that is inaccessible to the rest, admired at a distance, or venerated from the span of millennia.

The Mary Magdalene of the Bible believed in Jesus. And as we saw in John's gospel account, she was the first human in the entire world to see the resurrected Jesus. And it was she who in turn would spread the good news: "Mary Magdalene found the disciples and told them, 'I have seen the Lord!' Then she gave them his message" (20:18 NLT).

The two views about Mary sum up all the differences that exist between the two gospel stories: the gnostic Mary is the hidden, secret one. She is the queen of the historic quest, before whom only a few worthy souls—those fortunate few with all of the right "stuff"—may one day bow. But they must prove themselves worthy; they must earn the right to worship before the silent, unknowable, progenitor of the yet-deeper secret of Jesus' bloodline, to which only an even more select few might (just possibly) lay claim.

The other Mary—the Bible's Magdalene, is the woman who first met the risen Jesus, and she along with a few other women, proclaims the very good news to her fellow disciples. She is among the first of a long line of gospel proclaimers—what she bears is not a hidden knowledge; it is the broadcasted truth for all who have ears to hear.

In that sense, it could be said that the Bible's Mary Magdalene was the first Christ follower. She was much more than some co-regent wife who bore his bloodline baby. She was a Christian bearing the good tidings of great joy to all the world—the completion of the story of the baby Jesus, born Christmas Eve of a virgin Mary, grown up in a world that rejected him, died, and rose again.

Character Sketch: BEZU FACHE

Captain of the Central Directorate Judicial Police, Fache wears a dark double-breasted suit that strains to cover his wide shoulders (19). Stocky and dark skinned, he is known by his colleagues as the "Bull," carrying himself "like an angry ox, with his wide shoulders thrown back and his chin tucked hard into his chest" (21). He advances with "unmistakable authority on squat, powerful legs" (19). His voice has a "guttural rumble … like a gathering storm" (20). Fache wears a *crux gemmata*—a silver crucifix tie clip with thirteen embedded pieces of black onyx (25). His intuition is almost supernatural at times: *"God whispers in his ear*, one agent had insisted after a particularly impressive display of Fache's sixth sense.... The captain attended mass and confession with zealous regularity" (47). From the beginning, Fache is decidedly antagonistic with sexist overtones toward Sophie Neveu (49–50).

The Da Vinci Code Novel and Movie

(**Spoiler Warning**—endings of the novel and movie are revealed on the next page.)

Communicating through film is powerful, but it often can't capture the length, breadth, and depth of a five-hundred-plus-page novel. Plot elements and characters must be cut, exposition must be simplified, and difficult editing choices must be made. So it is to be expected that *The Da Vinci Code* movie would have to leave out key elements.

The movie plot did vary from the original novel in ways that seemed curious, if inconsequential, while at other times these changes represented an almost profound shift. We've compared and contrasted some of the more consequential variations between the novel and the movie, citing where appropriate from *The Da Vinci Code Illustrated Screenplay* by Akiva Goldsman.

- Instead of being awakened in his hotel room late after the lecture on symbolism, in the movie Langdon is interrupted by Officer Collet during his book signing immediately after his lecture.
- In the book, Langdon is at first distracted by the deceased Saunière's having employed pagan symbolism, not recognizing the Vetruvian Man. But in the movie, he immediately realizes the Da Vinci connection.
- In the movie, when Langdon explains the Priory of Sion to Sophie while driving to the embassy, Langdon shows his skepticism of the Priory's reality: "It's a myth. The Priory is history's version of Santa Claus. Santa has his house at the North Pole, his reindeer, and his flying sleigh. The Priory has their oath, their chalice, their crest of fleur-de-lis" (74). He also refers to the history of the Knights Templar as a "myth" (84).
- The entire movie scene in the park during which Sophie confronts the junkie replaces the scene in the novel where Sophie commandeers the taxi. There was no scene in the novel of a supposedly Christlike intervention by Sophie with a drug addict.
- Sophie's healing touch to the claustrophobic Langdon in the tight circumstances of the armored truck is another Jesus allusion unique to the movie.
- When Langdon presses Sophie as to what happened between her and her grandfather, she recollects the sound of "a familiar slap" and "her own younger scream" (105). Later, she further recollects in her childhood shouting at her grandfather and his apparently abusive response as he "swings to strike" (163).
- The movie's Langdon is a far cry from the somewhat embarrassingly doting Langdon of

the novel, who repeatedly nods his head in approval whenever Sophie looks over to him for a confirmation of Teabing's gnostic apologetic. In the movie, Langdon remarkably serves as the voice of skepticism. During the famously provocative scene at Leigh Teabing's home

- ○ Langdon responds to Teabing's insistence of a historical Priory: "Philippe de Cherisey exposed [the Priory] as a hoax in 1967." Teabing fires back, "This is what they want you to believe" (113).
- ○ To Teabing's allegation that Christians started a religious war against the pagans, Langdon retorts, "Or it was the pagans who commenced making war against the Christians. We can't be sure who began the atrocities of that period, Leigh" (116).
- ○ When Teabing argues that Jesus was deified at Nicaea, Langdon qualifies: "Constantine didn't create Jesus' divinity, Leigh. He simply sanctioned a widely held idea" (117). Teabing responds, "Semantics." To which Langdon presses further: "No, it's not semantics. You're interpreting facts to support your own conclusion."
- ○ When Teabing begins to make his case for Mary Magdalene appearing in *The Last Supper* painting, Langdon responds, shaking his head: "Leigh, not this old chestnut" (122). And when Teabing indignantly insists Mary was no prostitute but Jesus' wife, "Langdon covers his eyes with his palm and shakes his head again" (123). He even retorts, "It's an old wives' tale, Leigh—" (123).
- ○ When Teabing proclaims, "And this is from the gospel of Mary Magdalene herself," Sophie begins to query, "She wrote a ..." Langdon interrupts, "She may have."
- ○ As Leigh leads Sophie to the conclusion that "Christ had a child" and that "Mary was pregnant at the time of the crucifixion," Langdon objects, "Now come on, Leigh."
- ○ Langdon provides a more realistic perspective to the novel's error in fact, suggesting that "In three centuries of witch hunts they burned over fifty thousand women at the stake." However, Teabing still protests, "At least. Some say millions" (129).
- The movie uniquely has Sophie confronting the bound Silas in Teabing's plane. When

213

Silas remains defiant when she demands to know if he killed her grandfather, she concludes, "You believe in God? He knows you. Your God doesn't forgive murderers. Your God burns them" (139). While this scene arguably lapses into a moment of gratuitous angst, it also begs the question of whose God doesn't forgive. Perhaps Sophie's ironically right that Silas's false god won't forgive, but the Christian God forgives all who want to be forgiven, even murderers.

- The cynical discussion between Aringarosa and the prefect at the Castle Gandalf never occurs in the novel. This discussion reframes the character of Aringarosa significantly into a transparent antagonist. With the promise of destroying evidence of Jesus' lineage, even if it means killing living heirs, Aringarosa reasons, "Christ sacrificed his life for the betterment of humanity.... Why shouldn't his seed?" (140). Brown's "red herring" Aringarosa of the novel is, in the movie, anything but. He is an irredeemably clichéd religious villain with little if any virtue, who only is outwitted in the end by the Teacher.
- Both Fache and Aringarosa are significantly altered characters from the novel. The movie has Fache finally giving an answer to Collet's queries about his monomaniacal pursuits. Fache explains that Bishop Aringarosa broke his vows to impress upon him Langdon's evil: "I could not imagine the evil in this man's heart. That he would keep killing. He said I had to stop him" (146).
- The entire scene in which Teabing recounts Langdon's childhood trauma of falling into a well never occurs in The Da Vinci Code novel. These specifics are revealed in Angels & Demons.
- When the decidedly less sympathetic Aringarosa of the movie is shot, he can at best only muster a regrettable, "I am sorry, son. We are betrayed." It is a far cry from the poignant plea of the novel's Aringarosa to a Silas bent on revenge: "'If you have learned nothing from me, please ... Learn this.' He took Silas's hand and gave it a firm squeeze. 'Forgiveness is God's greatest gift'" (418). It's also worth noting that when Silas dies in the movie, the scene likewise lacks the poignancy of his death in the novel.
- The final scene at Rosslyn Chapel represents some of the most significant divergences from the novel:
  ○ There is no indication in the movie that the docent is Sophie's brother. In fact, all

indications are that Sophie is the "last living descendant of Jesus Christ" (199).
○ In the chapel's lower chambers, Langdon finds ancient documents that "date back to the death of Christ" (196)—implicit proof that the myth of the Mary Magdalene Grail must be historical fact. The concluding messages of the movie would proclaim the gnostic history to be factual.
○ Sophie reveals that the cause of her estrangement with her grandfather was over her desire to know her family's history: "He was always such a gentle man. He started shouting at me. I shouted back. And he hit me, Robert" (198). While the novel's Sophie has separated from Saunière because she accidentally witnessed his participation in a Hieros Gamos sex ritual (only vaguely alluded to in the movie, though not in the screenplay), the movie's Sophie simply cannot get over her grandfather's aberrant behavior when she got too nosy about her past.
○ Inexplicably, the movie's account of Saunière is that he actually was not Sophie's grandfather, which is interesting because the published screenplay does not recount this variation.
○ The novel has none of Langdon's philosophizing nor the overt attempts at drawing parallels between Sophie and Jesus. But in true monistic form, Langdon's parting wisdom in the movie smacks of good old-fashioned pantheism: "Why is it always human or divine? Maybe human is divine. ... What matters is what you believe" (203).

- It is especially significant that the final scene of the movie goes beyond the novel. With Langdon kneeling at the Louvre pyramid, the novel implies a faith in a revelation that has come to Langdon—the gnosis has been revealed, but he must still choose to believe.

But in the movie, we follow the camera down into the depths below the pyramid, and with dramatic irony we are allowed to see Mary Magdalene's sarcophagus itself with its "finely etched face staring upward. Familiar. Sophie's face" (205). In the novel we never are allowed to actually glimpse evidence such as documents or a sarcophagus, and Teabing's insistence that we must choose our history based upon faith rings a little truer in the end. But the movie would leave no doubt and no room for faith. It declares much more dogmatically, *this gnostic history is the true history—and there is no denying it.*

11

Out of the Gray

We hope you've enjoyed this examination of Dan Brown's novels. We began by saying that we don't hate Dan Brown. We still don't, and we don't want you to either. We're grateful for the opportunity to look at Brown's philosophies with you. He has written entertaining novels that have stirred much-needed discussion both inside and outside the church. While we disagree with Brown in a number of areas, we're glad he raised these issues. It's good to have to wrestle with our beliefs.

As we conclude our discussion of the gospel according to Dan Brown, we have just a few final things we want to say—some personal remarks to specific people. We'll be addressed our remarks to

- The Christian
- The non-Christian
- Dan Brown

You'll definitely fit into one of these categories, and you're welcome to read the other messages as well.

A Look Back

Before we get to these final thoughts, we need to take a step back in time—a big step back about two thousand years. If you think Dan Brown has stirred up controversy with his ideas about religion, remember what Paul did. Paul was first known as Saul and was a man of great religious passion. He fought for his beliefs, and as an elite Jewish teacher, those beliefs did not allow for followers of Jesus. Saul hunted them from town to town, handing them over to be tortured and killed. But one day he had a dramatic encounter

with the One he was persecuting—the risen Jesus—and was converted. From that time on, Saul became known as Paul—still
extremely passionate, but this time about spreading the good news
of Jesus' sacrificial death and resurrection.

Paul traveled with companions throughout parts of Turkey,
Greece, and Italy, sharing the gospel and planting churches. And
while he was very successful at this, he wasn't always greeted with
open arms by all who heard him, especially other Jews. He often had
to flee to save his life. Such was the case when he set out for Athens.

Paul had been speaking throughout Greece, stirring up trouble
with his message of a Messiah who had been executed but was no
longer dead. With an angry mob at his heels, Paul was hastily
escorted from Berea to Athens. He was to stay there until his colleagues Silas and Timothy could catch up with him, and then they
were to head out for Corinth.

Corinth was the seat of political and military power in Greece,
but Athens was still an educational and cultural center, the ancient
home of Socrates, Plato, and Aristotle. Sophocles and Euripides were
taught in its streets. If you wanted to learn the latest philosophy,
you went to Athens.

Paul strolled the streets of Athens, and what he saw really upset
him. Everywhere he turned were icons, statues, and other artwork
depicting various gods. The Athenians worshipped tens of thousands
of gods, inventing new ones almost daily. Once when a sickness
swept through the city, they erected statues to the "unknown god,"
just in case they had missed one.

Paul couldn't just sit quietly after everything he'd seen in the
city. He found the synagogue and met with the Jews there, but he
also spent time in the marketplace, speaking to anyone who would
listen. Workers, artists, slaves, teachers, philosophers—they all
went to the marketplace and were especially interested in the new
gods Paul seemed to be advocating—Jesus and something called
the resurrection.

Two groups in particular, the Epicureans and the Stoics, wanted
to hear more. The Epicureans lived by the motto "Eat, drink, and be
merry—for tomorrow we die." The Stoics were pantheists who
believed that some great Purpose was behind all life, and this

Purpose was seen in all living things. These men invited Paul to speak to them at Areopagus, or Mars Hill. This was the place where judges heard cases involving religion and education. What would Paul say to these philosophers? Would he berate them for following false gods? Would he condemn them for not being Christians? Or would he refuse their invitation and boycott their meeting?

Paul, of course, welcomed the opportunity to speak. Addressing the crowd at the Areopagus, he began his eloquent discourse:

> Men of Athens! I see that in every way you are very religious. For as I walked around and looked carefully at your objects of worship, I even found an altar with this inscription: TO AN UNKNOWN GOD. Now what you worship as something unknown I am going to proclaim to you. (Acts 17:22–23)

And proclaim he did. Paul started by presenting God as Creator, not a created being. God doesn't need anything from us, said Paul, but gives us everything we need to live. God does this, he explained, so that we will reach out to him. Paul even quoted an Athenian poet: "We are his offspring" (17:28).

Then he threw his audience a curve by proclaiming that God raised Jesus from the dead. Some scoffed at his ideas; others said they wanted to hear from him another day. And some became believers in Jesus. All in all, it was a good stop in Paul's travels.

What does all of this have to do with Dan Brown and, more specifically, you? A lot. To understand just how much, let's proceed to what we promised would be our final words on the gospel of Dan Brown.

Final Thoughts for the Christian

If you're like many other believers, you may not have read *The Da Vinci Code* or seen the movie because you heard it was full of lies about your Savior. You may even react angrily when someone tries to engage you in conversation about the subject. "Why," you ask, "should I be interested in a story that's full of heresy?"

Remember when Paul was in Athens. He was passionate for Jesus, and his life's mission was to tell the good news to as many people as possible. So why did he take an interest in the Athenians' idols? Could it be that he saw the great interest in spiritual matters as an open door for him to share the Truth, just as the interest created by Brown's books can be an open door for you to share the Truth with those around you?

Look at what Paul said when invited to speak at Mars Hill: "Men of Athens! I see that in every way you are very religious" (Acts 17:22). The Greek word Paul used for "religious" here means "firm in one's reverence for deities." He started by complimenting the men for being reverent and for their devotion to their faith. He didn't criticize them for following false gods or for being misled. He started where they were. For hundreds of years the Greeks had worshipped these gods. Paul knew he couldn't dismiss their beliefs and still have their attention.

If you were to tell someone who enjoyed *The Da Vinci Code* or Brown's other books that he or she was wrong to take pleasure in books that portray Jesus and God the way they do, would that person then be open to hear you share the Bible's story of Jesus? Oftentimes, Christians want to out-shout those who disagree with them rather than honoring the faith of nonbelievers and using that as a starting point in developing relationships that can lead to true conversion.

Dan Brown has given Christians a great opportunity. His fans love mysteries and looking for that which is hiding in plain sight. And we Christians believe we're the recipients of the greatest mystery of all—the incomprehensible fact that God, the Creator of everything, chose to become human and die in order that we can live. In his letter to the church at Ephesus, Paul wrote that God had given him the task of sharing this great mystery with everyone, insider Jews and formerly outsider Gentiles. (See Ephesians 3.) That same task is before Christians today: to share the mystery of Jesus with everyone. And thanks to Brown, many agnostic, gnostic, and pagan "outsiders" are excited to have the mystery unveiled for them.

Brown has created an atmosphere in which many who previously had no interest in discussing spiritual things are now buying books, attending workshops, and listening to those who have something to share. Entire sections of bookstores are now devoted to books dealing with Leonardo da Vinci, secret societies, and so-called religious cover-ups. You can practically hear people screaming out that they're hungry for the truth.

Have you read any of these books? Can you discuss these topics and reason with readers who are now wondering if the books' claims are true?

When Paul spoke on Mars Hill, he quoted poetry, not Scripture. He was familiar with what the people of that culture read. You can do the same. Take time to read Brown's books and other books that deal with issues raised in his novels. Then search the Scriptures to see if the claims Brown makes are true. You also need to study so you'll be prepared to answer Brown's claims and to give an answer to those who want to know whether his gospel is true. This is your time, Christian. Make the most of the opportunity God has given you.

You should be ready to discuss any of the following topics or points:

- *Stories* and why they matter more than most of us give them credit.
- *Facts and truths* and the differences between them. They're not the same thing. Truth requires choice and faith.
- *Jesus is Truth.* He didn't just claim to *have* the truth; he claimed to *be* the Truth.
- *No history account is fact.* As Sir Leigh Teabing said, you have to choose in faith.
- *Conspiracies abound.* For every history, there's a contradicting one.
- *Life has a purpose.* There has to be more to it than survival of the fittest.
- *Secret knowledge* and the differences between gnosticism and Christianity. Gnostics teach an exclusive knowledge; Christians are about open and inclusive faith in the one true God.
- *The yin-and-yang worldview.* Yin and yang seek to balance good and evil; Christians seek only the one true God, in whom is goodness and light.
- *The relationship between Christianity and science.* God is the supernatural Creator of science.

- *Paganism.* Why is it relevant in today's world, and in what ways is it different from Christianity?
- *Gnosticism.* What is it, and where do we see it in religion today?
- *The origin of the Bible.* How can we be sure the books that make up our Bible are the right ones?
- *The divinity of Jesus.* Was it a political maneuver by Constantine? Why can't we just believe that Jesus was a good teacher who taught us to live in peace?
- *The sacred feminine.* Does the Christian Bible teach hatred for women? Is spirituality only to be found through sex?
- *How to reach God.* Are all paths to God equal? And is one's religion primarily based on the culture each of us was born into?

Just before Paul traveled to Athens, he spoke in Berea. Here, we're told, "The Jews received Paul's message with enthusiasm and met with him daily, examining the Scriptures to see if they supported what he said" (Acts 17:11 MSG). This is our request of you, Christian: Check the Scriptures to see if what we've presented in this book is true. Prepare to answer those who have questions. And when the topic comes up, even if it's raised in a confrontational way, take advantage of this opportunity to proclaim the message of Jesus boldly. You may not have a chance like this again.

Final Thoughts for the Non-Christian

You no doubt figured out early on that we, the authors of this book, are Christians. But regardless of this fact, we have tried our best to present Brown's ideas as fairly and reasonably as possible. Although we may not agree on the issues Dan Brown presents in his books, we want you to know that we respect your beliefs, whatever they are. As we set out to present our views on Brown's gospel, we made some assumptions about you, the non-Christian reader.

We assumed you've probably read one or more of Dan Brown's books. And by now, you've probably even seen Tom Hanks portray Robert Langdon on the big screen (maybe more than once). And when you heard Leigh Teabing say, "Almost everything our fathers taught us about Christ is *false*" (235), you likely wondered whether this statement is true. Perhaps you've even read books like *Holy Blood, Holy Grail* and *The Templar Revelation* to learn more about these theories. The idea that people are secretly controlling things around you may excite you, and you want to solve the mystery. "Life is more than it seems," you say.

And you're right.

You're on a quest to find this hidden, abundant life, a search that starts with trying to discover if what Brown has written is true. The quest has a deeper meaning for you. As a writer for the *Boston Globe* put it, you're wondering if "perhaps the quest is to solve one's own problems, to decipher not the Da Vinci code, but the in-law code, the job code, or the teenager code—to find a new answer to the question, What's next?" ("Code of one's own," par. 8).

To solve these puzzles, you turn to your gods. Yes, just like the Athenians, you worship many gods, although they aren't made of wood or stone. You may not even realize they're gods. Still, they control your life. You may argue that you don't worship money, but can you honestly say you don't use it to buy an "image" for yourself? Clothing, cars, music, your house, even your friends—all of this makes up who people perceive you to be.

There is the god of self-gratification, better known by the nickname "I deserve this." There is the god of pleasure—"I long for this." There is the god of greed—"I want this." And the god of addiction—"I need this."

In the midst of all these gods, you see another altar, one dedicated to the Unknown God. You're drawn to this mysterious god by something deep inside you. "Maybe," you say, "this god won't disappoint me. Maybe this one won't leave me. Perhaps this god is the one who can help me crack the codes of my life. Maybe, just maybe, this one is real."

Paul talked about the gods the Athenians were familiar with, the gods of wood and stone that seemed to spring up like mushrooms after a hard rain. He said he could see that the Athenians were very interested in religion. He then focused on the Unknown God to make him known to his audience. This God, said Paul, created all there is. He doesn't live in man-made temples, nor does he need anything from us, his creation.

Dan Brown has attempted to capture this god within the confines of the pages of his books. This god, like the supercomputer TRANSLTR, may be able to see into people's lives, but this invasiveness is his ultimate undoing. We can parade this god on television and in the press as being from outside our world, according to Brown, but further investigation will show that he, like a false meteorite in the ice, was manufactured on earth after all. Brown's god cannot trump science; he can only cooperate with it. And this god, in the form of Jesus, can be manipulated by politicians and theologians, as the Council of Nicea proved.

This is how Brown pictures this Unknown God. And if this is true, then the Unknown God is no better than the gods of wood and stone. He would be unable to save, unable to help, unable to cure. He wouldn't be able to help you solve the puzzles and mysteries in your life.

But that isn't the God Paul proclaimed. This Unknown God, said Paul, isn't far away from us, for in him we live, we exist, we draw our every breath. (See Acts 17:28.) This God isn't chiseled out of stone or carved from wood. This God is above all other gods. He cannot be manipulated by us, and he doesn't need us in any way.

Before you is this Unknown God. Why won't you get to know him? None of your other gods have been able to help you. They can't stand in his shadow, let alone in the light of truth. Maybe you say you were never told about this God. Perhaps you were led to believe that Dan Brown's portrait of a man-made god was the right one. You would have been in good company with the Epicureans and Stoics of Paul's day. But Paul had this final word for them: "In the past God overlooked such ignorance, but now he commands all people everywhere to repent" (Acts 17:30).

You've lived your life as you thought best—until now. Maybe you gave a casual nod to God, admitting that there is a God, and perhaps even uttering a prayer for help or of thanks now and then. But that's not enough any longer. The unknown is now known. A radical change is necessary. And that change begins with a change in how you think about God and yourself.

Picture it like this: Until now you've been sitting in the driver's seat, using the gods of wood and stone as fuel. Now the true God is calling you to abandon your car and climb on his back. He'll carry you where he will and will provide all you need on the journey. It won't always be easy or fun, but this journey ends in life. Your way will only end in death.

The code is broken. God exists as the one person you really want to get to know, and he's been saying this all along through his creation and through his love letter to us—the Bible. Real, abundant life is within your reach.

Which gospel will you choose?

For Dan Brown

We really hope you read this, Dan, because we sincerely thank you for bringing important topics to the surface. For too long we Christians have coasted in our faith. We've been told what we're supposed to believe, and we sort of believe it—most of the time. But when push comes to shove, most of us would have a difficult time defending our faith. And now you've given us a reason to break out of our apathy.

You've made us think, Dan. Again, many of us have been content with swallowing what we're fed without analyzing it. Now you tell us in *The Da Vinci Code* that "almost everything our fathers taught us about Christ is *false*" (235), and we're forced to ask, "Is this true? Is what we learned about Jesus from our fathers—and mothers, pastors, and Sunday school teachers—real, or is your approach the real truth? Can we even know what's true?"

You seem to like middle ground—areas that aren't in one camp or the other. As you explained when *The Da Vinci Code* released, "I am fascinated with the gray area between right and wrong and good and evil. Every novel I've written so far has explored that gray area" (Brown, "Explosive," par. 7).

But the middle won't support any of us for long. We must choose between white (the presence of all colors) or black (the absence of color). In your books, you take your readers to the gray area and leave them to find their own way to either a colorful shore or one sheathed in complete darkness. But there's no life for long in the land of gray.

Dan, you've said you grew up in a household in which solving puzzles was a favorite pastime. Now you've presented us with a puzzle in which the clues are hidden in your four novels. But as Christians, we believe the mystery has already been solved. The answers are available to everyone, though it does take a little effort—spiritual, mental, and physical—to find them. They don't have to remain hidden, unless we choose not to search for them. They can be found between "In the beginning" (Gen. 1:1) and "Even so, come, Lord Jesus" (Rev. 22:20 NKJV).

You say you're a Christian. And when you testified in England in your plagiarism trial, you said you didn't use the main thesis from *Holy Blood, Holy Grail* as your own—that Jesus' death was faked and that he came down from the cross and lived out the rest of his life in another country—because that went against the very tenets of Christianity.

Thank you for proclaiming this to the world. You're absolutely right in saying that without the sacrificial death and resurrection of Jesus, there would be no Christianity. And yet the main character in your biggest-selling book, the character you most associate with, says that Jesus was just a good teacher.

Dan, we want to ask you to consider this once again. Has Christianity survived all these centuries because of the teachings of someone who was only a good man? Have millions of believers willingly given their lives for the sake of a teacher or for a great big conspiracy? Or could there be something more to this than a cultural phenomenon?

We invite you now to think this through with us. You've given us cause to reflect, to search within ourselves to see what we really believe. We ask that you do the same. Is gray the shade you prefer to wear as the color of your life?

We believe if you ask God to reveal to you which gospel is true, he promises he will make clear what has been hidden, because he is the light, the source of all color. Perhaps then you will swim with us toward his shore of infinite color. There, and only there, are we going to find peace, joy—and life. Because there we will find God the Son—the way, the truth, and the life ... the light, in full color, and in person.

Works Cited

Armstrong, Karen. <u>A Short History of Myth</u>. Edinburgh, Scotland: Canongate, 2005.

<u>The Barna Update</u>. Ed. George Barna. Vers. 3.0. "Da Vinci Code Confirms Rather Than Changes People's Religious Views." 15 May 2006. The Barna Group. 24 May 2006 <http://www.barna.org/FlexPage.aspx?Page= BarnaUpdate&BarnaUpdateID=238>.

Berzins, Alfred. <u>The Two Faces of Co-Existence</u>. New York: R. Speller, 1967.

Bock, Darrell L. <u>Breaking The Da Vinci Code: Answers to the Questions Everyone's Asking</u>. Nashville: Nelson, 2004.

Briggs, Robin. <u>Witches and Neighbors: The Social and Cultural Context of European Witchcraft</u>. New York: Penguin, 1998.

Brown, Dan. <u>Angels & Demons</u>. New York: Simon & Schuster, 2000.

——. "A Conversation with Dan Brown, author of *The Da Vinci Code*." Interview. <u>BookBrowse</u> 2001. 26 May 2006 <http://www.bookbrowse.com/ author_interviews/full/index.cfm?author_number=226>.

——. <u>The Da Vinci Code</u>. New York: Doubleday, 2003.

——. <u>Deception Point</u>. New York: Simon & Schuster, 2001.

——. <u>Digital Fortress</u>. New York: St. Martin's, 1998.

——. "Explosive new thriller explores secrets of the church." Interview by Edward Morris. <u>BookPage</u>. Apr. 2003. 30 May 2006 <http://www.bookpage.com/0304bp/dan_brown.html>.

——. "NH Writer's Conference." Concord, NH, 2004. Danbrown.com. <http://www.danbrown.com/novels/davinci_code/breakingnews.html>.

<u>CERN Spotlight On</u>. "Spotlight on Dan Brown's Book *Angels & Demons*." CERN. 26 May 2006 <http://public.web.cern.ch/Public/Content/ Chapters/Spotlight/SpotlightAandD-en.html>.

"A code of one's own." Editorial. <u>Boston Globe</u> 24 Apr. 2006. 30 May 2006 <http://www.boston.com/news/globe/editorial_opinion/editorials/ articles/2006/04/24/a_code_of_ones_own/>.

Daly, Pete. "Polke pleads guilty to 2002 shooting." Trentonian.com 27 Apr.
    2005. 26 May 2006 <http://www.trentonian.com/site/index.cfm?newsid=
    14421873&BRD=1697&PAG=461&dept_id=44551&rfi=8>.

"Dan Brown Witness Statement in Da Vinci Code Case." Times Online 14
    Mar. 2006. 6 May 2006 <http://www.timesonline.co.uk/article/
    0,,923-2085827_1,00.html>.

Dickens, Charles. A Tale of Two Cities. New York: Barnes & Noble Books,
    1993.

Einstein, Albert. Out of My Later Years. 1950. New York: Gramercy, 1993.

Garlow, James L. The Da Vinci Codebreaker. Minneapolis: Bethany, 2006.

Garlow, James L., and Peter Jones. Cracking Da Vinci's Code. Colorado
    Springs: Victor, Cook Communications, 2004.

Glaister, Dan. "The Guardian profile: Dan Brown." Guardian Unlimited. 6
    Aug. 2004. 6 Mar. 2006 <http://books.guardian.co.uk/departments/
    generalfiction/story/0,,1277339,00.html>.

Goodstein, Laurie. "Week in Review." New York Times. 21 May 2006.

Herrick, James. The Making of the New Spirituality. Downers Grove, IL:
    InterVarsity Press, 2003.

Hoeller, Stephan A. "A Brief Summary of Gnosticism." The Gnostic World
    View. The Gnostic Archive. 26 May 2006 <http://www.gnosis.org/
    gnintro.htm>.

Irenaeus. Against Heresies, Book III. The Gnostic Society Library. 19 July
    2003. 26 May 2006 <http://www.gnosis.org/library/advh3.htm>.

Jones, Peter. Stolen Identity. Colorado Springs: Victor, Cook
    Communications, 2006.

Ladd, George Eldon. The Last Things. Grand Rapids: Eerdmans, 1978.

Lambdin, Thomas O., trans. The Gospel of Thomas. The Gnostic Society
    Library: The Nag Hammadi Library. The Gnostic Archive.
    <http://www.gnosis.org/naghamm/gthlamb.html>.

Lewis, C. S. God in the Dock. New York: HarperCollins, 1979.

——. Mere Christianity. New York: MacMillan, 1952.

——. Miracles. New York: MacMillan, 1960.

——. Of Other Worlds: Essays and Stories. New York: Harcourt Brace
    Jovanovich, 1966.

——. The Screwtape Letters. New York: MacMillan, 1970.

——. Surprised by Joy. London: Collins, 1955.

Lutzer, Erwin W. The Da Vinci Deception. Carol Stream, IL: Tyndale, 2004.

Machiavelli, Niccolò. The Prince. Trans. W. K. Marriott. 1908.
    <http://www.constitution.org/mac/prince00.htm>.

"Myth." Webster's Third New International Dictionary. 1976.

"New Orleans will force evacuations." CNN.com. 7 Sept. 2005. 30 May 2006
    <http://www.cnn.com/2005/US/09/06/katrina.impact/index.html>.

Pangyanszki, Jennifer. "3 days of death, despair and survival." CNN.com. 9
    Sept. 2005. 30 May 2006
    <http://www.cnn.com/2005/US/09/09/katrina.survivors/index.html>.

Peel, Malcolm L., trans. The Thunder, Perfect Mind. The Gnostic Society
    Library: The Nag Hammadi Library. The Gnostic Archive.
    <http://www.gnosis.org/naghamm/thunder.html>.

——. Treatise on the Resurrection. The Gnostic Society Library: The Nag
    Hammadi Library. The Gnostic Archive.
    <http://www.gnosis.org/~gnosis/naghamm/res.html>.

Rogak, Lisa. The Man Behind The Da Vinci Code. Kansas City: Andrews
    McMeel, 2005.

Ryrie, Charles C. Basic Theology. Electronic media. Wheaton, IL: Victor
    Books, 1987.

Sagan, Carl. The Demon-Hunted World: Science as a Candle in the Dark.
    New York: Random House, 1995.

Shakespeare, William. Romeo and Juliet. New York: Dorset Press, 1988.

Siegel, Marc. False Alarm: The Truth About the Epidermic of Fear. Hoboken,
    NJ: John Wiley and Sons, 2005.

Strauss, Richard L. "The King of Glory." The Joy of Knowing God. Neptune,
    NJ: Loizeaux Brothers, Inc., 1984. 30 May 2006
    <http://www.bible.org/page.asp?page_id=244>.

Thoreau, Henry David. The Journal of Henry D. Thoreau. Eds. Bradford
    Torrey and Francis H. Allen. New York: Dover Publications, 1962.

Valentinus and the Valentinian Tradition. Ed. David Brons. The Gnostic
    Society Library. The Gnostic Archive.
    <http://www.gnosis.org/library/valentinus/index.html>.

Walvoord, John F., and Roy B. Zuck. The Bible Knowledge Commentary,
    New Testament Edition. Colorado Springs: Victor, Cook Communications,
    1983.

Wikipedia: The Free Encyclopedia. Wikipemedia Foundation, Inc.
    <http://en.wikipedia.org/wiki/Main_Page>.

Index

You've read the fiction.
You've seen the movie.
Now Read the Truth.

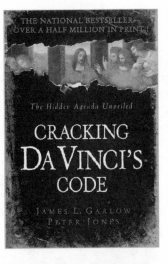

Cracking Da Vinci's Code
by James L. Garlow and Peter Jones

In the fiction bestseller *The Da Vinci Code*, Dan Brown presents a compelling case that Jesus and Mary Magdalene were not only married, but that they had a child. In *Cracking Da Vinci's Code*, Garlow and Jones trace Brown's misguided and false teaching back to its roots—which, surprisingly, are still active in our culture and churches today.

ISBN-13: 978-0-7814-4165-0 • ISBN: 0-78144-165-X
Item: 103795 • $14.99 • Paperback • 5.5 x 8.5 • 256 pages

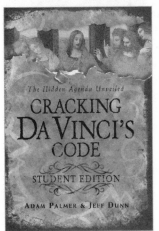

Cracking Da Vinci's Code, Student Edition
by Adam Palmer and Jeff Dunn

Teens can be someone "in the know." Help them discover the true truth about *The Da Vinci Code* by Dan Brown. But, brace yourself for the fact that the novel isn't just historically inaccurate–it may just contain a hidden agenda, too!

ISBN-13: 978-0-7814-4363-0 • ISBN-10: 0-78144-363-6
Item #: 104689 • $9.99 • Paperback • 4.5 x 6.25 • 160 pages

To order, visit www.cookministries.com,
call 1-800-323-7543, or visit your favorite local bookstore.

Timely and Relevant
Titles from Victor

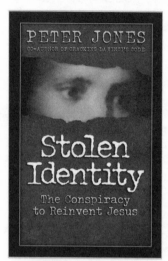
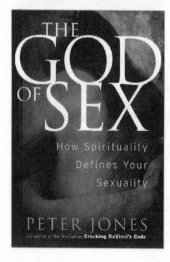